The Hous
Commons

The House of Commons

An Anthropology of MPs at Work

Emma Crewe

Bloomsbury Academic
An imprint of Bloomsbury Publishing Plc

B L O O M S B U R Y
LONDON • NEW DELHI • NEW YORK • SYDNEY

Bloomsbury Academic

An imprint of Bloomsbury Publishing Plc

50 Bedford Square	1385 Broadway
London	New York
WC1B 3DP	NY 10018
UK	USA

www.bloomsbury.com

BLOOMSBURY and the Diana logo are trademarks of Bloomsbury Publishing Plc

First published 2015

© Emma Crewe, 2015

Emma Crewe has asserted her right under the Copyright, Designs and Patents Act, 1988, to be identified as Author of this work.

British Library Cataloguing-in-Publication Data
A catalogue record for this book is available from the British Library.

ISBN: HB: 978-1-47423-458-0
PB: 978-1-47423-457-3
ePDF: 978-1-47423-460-3
ePub: 978-1-47423-459-7

Library of Congress Cataloging-in-Publication Data
A catalog record for this book is available from the Library of Congress.

Typeset by Fakenham Prepress Solutions, Fakenham, Norfolk NR21 8NN
Printed and bound in Great Britain

To Scarlett

Contents

List of tables

Acknowledgements

The Leverhulme Trust generously funded a Research Fellowship, which allowed me to undertake initial fieldwork in the House of Commons between 2011–12. My thanks are due to colleagues at SOAS, University London for keeping me rooted in anthropology and at the University of Hertfordshire for shaking those roots.

My gratitude to the natives of Westminster is enhanced by amazement. Parliamentary officials, MPs, MPs' staff and visitors to the Palace were unexpectedly open and patient about answering endless questions and letting me observe them at work. Parliament is far more transparent as an institution than the NGOs I have worked with. My thanks go to the Justice Select Committee, its Chair Sir Alan Beith MP and its Clerk Nick Walker, as well as the Clerk of Committees Andrew Kennon, for allowing me to listen to their private deliberations and read draft reports. The Speaker and Deputy Speakers kindly let me observe their morning meeting with the Clerks, for which I thank them, and the Clerks allowed me to lurk in their various offices so that I could watch how they advised MPs. Thanks also to the Returning Officer at Eastleigh for giving me permission to watch the count.

My particular thanks go to Sir Robert Rogers, Clerk of the House (2011–14), and his predecessor Sir Malcolm Jack, for issuing a parliamentary pass, encouraging all concerned to talk to me and explaining aspects of Parliament that no one else could, and to the following Clerks and officials for their insight and guidance – David Natzler, Matthew Hamlyn, Tom Goldsmith, John Benger, Roy Stone, Paul Evans, Oonagh Gay, Philippa Helme, Andrew Kennon, Eve Samson, Ben Williams, Kevan Mayor, Abbi Hobbs, Liam Laurence-Smyth and Sarah Petit, as well as the BBC journalist Mark D'Arcy. My thanks also to the MPs who gave me their time and made this research possible and fascinating; and to all those in this book, whether named or not. Sir George Young MP and my own MP Andy Slaughter were especially patient, Richard Graham MP showed me his alarmingly packed diary (see Table 2.1), and the Deputy Prime Minister, Nick Clegg MP, Minister of Children and Families, Edward Timpson MP, civil servants and various whips were particularly kind to talk to me, given their other responsibilities. My sincere thanks to the MPs and their staff who facilitated visits to their constituencies and the peers involved in the Children and Families Bill, especially Baroness Butler-Sloss. Thank you to the consortium of NGOs, and especially Carolyn Hamilton and Hazel Kent at the Coram Children's Legal Centre, who allowed me to attend their meetings. Without all these people I would have understood far less about what goes on behind the scenes.

I would like to thank Mukulika Bannerjee for introducing me to Bloomsbury and to commissioning editor Jennifer Schmidt at Bloomsbury for her enthusiasm and for being a pleasure to work with. Without the comments of various academics and Clerks on earlier drafts, this book would have been weaker in so many ways. So, thank you once again to Robert Rogers, David Natzler, Tom Goldsmith, John Benger, Nick Walker, Helen Kinghorn, Kevan Mayor, Carolyn Hamilton and various MPs for their contributions to the text. I am also grateful to the Bloomsbury reviewers and to Mark Geddes, Jonathan Spencer, Peter Hennessy, Shirin Rai and Doug Griffin for their responses to drafts.

My family deserve thanks like no others. Nicholas, Cleo and Scarlett gave me encouragement, advice and comments without which I would have sunk. In almost daily conversations with Nicholas about politicians he sharpened up my arguments. My daughter Scarlett's grasp of paradox made me realize both its importance in politics and that I have yet to tackle this aspect of democracy. But that is for another day.

Introduction

Stalking MPs: The research

Parliament has everything an anthropologist loves. Conflict sits with co-operation. Friends and foes argue, sooth and perform curious rituals, and hierarchies shift around. The Westminster Parliament is famous, changing and misunderstood; perpetually in the news but always mysterious. The inmates are loathed as a group, but often loved as individuals in their constituencies. I wanted to see what parliamentary work looked like from the viewpoint of parliamentarians themselves.

Anthropologists need the trust of gatekeepers. In Parliament these are the Clerks. When I was studying the House of Lords in the late 1990s, I relied on the insights of the Clerks in the Upper House. Like a politician looking ahead to the next election, I knew there would be no harm in catching the attention of Commons Clerks too, in case I ever chose to study the Lower House. So I invited the then Clerk of the Journals, Sir Malcolm Jack, to a conference on ritual in Parliament I was co-organizing in Hamburg and he graciously accepted. Subsequently I watched as he rose up the Commons clerkly hierarchy. My respect for our Parliament, in part born of the experience of working in countries where governance has been disrupted by colonial rule and conflict, made me hesitate. By the time I had summoned both the courage and the finance,[1] Sir Malcolm had become the top Clerk and CEO of the House. He seemed relaxed about the prospect of an anthropologist embedded in the Commons. On the other hand, when I added my signature to a letter to *The Times* backing Tony Wright's proposed parliamentary reforms, he emailed: 'Better to refrain from any more public support of political reform on your part. M.' I quaked.

Making this connection was essential for the research and yet it was nerve-wracking. Sir Malcolm was the great panjandrum in the palace, known as Three Brains to his friends. Sir George Young said about him:

> He cuts an elegant figure ... Indeed, when he was Clerk of the Agriculture Committee he was known as 'the most elegant man ever to don Wellington

---

[1]Leverhulme Trust generously awarded me a Research Fellowship for this research from October 2011 to December 2012.

boots' … By profession Sir Malcolm is a philosopher as well as a Clerk and has published learned books and articles on philosophical subjects. He has put this into practice here. When he was a Clerk in the Table Office, a Member trapped his hand in a filing cabinet. Others present in the room looked on with interest. 'Can't you do something?' the unfortunate Member asked, 'I'm in physical pain.' Malcolm decided to be helpful: 'Ah,' he said, 'metaphysical pain is far worse.'[2]

When I next saw him I sat feeling nervy and scruffy in the dignity of his panelled office. He reassured me with clerkly counsel. Such advice from Clerks is rarely merely a matter of procedure; they are also shrewd about politics. 'Don't get too close to anyone – if you do you will alienate others', he advised. 'If a group of MPs came into this room and we sat at that table, they would all notice where they were sitting in relation to each other, you and me.' MPs are in competition; status exercises most people, but MPs have the dial turned up higher than others. I realized over time that there is more at stake for them, and closeness is also marked by party allegiance, so I took care to avoid revealing any views that might place me close to any one of the political gangs.

The day before I was due to start on 1 October 2011 Sir Malcolm retired. Somehow he managed to find time to issue me with a pass despite dealing with the fallout of the expenses scandal, encroachment on parliamentary privilege and arrests in the Palace. I signed a form confirming that I had not tried 'to overthrow or undermine Parliamentary democracy by political, industrial or violent means', and he handed me over to another Clerk as my sponsor. At our first meeting I asked my sponsor whether Sir Malcolm backed the project because he is an historian and understands the sister discipline of anthropology or was responding to the need for public education about Parliament. He smiled: 'I infer it is his sense of mischief. He is lighting the fuse and running for cover.'

The project could have been stopped by Sir Malcolm's successor. The new Clerk and CEO of the House, Sir Robert Rogers, has an appearance at odds with his character, like so much in Parliament. He looks like a terrifying and austere Victorian statesman. But if you talk to him at length, you appreciate his warmth, ingenuity and love of Parliament's strange mix of old and new, qualities that are not easily discerned if you just glance at the magnificent beard,[3] low spectacles and court dress. He backed outreach and engagement to the point that the UK Parliament probably outperforms all others and he supported the idea of my project with enthusiasm. Many Clerks at all levels allowed me to

---

[2] Sir George Young MP, *HC Debates*, 12 July 2011, col. 200–1.
[3] According to Leader of the House, the Rt Hon William Hague MP, he preserves this beard by royal command as he was encouraged to keep it by the Queen of Denmark (*HC Debates*, 16 July 2014, col. 887).

watch meetings, explained their work and chewed over the niceties of the culture and work of parliamentarians. As part of their everyday work, Clerks have to be astute observers of human behaviour but also to be seen as utterly discreet. On the other hand, if they trust your discretion, they will reveal more about MPs than a shelf of scholarly books. Their perspectives are in part shaped by when they began working in Parliament, and which department has claimed the majority of their time, so Clerks have multiple views. But listening to as many as possible is the fastest crash course on Parliament and its cultures.

One piece of guidance by a former Chief Whip stood out from an interview I held some years earlier:

> If I learnt one thing when I was Chief Whip in the Commons about politicians, like many other people, is that a politician has, by and large, an infinite capacity to absorb flattery … They can be persuaded of virtually anything if it's skilful enough. If they see it and think you're just flattering them, then it's no good at all. But if you can actually find the key to making them feel really loved and good, they'll do it.

I applied this advice with gusto. Flattery tends only to work if you believe it, otherwise even an arrogant person will see through you. 'What is it like being famous for being such a terrific constituency MP?' I'd ask. Or I went in for indirect flattery: 'That report on transport policy by your Select Committee was amazing. Did you get good feedback?' But it was only to warm them up – once reassured, I tried not to express any distracting opinions. I passed messages through others too. I told everyone of my admiration for Sir George Young, which was true but I wouldn't normally be brazen enough to say so. Sir Malcolm advised me not to get close to anyone, but I made two exceptions – Sir George and my own MP, Mr Andy Slaughter. I'm not sure they would say we were close: Sir George asked whether I was stalking him and Andy threatened to take out an injunction against me. But I enjoyed following them around in any case.

Sir George Young was the Leader of the Commons and then Government Chief Whip in the 2010–15 Parliament, a Conservative, known as the Bicycling Baronet.[4] Everyone thinks he is rich and while he is clearly not slumming it in his lovely village house in Hampshire, he relies exclusively on his salary as an MP. Whether canvassing together at a by-election, listening to constituents talk about their problems or attending a prize-giving ceremony for the best allotments, Sir George explained what was going on with patience.

---

[4] Sir George entered Parliament in 1974 and became Financial Secretary to the Treasury in 1994. He has also been Secretary of Transport (1995–7), Shadow Secretary of State for Defence (1997–8), Shadow Leader of the House of Commons (2009–10), Leader of the House of Commons and Lord Privy Seal (2010–12) and finally Government Chief Whip in the Commons and Parliamentary Secretary to the Treasury (2012–14), before retiring in 2015.

The other person I followed closely was my own MP, Andy Slaughter (Labour MP and Shadow Justice Minister). My then ten-year-old daughter Scarlett had been emailing him about forests and badgers for some years. Some months before I interviewed him he called on our home to see her and when he found us out, he left a handwritten postcard saying he would visit again. She was incredulous. When I told him during our first interview that he was spending time winning the support of people too young to vote, he looked amused. I followed Andy Slaughter as he spoke as a Shadow Minister for Justice, in the constituency as he listened to problems or campaigned to save Charing Cross hospital, and in Eastleigh as he canvassed at the by-election. I listened to him talking to small business owners about the recession, vicars about gay marriage, and housing association workers about hot water. In July 2012 Andy opened a fete in Stamford Brook and the major institutions of British society were represented on one small green: the residents' association organized it, the army processed, the vicar spoke on behalf of the church, Andy represented Parliament, local businesses funded it, and we all raised our glasses to the Monarch to celebrate her Jubilee. 'Bet the MP didn't buy your drink?' said a resident. 'He did actually', I countered defensively.

Andy Slaughter represents a seat with high deprivation and middle-class activists like my daughter; he gets 300 emails a day after spam, has been assaulted and repeatedly phoned in the middle of the night, but he doesn't like to complain. He is in a highly marginal seat, so he is under pressure to appear relentlessly positive. But also, as he says: 'I could work less and earn more as a lawyer. But no one asked me to be an MP.' So why does he do it? Like most MPs, for a mixture of reasons – prominent at different times: excitement, to change things, to get the other lot out, and because it is addictive. This book is partly about the nature of that addiction.

I picked up my grey pass in October 2011. I asked a policeman: 'Where can I go exactly?' He answered in a reassuringly ad hoc British fashion: 'If you have a good explanation for what you are doing there, anywhere except private areas for MPs, peers and officers.' So I wandered about the Palace and outbuildings. Initially it was lonely and worrying. I was accustomed to the intimacy of the House of Lords. Peers work in a parliamentary village, like an Oxford college, plodding down panelled corridors, enjoying a fabulous library and eating at a long table with whoever they find there. The pressure is slight and the ethos is shared – peers are equals to each other, socially superior to others and politically underneath the commoners – even if everyday practices belie this.[5] Their audience is parliamentary and most are ambitious only to irritate the government and revise draft bills. So peers are perfect informants: leisurely, candid and

---

[5]Emma Crewe, *Lords of Parliament* (Manchester: Manchester University Press, 2005).

reflective. MPs are the opposite in every possible way. While the Lords is a gilded village, the Commons is a new and manic town.[6]

Table i Job and gender of MPs interviewed

	M	F
Backbenchers	10	7
Former Ministers	3	0
Minister/whip – government	5	2
Minister/whip – opposition	3	2
PPS	4	1
Committee Chair	4	2
Speaker	1	0
Total	30	14

For the first months in the Commons I knew few, and no one well, and had the perpetual feeling that I was in the wrong place at the wrong time. The Palace of Westminster and its Estate has up to 5,000 people working in over 1,100 rooms, walking up 100 staircases and down three miles of passageways, so rumour has it. It welcomes a million visitors a year. When Parliament is sitting between Monday and Thursday there are debates in the main Chamber and Westminster Hall, inquiries and scrutiny in committees rooms, endless All Party Parliament Group meetings, and multitudes of private conversations. How should I decide where to go? I would bump into the BBC parliamentary journalist Mark D'Arcy in the Portcullis atrium and he would explain where the heated action was likely to take place that day. But I couldn't always find him. I signed onto Twitter and various blogs[7] which not only revealed where controversy could be found but also what was being said (often live), if I was not able to get there. Gradually I developed a sense of where to find my main story.

When not dashing from debate to committee room, I had conversations. They took the form of formal interviews with 44 MPs and 41 staff working for MPs, party workers, parliamentary officials, special advisers, civil servants, peers and journalists. I interviewed 24 former MPs; 20 of them were peers I interviewed during an earlier study between 1998–2002. I also watched the Chamber, committees and other meetings; followed media stories, the Leveson Inquiry and Twitter; visited seven constituencies, talking to more

[6]Former MP and peer Lord Cranborne, now the Marquis of Salisbury, suggested this analogy in an interview with the author on 23 February 1999.
[7]As examples of blogs: Iain Dale's, Conservative Home, Guido Fawkes, Labour List, Andrew Sparrow's at the *Guardian*, Politics Home, Liberal Democrat Voice, Mark D'Arcy's at the BBC.

staff as well as MPs and constituents; tracked pre-legislative and legislative scrutiny of one bill; canvassed during the Eastleigh by-election with MPs and activists from the three major parties; attended consultation meetings at IPSA (Independent Parliamentary Standards Authority) as a member of their external panel of experts; advised officials about getting feedback from MPs on services provided by the House; and assisted a friend who happened to unexpectedly stand as a potential candidate in a selection. I wrote up all the interviews and discussions and recorded them in a 355-paged log. To protect the anonymity of some, not all views and information are referenced, but mostly the source and/or the date of the interview is explained in footnotes.

Table ii Party and gender of MPs interviewed

	M	F
Conservative	11	5
Labour	10	6
Lib Democrat	7	2
Small party	1	1
Speaker	1	
Total	30	14

Good participant-observation research, as anthropologists call it, depends on an open sense of relevance, the suspension of judgement (or at least slowing it down), skill at asking questions, listening and watching with rapt attention, uncovering assumptions and then finding connections and patterns. As American anthropologist Clifford Geertz explains, fieldwork is about getting access to strangers, establishing rapport and trying to fathom their puzzling conceptual worlds: 'understanding a people's culture exposes their normalness without reducing their particularity.'[8] I was interested in MPs' work, but since everything they do in the Palace and in constituencies has at the least some remote relationship with their job, how did I decide what was relevant? I had a rough idea of lines of enquiry, but these questions were only a guide (see Table iii).

---

[8]Clifford Geertz, *The Interpretation of Cultures* (New York: Basic Books, 1973), p. 14.

Table iii Checklist of questions for interviewing MPs

1 What motivates them in becoming and being MPs? What are their aspirations and why?
2 How has Parliament changed since they started?
3 What is their average day/week like? How do they prioritize time?
4 How do they learn and become skilled in different sites?
5 How do they judge their own and each other's performances?
6 Who are their adversaries and opponents, allies and friends? What alliances, networks and tactics do they use to advance their goals?
7 Where do their loyalties lie and why?
8 How is the work affected by their identity and background? By party and being in opposition/government? By length of service?
9 How does whipping work in their party?
10 How can MPs and Parliament gain respect?

Any group of informants has a varied experience of work and life, so the same question will not necessarily be relevant or will at least produce wildly different responses. For most MPs the questions above are too abstract, compromising or embarrassing to answer honestly or with anything more than bland platitudes. So I broke these broad questions down: 'What motivates you?' might become 'Why did you become a lawyer?', then 'How did you get into politics?', followed by a series of how/why questions, depending on what they say, disguised to sound like a normal conversation. Avoiding questions that can be answered with a yes or no, as well as leading questions so favoured by lawyers because they are seeking particular answers rather than people's perceptions of truth, anthropological interviews involve an intense focus on how you ask questions and interpret answers. Understanding meaning, discerning the links between what people say and your threads of interest, thinking up provocative questions, soothing people into candid replies and taking notes, is a skill that is learned, like any other, through practice. Because the ethnographic method requires attention on elusive, diverse and changing cultures, anthropologists write in as much detail as possible about what they have heard, seen and interpreted as they go along. As the 18 months progressed and the Commons became familiar, I became less of an idiot. Towards the end, some interviewees did not want the conversation to end. Despite repeated offers to leave, the last interview went on for three and a half hours and only concluded because the interviewee had to rush off to chair an All-Party Parliamentary Group (APPG). MPs' willingness to talk was revealing in itself; they become programmed to please and impress, but many seemed in need of a sympathetic ear.

Interviewing any informants entails a process of interpretation. People's articulation of their views cannot be read as a mirror of even their full reality because what they say comes through a filter of, for example, self-publicity, wishful thinking, or politeness. Partly for this reason, what people say they do or think is different from what they actually do, as anthropologists discern through observation and interpretation. French anthropologist Bourdieu points out there is much that people do not tell you because they take it for granted and no longer notice it: 'what is essential *goes without saying because it comes without saying:* the tradition is silent, not least about itself as a tradition.'[9] Or, as one of T. S. Eliot's characters, a psychoanalyst, put it: 'I learn a great deal by merely observing you, and letting you talk as long as you please, and taking note of what you do not say.'[10]

To get beneath the surface appearances of social life, anthropologists have to observe and make sense of multiple views, from a detached or semi-detached, and sometimes lateral, angle. When interviewing politicians, whose work is so much about the representation of themselves, their achievements and their ideas, you have to continually ask yourself: 'Why is she saying that?', 'What does he mean by that?', and 'Is she saying that to put her party in a better light?' Like anyone else, MPs' statements are produced by their specific social context – a mix of cultural values, pressures, ideologies, emotions and aspirations. Unlike others, they have extraordinary skills of persuasion. The more controversial or contested the statement, the more I investigated it. If someone told a funny story which nicely illustrated a point made by many, I did not agonize about verification. But if someone made a claim that would be, or was, hotly disputed by others, then I checked with others – the more contested, the larger the number of informants. Getting to the bottom of the votes against House of Lords reform and boundary changes, and the links between them, involved many conversations over months.

Some interviews shone a feeble glow on MPs' work; others felt as if someone had turned some high-intensity floodlights onto the world of politics. One of the latter took place with the Principal Private Secretary of the Chief Whip. I was introduced to him by a young woman from a whips' office and the three of us got talking about smoke and mirrors. The PPS rarely talks to researchers so I was amazed when he agreed to meet the next day. After the interview – during which he told me a great deal about what goes on in Parliament behind the scenes, but no political secrets – he emailed me to recommend I read *The Servant* by Lord McAlpine. On the blurb it says that this book is partly about 'how to ensure a piece of news spreads (tell it to another in confidence)'. Was he allowing a

---

[9]Pierre Bourdieu, *Outline of a Theory of Practice* (Cambridge: Cambridge University Press, 1977), p. 167.
[10]Maurice Zolotow, 'Alec Guinness discusses his role in play by T. S. Eliot, *New York Times*, 26 February 1950, http://www.nytimes.com/books/97/08/24/reviews/guinness-party.html [accessed 11 October 2014].

little light to shine on the whips' office by telling me what goes on there because he did or did not trust me? Perhaps both. Like Cromwell in Hilary Mantel's version of his relationship with King Henry, the PPS's power is rooted in people's assumption that he has power, so they tell him things and he ends up knowing more than anyone else. Even when a whip does not realize his importance at first, people soon discover that if they don't take his advice, it ends badly, so both MPs and Clerks explained to me. If the Chief Whip is close to the PM then he is more powerful as a consequence. In short, his power rests on his access to people's ear and secrets and their trust in his complete discretion. I realized that the only way to get people to talk to me was to convince them that not only could I keep secrets but I could judge what was a secret in the first place.

What this book is about

In this book I aspire to contribute to the debate about politicians with a many-faced portrait rather than a definitive history. In addition to conducting anthropological fieldwork during the 2010–15 Parliament, seeking comments from MPs, former MPs, officials and academics on the draft of this book during 2014 was no trivial exercise in the process of understanding multiple perspectives. It was an integral part of the research to invite a range of informants to respond to my descriptions and interpretations, not merely correcting inaccuracies but challenging the way I made sense of what I saw.

This is the first time an anthropologist has written a book about the House of Commons. While scholarly books about Parliament tend to strip out the excitement of politics, sometimes because academics are under pressure to appear scientific, this one has theatre, conflict and secrets at its heart. The secrets are neither scandalous nor even shocking – they are everyday revelations about how our Parliament really works, seen through the eyes of its main protagonists: Members of Parliament. The most closely guarded secrets tend to revolve around hostility within and not between parties. This book reveals how it works backstage from the viewpoint of the main actors.

This research follows in the tradition of ethnographies of politics by anthropologists such as Jonathan Spencer, David Kertzer and Marc Abélès. Anthropology starts from the perspective of the natives but then probes into what they take for granted; it is 'the art of distancing within the everyday'.[11] When Abélès wrote about local politics in France, he left no stone unturned in his investigation of the history and sociopolitics of a department in Burgundy. Like all anthropologists, he is less interested in individual motives – ambition

---

[11] Marc Abélès, *Quiet Days in Burgundy* (Cambridge: Cambridge University Press, 2007), p. 258.

or greed – and more interested in relationships between politicians and the communities in which they are embedded. Unlike political scientists, he 'peers into cracks between the overt statements or the coded social relationships that govern the world of political action and decisions'.[12] He paints a picture of politics and culture as intertwined differently in specific nations: in France, national politicians have to have a strong local political base; the Communist Party occupies a special cultural place, representing as it does a tradition of resistance; and history is important not just for understanding the past but people's political memories in the present. So anthropology of politics in France involves a toing and froing between the local and the national, between the past and the present, between individuals and collectives. Is it the same in the UK? To find out I will muse on relationships between MPs, electors, journalists and experts – some antagonistic, but others collegiate – on the moral judgements they make, on what they do in Westminster and constituencies. I aim to do no more than illuminate a tiny fraction of what went on in the House of Commons during a specific period in the 2010–15 Parliament, partly for those interested in the workings of politics and partly to provoke other ethnographers to continue the investigation.

This book's main focus is on MPs' work. The departure from previous studies of MPs' work arises from my different intentions, methods and theoretical starting point. Political scientists have tended to adopt a positivist scientific method to the study of the outputs of votes or scrutiny; political sociologists have described MPs' roles and invited MPs to rank them; and feminist scholars have grappled with questions of representation, rules and inequalities. How is my approach different? My aim was to analyse MPs' work in ways that take account of the views of a range of MPs; differences between MPs; changes within Parliament and wider society; the gaps between rhetoric, rules and practices; and the contradictory nature of politics. These aims emerged from an anthropological approach to research. The method favoured by most anthropologists is participant-observation – a mix of interviews, watching and immersing yourself in the daily activities of informants – to produce an ethnography, a detailed picture of the cultural and social life of a defined group of people. In this approach the method and theory are intimately bound up with each other. To decide what questions to ask, and to make sense of the conversations you have with informants, you need open, emergent and iterative theorizing about what is going on in both your research and in your informants' lives. Or in my case, MPs' work. You continually ask yourself why that informant sees their world in that way, and how you are having an influence on your research, seeking both connections and contradictions between ideas, statements and practices. The

---

[12] Abélès, *Quiet Days in Burgundy*, p. 258. For the following points see pp. 103, 174, 209, 227.

result is a book that provides an overview of MPs' work that looks at different roles – party politics, constituency work, governing and scrutiny – but also the relationship between them for different MPs.

The first chapter of this book considers why and how MPs become MPs. People aspire to become politicians to change the world, to campaign on particular causes, to help their party win, or because someone encouraged them. Like any form of work, people are drawn to it for a mix of reasons. Winning support from your local party members means assuring them that you are electable and will represent their views. Endorsements from party leaders improve your chances; it gives the impression that you are already somebody important if you are backed by political heavyweights. Before you will be accepted as their candidate you will usually have pounded the streets, and canvassed for others in local and national elections. Excuses about having to hold down a job or look after children or parents are not accepted by local party organizers. The consequence is that local parties depend heavily on men and either very young or retired people.

Once the aspiring MP has been selected as the party's candidate, their experience of elections will depend on the party. The three main ones will have excellent information about people's voter intentions in the seats they have a good chance of winning. The Liberal Democrats are famous for efficiency in elections. Employing a mix of the latest data-crunching software, charm on the doorstep and military-style organization of volunteers, in the by-election I watched their efficiency left me awestruck. Robert Halfon suggests that MPs only succeed if they show the voters that they are different from other politicians, so candidates need to present themselves as like the voters and unlike each other (or they think they do).

Chapters 2 to 6 of this book investigate different aspects of MPs' work. Chapter 2 is about party work. I explain that you are already part of a political gang as a new MP – one of the three main or smaller political parties – but Labour, Conservative and LD will also draw you into various factions on different topics and at different times. If you are in government, the tensions within parties – or even more so, between parties in a coalition – crackle and sometimes explode into media spats, whereas there is less at stake when in opposition. At the same time, friendships and co-operation across parties goes on far more than the public think. Jack Weatherill (Conservative) told me a story about how he and another deputy whip, Walter Harrison (Labour), both put honour in friendship above party interest, with the result that the Labour government fell from power in 1979. In a more recent example, co-operation between parties has become an automatic feature of the work of the Backbench Business Committee, leading to some of the best debates in the 2010–15 Parliament. So highly visible party political tribalism runs alongside the less visible factions and cross-party co-operation, making political alliances and divisions far more complex and fluid than may be apparent to those who rely on the TV for their political news.

Scholars, too, tend to see politics as a charged arena where friends combine to compete against foes. In our British adversarial system, politicians provide voters with clear choices by taking opposing sides and doing verbal battle. That is the received wisdom about political tribalism – but how does it work in practice? Party rhetoric implies that Conservatives champion individual aspiration, Labour argue the state should protect the vulnerable, and the Lib Dems fight for equality and human rights, so differing ideology does remain important. But the social and cultural push-and-pull within these gangs has been neglected by both scholars and other observers. These ideological blocs are straining more than ever in the face of internal disagreements and declining party membership. MPs do not have two political sides to choose from, but a multitude. The competition is intense. The coalition means that bitter disputes within government that might have been kept quiet pre-2010, or leaked in clandestine embarassment, are openly aired in public. Parties use the only means they have left to galvanize team support: gladiatorial battles at Prime Minister's Question Time (PMQs), BBC's news and political programmes, the showpiece party conferences, collective campaigning at elections, and social media and networks. Cross-party alliances are becoming more common, and the most significant secret at the heart of Parliament is that political work is less antagonistic than it appears. This challenges existing scholarship on party politics by describing the daily contra-dictions created by competition and loyalty that MPs experience when working with colleagues in their own and other parties.

Chapter 3 looks at constituency work, specifically the interaction between MPs and their constituents. The public loathe MPs as a group but often love their own representative. MPs strive to keep their local association and party members sweet, vital for staying put as the candidate and for getting help with canvassing at elections. Meanwhile they keep winning the approval of their constituents by appearing busy, achieving results for the community and by making themselves available at all hours. All MPs have a small team of staff working for (and usually in) the constituency, but very few dare delegate everything to staff. Nearly all hold 'surgeries' where they spend a few hours or half a day meeting constituents to discuss either policy issues or grievances they have with government or companies. MPs and their staff accumulate an encyclopaedic knowledge of their locality – its services, efficient characters in the council, charities who might help and people to avoid. The MP develops a sense of belonging to this locality, or deepens it if she came from there, and acts as a bridge between local and national for those she represents. She or he represents the multitude of voices in this locality, some of whom are heard and most of whom remain silent except through their vote, inevitably privileging some above others.

Some MPs, particularly women, excel at this mix of advice and advocacy for individuals and families, helping those at the end of their tether deal with a faceless bureaucracy. The demands can become overwhelming and the more energetically MPs respond, the more their reputation grows and the more requests they receive. Our champions can never fully satisfy those they represent, and yet those that are seen to belong to their locality command considerable respect. Often dismissed as 'mere social work' by academics, I argue that this neglected area of MPs' work is socially and politically significant.

In Chapter 4 I write about the work of government in Parliament. To get into government as an MP your party needs to win a majority, or form a coalition, and you probably need a patron at the top of your party hierarchy to persuade the leader to put you on the frontbench. All three main party leaders were previously special advisers to senior Ministers. As the leader of the party, you can only maintain support within your party if you command the loyalty of your rivals, whose supporters will then fall in line. Increasingly senior party leaders may get a public show of loyalty from their fellow Ministers/spokespeople while their rivals leak poison to the press about them. The Freedom of Information Act, a hyperactive and aggressive media and the indiscretion of MPs means that exposure of government blunders increases by the day. This creates tension between Ministers and civil servants, with the former more inclined to blame the latter than was once considered polite. Backbenchers strive to nobble Ministers, especially if their party is in government, while Ministers in turn expect their support in the division lobbies. The relationship between whips and their flocks is changing beyond recognition. The influence of constituents on MPs grows, and the clout of Select Committees swells, in parallel with a decline in the power of the whips. The story of the Sensibles, Conservative rebels who defied the whip to defeat the House of Lords bill 2012–13, illustrates how backbenchers in this Parliament continue to be in their new feisty mode.

The tectonic plates of power are shifting in Westminster. Ministers struggle for credibility as blunders are exposed by 24-hour media scrutiny and only survive if they have wide support within the party in Parliament. Most critiques of government pay too much attention to the failings of individual ministers or civil servants, whereas an anthropological perspective points to culture, hierarchies and relationships. The cult of modernization, social distance between policymakers and those affected, and poor working between departments are more to blame for government failures than the inadequacy of individuals. But Parliament is putting government under increasing pressure to consult and explain.

Chapter 5 looks at what happens when MPs put government under scrutiny. The scrutiny of government administration, policy and lawmaking is accomplished across a variety of sites within Westminster through debate, inquiries and meetings. The tumultuous show of PMQs contrasts with sleepy committee evidence sessions and MPs adjust from one to the other in a matter of minutes. There are three processes that provide some continuity for MPs between and across the diversity and dynamism of their work. First, MPs create riffs communicated as policies and arguments, each improvised for different audiences. The second are rhythms that organize the work of MPs by creating repetition in time and space, again allowing for adaptation and variation where necessary. The third are the rituals, whether debates in the Chamber, interviews in TV studios, or speeches at party conferences. These events punctuate the daily routine. They are far less trivial than they appear; they are charged with political, social and cultural significance and achieve policy innovations without a permanent breakdown in relationships.

The public disdain for showy political tribalism distracts us from the most troubling aspect of contemporary British politics; it is the secret conversations with pet journalists that lead to real trouble between politicians. When MPs decide to cause trouble for the other side, or – even more painful – for a rival or enemy in their own party, hacks collude in bringing them down with articles about their failings, their bad behaviour or their terrible taste in clothes. While journalists mimic the adversarial tone of politicians by attacking individuals on conventional and social media, MPs grapple with a new and violent Wild West of the web and Twitter, excited by their direct connection to the public but bruised by the abuse of the deranged. This chapter offers an analysis of different forms of scrutiny and exposure and how they are changing.

Chapter 6 continues on the theme of scrutiny with a story about one clause of the Children and Families Act 2014. The characters involved in drafting, campaigning and debating these 250 words ran into thousands. It was controversial partly because hundreds of thousands of families could be affected by a bit of text that states that if parents go to court on separation then it should be assumed that children would see them both. It was also the executive entering into a private social domain – the family – and making a pronouncement about relationships between parents, children and the courts. Unsurprisingly emotions ran high. The government changed the wording as a result of persuasive arguments by the Justice Select Committee and the House of Lords in conversation with outsiders. So looking under the text of law, the public script, we find layers of complex social life in its underbelly.

It can be those in the shadow of the law, rather than those who go to court, who are often most affected by new legislation in unexpected ways. Simplistic claims that lawmaking should be 'evidence-based' gloss over the complex nature of different types and sources of evidence, as well as the social relationships and varied forms of communication that can be found under the legislative performances. Rather than judging scrutiny merely by its rules or outputs, such as amendments to bills, I describe the processes of public and private debate and contestation that are so vital for democracy.

In the final chapter I consider what it means that the various strands of MPs' work create such contradictions and conflicts. MPs have no choice but to seek popularity and the support of political parties and yet, at the same time, we demand authenticity, evidence and conscience. Day-to-day work for MPs attains some consistency, and MPs manage therefore to maintain a sense of coherent self, through riffs, rhythms and rituals. But underlying our parliamentary democracy is a paradox when you consider the representative role from the perspective of MPs. MPs' identity is bound up with their constituency – they embody a locality and an invented political community – so that when they represent themselves, they represent their constituency at the same time. It is this paradox that gives democracy its dynamism.

1
Joining the House

How I came to be studying MPs, the puzzling question of why people wish to enter Parliament to face scrutiny and vilification, and how they win selections and elections by making friends and gathering intelligence.

****

Like every MP, I want to change the world.

Peter Bone MP (Conservative)[1]

Why do people become MPs?

'People enter politics to achieve power or control' – or so goes the cliché. Even some MPs make this claim.[2] Maybe it is partly true. At the same time, most MPs are drawn by their desire to do public service, to 'change the world' or correct the damage done by others. Chris Bryant MP (Labour) received help as a child so he wanted to give something back, as an act of indirect reciprocity to those who inspired his gratitude.[3] Many of the 2010 intake wanted to either improve Britain and the way it is run, or revive Parliament after the opprobrium into which it had fallen following the expenses scandal. Several new MPs, Mary Macleod, Priti Patel and Thérèse Coffey as examples, claimed that they went into Parliament in 2010 inspired by Margaret Thatcher.[4] Another said that he did not want to be an MP, he wanted to be a Minister: 'I was interested in making things happen', and getting into Parliament was the only route to government.

Some are galvanized by what they see as a mess created by the opposition. In the 1960s Jack Weatherill (later a Conservative MP) was complaining about the state of the nation and a friend said: 'Well, go and do something about it.' Although his father was Labour, as a businessman with a tailoring outfitters in

---

[1] Interviewed by Emma Crewe, 26 March 2012.
[2] Bob Marhsall-Andrews, *Off Message* (London: Profile, 2007), p. 1.
[3] Interviewed by Emma Crewe, 25 January 2012.
[4] *HC Debates*, 10 April 2013, col. 1702, 1707 and 1711.

Savile Row, Jack made contact with the local Conservative Party. When he was first elected as an MP, his wife burst into tears and said: 'You have ruined our marriage.'[5] I asked one former MP whether he went into Parliament to follow his long line of parliamentary ancestors. He replied that he became an MP by mistake. He, too, was talking about how frightful things were in the country in the 1970s. An American friend suggested he should do something rather than merely complaining. He put his name down for selection in a safe seat, which he knew was going to be won by a man called Jock, a favourite with the local party. Jock said something inappropriate about military widows' pensions and it was all over for him. My informant was selected and then elected.[6] On the other side of the political spectrum, a Labour MP agreed to stand in the mid-1990s, even though he hated MPs and had no interest in politics, because he said he had witnessed Mrs Thatcher strip the country of its assets and he thought he should get involved. Another Labour MP said: 'It is anger that gets people into politics.' In 2013 one potential candidate was roused by what she saw as the lack of compassion in the Coalition government.

Some had particular causes. Paul Flynn MP (Labour) grew up in poverty; when one of his family fell ill, his mother was never sure whether they would have enough money for the doctor. His father then died young as a result of the First World War. He went into Parliament to fight against poverty and for peace.[7] Another former Labour MP got in to represent the interests of working-class people; he was one of several local councillors who might have stood and was chosen because he was reasonably popular and had no skeletons. Others were inspired by teachers; Karen Buck MP (Labour) was told by one: 'You're inter- ested in politics. You should be an MP.'[8] Some wanted to represent a specific area. Jonathan Edwards MP (Plaid Cymru) plans to cut his teeth in Westminster, argue for stronger powers for Wales, and then stand for the Welsh Assembly.[9] Gordon Birtwistle MP (Liberal Democrat) wanted to improve things in Burnley.[10] When he stood as the candidate in 2010 – 'because someone in the party had to' – he assured his wife that he was bound to lose as the seat had been in Labour's hands for 78 years. He won. Behind many MPs you find exasperated spouses, partners and children.

Some were born into politics. Gwyneth Dunwoody MP went to her first Labour conference aged 3.[11] For Stephen Pound MP, politicians were the group

---

[5]Interviewed by Emma Crewe, 26 June 2000.
[6]Interviewed by Emma Crewe, 29 September 1999.
[7]Interviewed by Emma Crewe, 17 September 2012.
[8]Linda McDougall, *Westminster Women* (London: Vintage, 1998), p.17.
[9]Interviewed by Emma Crewe, 11 October 2011.
[10]Interviewed by Emma Crewe, 4 February 2013.
[11]McDougall, *Westminster Women*, p.12. She gives many examples of how older MPs' political roots can be found within their families.

he most hated in society, but his father's colleagues in the Communist Party encouraged him to get involved in the union and he was elected President in error. Later, like many I met, he agreed to stand as councillor as a favour to a mate and only because he was told it was unwinnable. For others, their father, mother or spouse had been in politics so having had a little experience, they wanted more. As a Conservative MP put it: 'Politics is in my genes, I'm from a political hierarchy'; but the genes do not necessarily dictate which party – three generations had managed to sit for Conservative, Liberal and Labour. Frank Field MP (Labour) told me that the source of his political ambition was his mother – she was determined that her son would do well.[12]

A few were attracted to the variety involved in a politician's job: advocacy, social work, debate and running things. Dick Marsh (Labour MP, then a Crossbench peer) described himself as opportunistic.[13] He left school at 14 and became a lathe operator. It was only because he was called up by the army that his horizons expanded. At the end of the war he became a trade union official and went from there into Parliament; his salary stayed the same at £1,500 a year but he thought being an MP sounded fun. He arrived with Margaret Thatcher, who joked about how she wanted to become Chancellor of the Exchequer.

A handful may have been attracted by the salary, but for most, if they have the energy and contacts required to be an MP, there are far easier ways to earn £65k a year. Over half the 2010 intake took a pay cut. 'The new MPs are certainly not in it for the money', found the UK's leading research institute on Parliament.[14] But one pull factor is visible on the faces of candidates at any election – excitement. Whether going into the fray, or returning despite terrible sacrifices that MPs have to make, the drama, the influence and the unpredictability all play their part in making the political arena entertaining and even addictive.

If you ask people about motivations they tend to give one, but motives are never singular. A few did give a bundle of reasons. Sir Malcolm Rifkind MP said that he thought about being an MP when one visited the Conservative Association at Edinburgh University and made the job sound fascinating and left him thinking 'I could be as good as him'. He also concluded it could be a way of pursuing his interest in foreign affairs. Dame Anne Begg MP, another Scot but in the Labour Party, was encouraged by her manager when she was a teacher; women at senior levels were still under-represented. She was already an activist through the teaching union and others in the party pushed her. She decided

---

[12] Interviewed by Emma Crewe, 29 May 2012.
[13] Interviewed by Emma Crewe, 17 March 1999.
[14] Matt Korris, *A Year in the Life: From member of public to Member of Parliament*, (London: Interim briefing paper, Hansard Society, 2011).

to do it because, like many, she thought she might regret it if she didn't.[15] But most MPs reduced their answer down to one motive; in conversation we are usually inclined to simplify. As Sir Menzies Campbell MP (Liberal Democrat) said: 'Motivation is complex. It can be a mixture of things that fluctuate and change over time.'[16] The point of these examples is to suggest that MPs were not seeking power or money for its (or their) own sake, but were drawn to the job by as many combinations of circumstances as there are MPs.

Winning a seat

How do candidates get onto the ballot paper? Entry into Parliament has moved down the class pyramid for candidates, patrons and voters. It was once the Monarch alone who decided when to take the advice of his nobles, until burgesses began to be elected and sent to 'Parliaments' from the thirteenth century. Until the nineteenth century over half the boroughs were rotten or pocket, controlled by landowners or other wealthy individuals, so that many candidates had to win the support of only one very powerful man (or exceptionally a woman) who then bribed or blackmailed the voters to back him. While the then large populations of Manchester and Birmingham sent no one, Old Sarum in Wiltshire and Gatton in Surrey had only seven voters but two seats each. With the redrawing of boundaries and the secret ballot in the great Reform Acts of the nineteenth century, corruption was stamped out of elections. But only men were allowed to vote. It wasn't until 1928 that women won the same voting rights as men, thanks to the Pankhursts, suffragettes and other feminists.

Selection, like election, is a mix of forging social relationships and navigating rules and rituals. The process has become more transparent; the Lib Dems even publish the rules and what to do.[17] They make it look as if it is like applying for any other job; you need to fulfil the six competencies of communication skills, leadership, strategic thinking and judgement, representing people, resilience and values in action. In practice, you need some other things too. You need contacts, to invest masses of time and cash to spend on leaflets, and probably to give up your day job.

Watching and even participating in a selection process gave me insight into the nature of British political networks. Towards the end of my research, a former colleague decided to throw her hat into the ring and mentioned it to me because

---

[15] Interviewed by Emma Crewe, 4 May 2012.
[16] Interviewed by Emma Crewe, 9 August 2012.
[17] http://www.libdems.org.uk/how_to_be_a_candidate.aspx#selection, and the rules in detail for England: http://www.libdems.org.uk/siteFiles/resources/docs/candidates/Rules%20for%20the%20selection%20of%20parliamentary%20candidates%20in%20England.pdf [both accessed 20 April 2013].

she knew I was researching MPs. Like me, she had worked for 20 years in the field of international development, mostly for non-governmental agencies and occasionally for official aid agencies. Her mother was actively involved in Labour Party politics and stood as a parliamentary candidate, so she had memories of campaigning as a child. Although she had been a member of the Labour Party all her adult life, she had not been active or even attended meetings, and took herself by surprise when she decided to stand. Why did she do it? Her work has always been making a difference to the lives of people who find life a struggle, whether those in poverty in the Third World or, more recently, as a visitor to prisons. She was increasingly horrified by the politics of the Coalition government, including those towards prisoners, and wanted to stop them destroying the welfare state, in her words. The final straw was their plan to confiscate prisoners' TV, in her eyes an act of foolish cruelty that would lead to unnecessary boredom and difficulties for the prison officers trying to keep order.

My colleague, who I will call Scarlett, began by submitting an application in her own constituency within a large English city. She did not progress onto the shortlist because her own ward decided not to put her forward, but the procedure secretary encouraged her to consider nearby seats. She resubmitted almost the same application to the neighbouring constituency and, armed with the list of Labour members in the constituency, we went canvassing. In this affluent city ward, we met leftist Labour members who were quick to probe where she placed herself. 'I'm on the left of the party with Old Labour, I agreed with our current MP – so where do you stand?' asked one, to which she replied: 'Oh yes, I am Old Labour in the sense that I am very strong on civil liberties and a great defender of the NHS …' Or another: 'So what is your politics then?', giving less away herself at first. At one house the wife of the local ward Chair came to the door. 'Oh you should talk to my husband', explaining who he was, and then to him: 'Come and meet one of the candidates, she is really interesting.' Scarlett did not know anyone in the local party so, unsurprisingly, she did not recognize him or know who he was. He came reluctantly to the door and looked at her with undisguised disdain. 'Who are you exactly?' he asked. While the wife was quick to realize she was a novice at this game and admired her bravery, the husband did not conceal his disapproval. After all, she was committing the greatest sin in politics – she was a total stranger locally.

After several hours of knocking on doors, and mostly receiving no answer, we stopped for a coffee.

'So are you Old Labour?' I asked Scarlett.

'In some ways and not in other ways. I'm not really that party political.'

'They are going to want to know how you stand on certain symbolic issues: the private sector, the unions, benefits, free schools … Are you a Blairite or a Brownite or one of them?'

'It's not really how I think!'

Since she may not align with the local party in ideological terms, I advised her to stress her local connections. She lived quite close to the boundary, although she never discovered exactly how close, so she could present herself as a local. But even living a few miles away was not necessarily going to be enough. She was also beginning to feel slight awkwardness about the gaps between her views, some of those of the local party and the stance of the national leadership.

'On the other hand, think what an incredible position you would be in to argue for better approaches to international development and to women prisoners. It's worth fighting for', I said.

Scarlett learned from the first process that it is expected that candidates send out a leaflet, so she printed a beautifully designed leaflet (pro-bono by a friend) stressing her more left-wing opinions with the following:

Putting people at the heart of politics again

Fighting for Labour, Fighting for x

Dear Labour Party Member
Weren't you relieved when x challenged the legacy of Thatcherism and reminded us of how she undermined education, health and support for those in need, setting the context for a get-rich-quick culture where the individual was more important than society?

I have lived locally for over 17 years and I am passionate about representing x, speaking out on issues that matter to you and putting people at the heart of politics. This desire is driven by an increasing sense of frustration with the Coalition and their policies, which lack insight, compassion and care and give relentless support for private contracts. My career so far has taught me how to give voice to the most vulnerable, especially on issues linked to health, environment and human rights ...

As the candidate for x, I would relish working with the local party to win the seat and campaign nationally for both local people and concerns that are close to theirs and my heart.

She listed some achievements, principles (including 'Society is changed for the benefit of all by collective action, not just individuals') and three priorities: health, jobs and equity. The canvassing had confirmed that nearly everyone minds about health, as does Scarlett, so she had included that with some confidence. You couldn't really argue with 'jobs' as a Labour priority and 'equity' was designed to signal a dose of Old Labour. I advised that she should say more about her campaigning priorities and working for the party and its causes.

Unlike most job applications, which focus on individual skills and experience, I stressed that she needed to convey her commitment to the local party and its demands. Others advised her that a photograph and strong design were essential. Nothing was untrue, but she left out various aspects of both past and present – that she once worked for a former Conservative Cabinet Minister, finds a sense of humour essential to everything she does, and runs a foundation for an oil company. She was all set, except that the three front-runners, as written up by the local newspaper, all had extensive party political experience and large numbers of 'endorsements' by senior party leaders, MPs, peers and party supporters. We discussed this. Should she try and rustle up a couple of endorsements somehow? She decided that it would look worse to have two relatively obscure party members as sponsors than none at all against these long lists of heavyweight patrons.

It was obvious that she needed to make friends fast. The leaflets of three other candidates had 'endorsements' from former Cabinet Ministers, and they were supremely networked. Since the endorsers were all New Labour, we hoped that might be a double-edged sword for the front-runners. But all three were local Labour councillors with decades of experience of campaigning and winning elections. We had intended to go canvassing for a second evening but what with holding down a job and the pressures of normal life, there wasn't time in the brief gap between application and the next stage – the shortlisting.

One chilly Sunday afternoon we joined members of the local party in a church for the shortlisting ordeal. Scarlett and I split up to work the room, reaching more people separately than we could together. A new member told me he had moved from a part of the city with very few Labour members and was excited to meet so many kindred spirits, so whoever would win the candidature would be getting a large donation from him. My eyes lit up on Scarlett's behalf and I took his email, already mentally composing a letter requesting his support as I began to believe my reassurances to her that she had a good chance of getting through because her experience was so much more valuable than the others (I should have known that wasn't necessarily the point). A famous comedian was waiting patiently for the proceedings to begin. I realized later that he was supporting one of the front-runners, but I sought his support for Scarlett should she become the candidate. He said politely that he'd support whichever one got through. In truth I realized by now that she was competing against three candidates who started fighting for this many years ago and who were, therefore, far ahead in the race.

The Chair of the Constituency Party called the meeting to order once over 100 people had arrived. The members, and candidates' assistants such as myself, sat at about ten tables of ten people each. The room seemed to be dominated by white, middle-class Labour party members with an average age of well over 50. The ten candidates were ready to speak to the assembled crowd. The Chair called on the first to start and each was given strictly only three minutes. Candidate 1 had only managed a few sentences when a member interrupted on a point of order, complaining that the speakers should proceed in alphabetical order. The Chair explained with considerable tetchiness that lots had been drawn and members should not interfere with the process. Various people shouted irritably that the candidates should speak from the stage, as they couldn't be heard from where they were standing, and so they were directed to move. By the time the first candidate walked onto the stage, the mood was charged with a strange taut and suspicious current; I was almost shaking with nerves on their behalf. Each spoke with considerable anxiety about why they were standing, what they could offer and why they would make a good candidate. The old hands stressed that they would win at the General Election and work with the local party; those new to politics treated it like a normal job and talked about their motivation and qualities. When I told the lady next to me I was a colleague of Scarlett's, she commented: 'She circulated the best statement but just now she talked too much about herself.'

Unusually the candidates then moved from table to table being questioned by the members for 5–10 minutes each. I stayed on the same table.[18] They asked the candidates questions about their politics, gauging where they stood on the symbolically important issues: 'What would you do about the privatization of the health service?', 'How would you pay for the reversal of cuts?'. 'What would you do about free schools?' To the latter, one of the front-runners replied: 'I don't like free schools and I wouldn't have supported them, but now that we have them, I don't think there is any point getting rid of them.' A member shot back, with a look of fury: 'So you would just let them be?' When the table decided the process was at an end, she turned to me panic-stricken to explain her position in more detail, as if I would in turn explain it to others when I had a chance. It made me realize how nerve-wracking it was to be judged on your views, and your performance in conveying them, at the same time.

A few days later the party members met and selected their shortlist. All three chosen were the same front-runners who were identified by the local newspaper some weeks before. They shared in common snazzy personal websites, endorsements by senior party figures, positions on councils and experience of elections. One was a journalist, stood for Parliament in 2010 and had the backing of many party figures, including a shadow frontbench spokesperson;

---

[18] Although I wanted to tell them about my research – after all, our ethics dictate that we should let people know we are studying them, if possible – I did not want to jeopardize Scarlett's chances. The loss of one vote – someone thinking 'why has she got a researcher spying on us?' – seemed an evil greater than relaxing my research ethics when I planned to anonymize everyone in any case.

one had worked for Labour MPs for her whole short career and had a string of endorsements, including one from a former party leader; and the third was special adviser to a senior MP with twenty years of campaigning for the Labour Party. Scarlett was told that she hadn't made it. I applied for permission to attend the final meeting, but was told that 'only voting party members are allowed. It is essentially a closed meeting.'

Since she realized that to have any hope of being a parliamentary candidate she needed to be a councillor first, Scarlett applied to stand for local government too. The assessment panel turned her down for lack of experience of campaigning and knowledge of government (see Table 1.1).

Table 1.1 Assessment of a local government candidate

Area of concern	Brief comments
Campaigning Knowledge of local government	We thought you have the potential to be an excellent candidate in the future given your extensive public sector experience. However, we would like you to get involved in the voluntary and campaigning aspects of the local Labour Party before standing for public office. We would also like you to research and learn more about local government structure.

Eligibility for public office from the perspective of officials in that Labour Party constituency means connections of a certain kind. To get onto the shortlist you need to be part of the local and national party network. If you study any local party list of activities, it is clear that this means at the least an exhaustingly time-consuming commitment over many years of canvassing on doorsteps, stalls and marketplaces. For the local party members it means being known, in relationships with other members, but also sharing their loyalties – in this case, to unions and the welfare state in opposition to the private sector – as signalled by the shared rhetoric. However, these processes of trying did finally pay off. Another local association was looking for a candidate to stand for a council seat that Labour had almost no chance of winning. Scarlett was asked if she would stand. It would require only one hour a week of knocking on doors and 'the party would be very grateful', meaning that eventually it might lead to selection for a more promising seat. Despite these assurances of minimal inputs, her fellow canvassers demanded her presence three or four evenings a week, exerting severe emotional blackmail if other work or family claimed her time. Gradually, as she learned the rules and established relationships with fellow candidates and canvassers, she became more of an insider. She very nearly won a seat.

Party members would argue that experience is necessary for individual candidates to succeed at political work, just as recruiters do in any job. But there is also a cultural dimension to this. Communities often distrust outsiders; they don't know how to behave properly and have a tendency to break rules, norms and taboos. The sociologist Elias explains how the established group often think that newcomers could bring disgrace to their group and threaten their status by association; he calls this a 'fear of pollution'.[19] In a community, established members may refuse to socialize with newcomers, engage in malign gossip, call them derogatory names and or even attack them. In political parties, outsiders find it hard to get selected as candidates until they have become accepted insiders. It is common in communities or organizations (and it was certainly the case in the House of Lords when I studied peers from 1998–2002) that older residents/members value highly the standards and way of life that have evolved among them over a long period.[20] They expect respect from newcomers.

This all changed when the 2009 expenses scandal destroyed MPs' self-esteem and dented their reputation. Abruptly everyone saw the need for change. So it was understandable that the tendency to recruit people with experience of the party was bucked by David Cameron in the run-up to the 2010 election, when he encouraged non-party political people to stand for Parliament and held open primaries to choose some of the candidates for the Conservative Party. The whole electorate, rather than just party members, chose the Conservative candidates in a handful of seats. In the view of a former whip, this, and Cameron's A-list of candidates for seats, has caused problems because 'they are national personalities, very clever and successful, but they don't know politics … It is only a united party that stands a chance of winning at the election. You get the feeling they are thinking, "I want to be famous".' So for some of those who run the parties, eligibility remains an issue of belonging to the party political network.

In all three parties MPs and activists have talked about how the patronage of big players in the party helps.[21] Those big players want to build up their support base; the presence of indebted, bright young new MPs can be extremely useful. Alongside patronage, some MPs want to encourage people from groups that are under-represented: women, ethnic minorities or disabled people. Local party members tend to be less concerned about equality; their attention is on getting what they see as the best representative for their constituency. Some party activists tend to reveal dinosaur attitudes during the Q&A sessions. According to

---

[19] Norbert Elias and John L. Scotsman, *The Established and the Outsiders* (London: Sage, 1994), p. xxiv.
[20] Crewe, *Lords of Parliament*, and Elias and Scotsman, *The Established and the Outsiders*, p. 148.
[21] For example, http://labourlist.org/2012/11/labours-selection-process-a-word-of-praise-a-word-of-caution/ [accessed 21 April 2013].

a Conservative colleague, when Leon Brittan was trying to stand for Cleveland and Whitby in the 1970s, one association member asked: 'Is he Jewish? And do we want a Jewish MP?' The secretary replied: 'When we are choosing the next vicar we can ask about religious affiliation but not while we are choosing our MP.' He was elected. As one former Lib Dem MP put it: 'Usually the problem for women getting into Parliament is not the electorate but the selectorate.'[22] Betty Boothroyd was told in West Bromwich: 'Well I don't think I'm going to vote for you because you're unmarried, you don't know anything about life, you don't have any children or know what it is to make ends meet on a low income. You don't know how to run a house. I'm certainly not going to vote for you.'[23] Women are still asked how they will cope with managing two homes if they have children, or what their husbands think about them running off to Westminster. A woman candidate in 2010 was not unusual in being told: 'I think you are evil. Your children will suffer.'[24] It is clearly extremely difficult to work as an MP, running two homes and workplaces if your constituency is outside London, with children or dependents, unless you have a large additional income or a spouse or relative who takes care of the family. Since that is less likely for women, the consequence is that only 28 per cent of women MPs have children, while 45 per cent of men are parents.[25] But rather than demanding more support for MPs with dependents in Westminster, some local party members reject women MPs.

If the parties parachute candidates in to overcome this kind of prejudice, they incur the wrath of local parties. So they attempt grander strategies, the most effective – but also contentious – being quotas for women. Thanks to the introduction of all-women shortlists by the Labour Party in 1997, women shot up from occupying one-tenth to one-fifth of parliamentary seats. Not only were some seats reserved for women only, but they were nearly all winnable in 1997 – of the 38 on all-women shortlists, 35 got in.[26] By 2010 the proportion of women winning was far smaller, but that partly reflects the result for the Labour Party and not just those selected by the quota system. Despite their success in what might be seen as a crisis in representation, some in the party resented quotas – claiming that meritocracy had been compromised – and other parties have firmly rejected them.

On the Conservative benches there were 13 women in 1931 and the same number in 1997, so by the late 2000s the party was determined to do something. Cameron said in 2006: 'Only if we engage the whole country in our

---

[22] Interviewed by Emma Crewe, 4 September 2012.
[23] McDougall, *Westminster Women*, p. 30.
[24] Interviewed by Emma Crewe, 14 November 2012.
[25] Rosie Campbell and Sarah Childs, 'Parents in Parliament: 'Where's Mum?'", *Political Quarterly*, vol. 85, issue 4, pp. 487–92.
[26] Richard Kelly and Isobel White, *All-women shortlists* (House of Commons Library Note, SN/PC/05057, 2012), p. 7.

party will our party develop ideas that benefit the whole country. The conversation we have in the Conservative party must reflect the conversation in the country, and the sound of modern Britain is a complex harmony, not a male voice choir.'[27] For the 2010 election the Conservatives had priority lists with at least 50 per cent women and a significant number of black, ethnic minority and disabled people. Representation improved, with women leaping to 49, but the pattern was still that local parties preferred men.[28] Most strange of all is the lack of success in Lib Dem attempts to diversify their MPs, ending up with only seven women out of 57 in 2010 and no ethnic minority MPs at all. For a party that has equality and fairness at its core, the white-male dominance of its MPs is curious. According to a Lib Dem Asian activist, the party compares unfavourably to the public sector, where he used to work. It is patronizing and paternalistic to those facing disadvantage. It wants to help women or black people get in, but it hasn't faced up to its own sexism and racism, he claimed. Others make similar comments about the other large parties, but it may be the Lib Dems' ethos of equality that takes the pressure off the subject, gives a false sense of action and, ironically leads to inaction, he told me.

The increase in MPs with a political background and decline in both the working class and professionals worries many. Manual workers dropped from 16 per cent to 4 per cent and professionals from 45 per cent to 35 per cent between 1979 and 2010, while political organizers, advisers and research assistants rose from 3 per cent to 14 per cent during the same period.[29] All the parties tinker with the rules to improve selection processes. While the Labour Party have improved their gender balance significantly, they are perceived to be losing working-class candidates. Despite intentions towards the opposite, according to Peter Watt, former General Secretary of the Labour Party, when Labour changed the rules again in 2013 they may have made it harder for working-class candidates. Candidates have to campaign for longer and give up work earlier, which he argues is only good for professional politicians and rich people.[30] One candidate complained that it was so torturously complicated that only someone with a huge tolerance for bureaucracy would get past the first hurdle.

The candidates that get selected tend to be well connected and with extensive experience of party politics. The professionalization of politics is clear and it has

[27] Ibid., p. 17.

[28] Jeanette Ashe, Rosie Campbell, Sarah Childs and Elizabeth Evans, '"Stand by your man": women's political recruitment at the 2010 UK general election', *British Politics*, vol. 5, no. 4, 2010, pp. 455–80.

[29] Feargal McGuinness, *Social background of MPs* (House of Commons Library, SN/SG/1528, 2010), p. 6.

[30] http://labour-uncut.co.uk/2013/02/08/labours-new-way-of-selecting-parliamentary-candidates-makes-a-mockery-of-calls-for-more-working-class-mps/ [accessed 10 September 2014].

partly come about due to changes in the rules of selection over a longer period. New Labour shifted the power in selection processes from the activists to the leadership with the backing of mass membership and the media, which allowed them to purge the party of the left wing. However, this also contributed to a decline in working class MPs in Parliament. When the union Unite initiated a drive to recruit more members and encourage them to stand for Parliament, Peter Mandelson complained that working-class identity and union membership were being conflated and selections were controlled by a small cabal. Len McClusky, general secretary of Unite, countered that candidates funded by Lord Sainsbury gave an advantage to candidates on the right of the party.[31]

During by-elections parties are tempted to parachute famous people in, as they are more likely to get elected. Clement Freud, well-known partly thanks to appearances in dog food advertisements, was put forward by the then Liberal leader Jeremy Thorpe MP at a by-election in the Isle of Ely in 1973.[32] He did not have much time to make friends in the constituency, but the Chair of the local party thought that such a national figure deserved a good attendance at the selection meeting, so she invited the residents of a local old people's home. When one of them stood up and denounced the declining quality of the local council houses, Clement replied in his own deadpan lugubrious voice: 'Madam, if you vote for me, I will build you an old Council House.'[33] Mr Freud told plenty of jokes and was voted in.

Once selected by your party, or deciding to stand as an independent, elections require relentless intelligence-gathering and making connections. I witnessed this at a by-election in Eastleigh in 2013. The town was once known as 'beastly Eastleigh' after its MP, Stephen Milligan asphyxiated himself accidentally while performing a complex sex act.[34] Misfortunate struck again in early 2013, when the sitting MP, Chris Huhne admitted to swopping driving penalty points with his wife, Vicky Pryce. She told the papers for vengeance, furious at his betrayal with another woman, but, like her husband, was sent to jail. (Danny Alexander commented on MPs having affairs: 'I just don't know where people find the time.'[35]) When Mr Huhne resigned, a by-election was announced. For three weeks the nation's eyes turned to this Hampshire town to watch the Liberal Democrats and Conservatives battle it out on the doorsteps. Only two

[31] Len McCluskey, 2013, 'Mandelson's argument is about politics not procedure', 21 May 2013, http://www.unitetheunion.org/news/unitenewsdigest/mandelsonsargumentisaboutpoliticsnot-procedure/ [accessed 29 May 2013].

[32] Former MP and Lib Dem Chief Whip Lord Tyler told me this during an interview held on 20 November 2012.

[33] Bishop Alan Wilson, *Clement Freud: unusual achievements*, http://bishopalan.blogspot.co.uk/2009/04/clement-freuds-extraordinary.html [accessed 18 April 2013].

[34] http://labour-uncut.co.uk/2013/02/05/beastly-eastleigh/ [accessed 1 September 2014].

[35] Danny Alexander MP, ITV 1's *Agenda*, 11 February 2013.

years from a General Election, loss would be a disaster for either party but also for their leaders. Leaders only remain at the top of their parties as long as their colleagues view them as an electoral asset. So both of them poured staggering amounts of time and money into their campaigns.

I began my campaigning for Mike Thornton with the Lib Dems. I walked into their HQ lodged in a business park as one of a constant trickle of volunteers. A friendly activist immediately slapped a white sticker onto my lapel – I had to choose 'Driver', 'Clerical', 'Canvasser', 'Deliverer' – alongside another orange one saying 'I like Mike'. I asked how the mood was, given the unfortunate fall of the outgoing Lib Dem. She said that by-elections often have a sad beginning, usually someone's death, so they are used to an accelerated jump into positivity. Then I looked around the LD election factory. On the first floor I found virtually the whole party's media machine shipped from London to Eastleigh – working the phones, producing materials, connecting with journalists, party people and activists. They politely tore themselves away to answer a few questions, but these election pros were working flat out with scarcely a moment to grab a tea. Downstairs there were teams of people stuffing envelopes and writing addresses – hardly talking, they were so focused on getting through thousands of names.

The shop steward of this incredible industrial mission explained to me what was going on. They sent out calls for volunteers by emails, blogs and Twitter and hundreds were arriving from as far as Aberdeen to help. The point about sending them out to knock on doors is not to convert the voters – most activists don't have the skills to do that – but to find out voters' intentions and priorities and then convert the waverers with leaflets. Canvassing has become a form of intelligence-gathering through conversations and the LD operation is highly sophisticated. Some of this intelligence was done by phone and some by visiting people's homes. I joined a contingent of LD Black and Ethnic Minority Group members, mostly parliamentary candidates, and we were tutored at lightning speed by an amazing US election strategist who had been lent by Simon Hughes MP. He explained that each day they had slightly different questions to pose on the doorsteps. Today it was: (1) Do you plan to vote LD? If no, forget the other two – they don't need literature. If yes, then ask the next two: (2) Do you have a postal vote? Have you sent it? (3) Are you willing to help? If they say no to (1) then you record their intentions – not only which party they might vote for, but what mix of affiliation they may tend towards, so LD leaning Tory is a yellow Tory, for example. Once we returned our forms, then the Clerical workers would put them in the database. This would then allow them to produce lists, which would be handed to the Deliverers for putting leaflets through letterboxes. The media team had meantime produced specific leaflets, different versions for different communities and for voters with different intentions. The scale was matched by the grit. Up to 400 activists descended on Eastleigh during each day and every five seconds a LD activist phoned an elector. One of the LD councillors was in hospital for an operation to remove a cyst on Tuesday and was back out canvassing by Wednesday.

I wandered around the market with LD candidate Mike Thornton. The steady warmth and enthusiasm of this former tax specialist was obvious. When I asked whether I could follow him, his minder looked doubtful, but Mike said 'Oh why not?', so she relented. When he decided to stand, he had just taken up a new job a few weeks before with a financial company, who were displeased when he announced his news. He was screened not only by the local party, who insisted on a resident of the constituency, but by a specially formed central party 'Star Chamber'. Once through these gruelling processes, the party took over, calling for volunteers on the local LD site: http://www.eastleighlibdems.org.uk and sending their MPs to support the campaign. Back at the HQ I chatted to MPs and activists in a festival mood, while waiting for Mike to arrive for a rally with the Leader. They appeared in a shiny black car and were swept upstairs to chat. A young women stood on a platform of boxes and began to whip up an atmosphere. 'We are up to 1,000 calls in 90 mins, 320 volunteers through the door today, 1,500 for the week, distributed 70,000 leaflets, 5,000 phone calls, and knocked on 10,000 doors.' She thanked and thanked and thanked colleagues for their hard work and success. The core campaigners were working from 8 a.m. to midnight every day but somehow they drummed up an excited buzz. And then suddenly Deputy PM Nick Clegg and Mike Thornton appeared, looking pale and red respectively. They gave rousing speeches about LD achievements, surrounded by euphoric organizers in a tight gaggle, vital for galvanizing their support but also for giving the impression on Sky News that the campaign had momentum and huge numbers of people at the core. It ended suddenly and an MP told me he had rarely known such an election high. Such a mood is normally confined to party conferences or General Elections, so a by-election is an unusual opportunity to create some precious communitas among the troops.

During my second visit I canvassed with the Conservatives in Hedge End. I went to the Conservative Club, an impressive mansion with cornices and plush carpets, thronging with MPs on the day I visited, and met up with Sir George Young MP, the then Government Chief Whip. He introduced me to an especially active tweeting MP. 'Much of Twitter is so boring so I want to thank you for being entertaining and funny', I said. He replied with a big smile: 'Don't say that in front of the Chief Whip, we are supposed to be boring.' We were given our forms, leaflets and a map and set off with a woman MP. At the 2010 election she knocked on 20,000 doors and won because she took nothing for granted, especially as her predecessor came unstuck by the expenses scandal. George and the other MP handed me the canvassing printouts and whizzed from door to door at a cracking pace, far faster than the LD canvassers. The printouts had

names and addresses but less information than the Liberals about voter intentions in this constituency. They went to the door and asked: 'Will you be voting
next week?' 'Yes.' 'Would you mind telling me how you plan to vote?' If they
revealed which party, then I wrote in the code: O for out, C for Conservative, L
for Lib Dem, S for socialist (i.e. Labour), U for undecided, DV for don't vote, A
for against Conservative, and UKIP for the UK Independence Party. UKIP did
not have a letter because they are relatively new and had not made a significant
enough impression before Eastleigh.

If he had an opening, George's patter was: 'I hope you will consider voting
for the Conservative candidate. Maria Hutchings is a local girl, I have known her
for 4–5 years and she will be a marvellous MP.' Then, like many MPs, he would
glance at the house and garden and work out what they might be interested
in: children's toys, he would talk about education; posh cars, he would discuss
fuel price freeze; or an affluent house, he might talk about tax. A young man
from Conservative Central HQ joined us for a while, but the woman MP was
unimpressed as he held back from knocking on doors: 'like all these chaps from
CCHQ, they are all mouth and no trousers.' He probably could not be a politician
– if you fear strangers you are not going to make it. To some women voters she
recommended that they vote for the Conservative candidate, Maria Hutchings,
because more women were needed in Parliament. Sir George understandably
thought this might sound less convincing coming from him, although he agreed
with the sentiment.

All Tory MPs were asked to do three stints but some were skiing or shooting,
one Conservative MP told me, so they were short-staffed. The shortage of
activists in this area was partly why even Cabinet Ministers had to get knocking
on doors. All parties, including the Conservatives, are in a serious decline.
With a shortage of money and volunteers, winning elections has become hard
graft. We bumped into a Secretary of State, so I asked him why MPs and even
Cabinet Ministers were knocking on doors. He said that the local party needs
the resources and it is important that the voters don't think you are taking them
for granted. I wondered whether their presence was also partly to win support
from colleagues in the party. Whether seen by fellow activists or photographed
by the media, perhaps when MPs, Ministers and even the PM are seen backing
the party, this supremely egalitarian business of electioneering is a rare opportunity to engender some party spirit and loyalty – some communitas, again (see
above).

Back at the Hedge End Conservative Club we had a drink and met Maria
Hutchings. The long days of campaigning, media attacks and lack of sleep had
left her exhausted. The sins of the Lib Dems had particular drama – Chris Huhne
being prosecuted and then Lord Rennard was accused of sexual harassment
only days before the Count – but the stories about the Conservatives were
embarrassing, too, in a smaller way. Maria was criticized for saying that one

of her children was too bright to go to a state school.[36] Large numbers of Conservative MPs posted identical negative tweets – saying: 'The Lib Dem Eastleigh campaign in turmoil as Party's candidate admitted he "voted for" 5,000 new houses on green spaces' – presumably from their media machine, which looked clumsy. And Conservative Ministers were reported to be encouraging their canvassers to remind Eastleigh residents that Chris Huhne was a liar, according to the unsympathetic *Guardian*.[37]

As is often the case with by-elections, the shortlist was drawn up by Labour's National Executive Committee rather than the local party. They knew that they were going to lose, so they picked a candidate who would at least get them some good press attention. It didn't go quite to plan. John O'Farrell was writing as usual in the London Library thinking that February looked a bit quiet when out of the blue a colleague suggested he stand. He braced himself for the strangeness of being a candidate: 'You can't just be your normal everyday self in democratic politics. You have to put on clothes you wouldn't normally wear – metaphorically and literally.'[38] Once selected, he announced on Twitter that he was off to the pub, but confessed the next morning that he had broken his first promise: the by-election machine did not allow him. By 14 February he feared he had turned into a political robot; his Valentines card to his wife read: 'Vote Labour in #Eastleigh for a One Nation alternative.'

John O'Farrell (mrjohnofarrell)

17/02/2013 15:09

Voter: 'I'll vote for you if you pay for a boob job.' Me: 'Not sure if that is an actual spending commitment, we'll look at economy in 2015.'

John O'Farrell is an author and comedy scriptwriter and was a candidate for Parliament in Eastleigh

---

Although he told the shortlisting panel that the only embarrassing thing in his past was that he once wrote for Hale and Pace, the *Mail* jumped on his

---

[36] Jason Beattie, '"You'll never be a surgeon if you go to a state school": Tory by-election candidate rubbishes education system', *Daily Mirror*, 16 February 2013, http://www.mirror.co.uk/news/uk-news/eastleigh-by-election-conservative-candidate-maria-1712534 [accessed 12 April 2013].

[37] http://www.theguardian.com/politics/2013/feb/22/eastleigh-byelection-tories-chris-huhne [accessed 22 February 2013].

[38] John O'Farrell, 'Why I'm standing for Labour in the Eastleigh byelection', *Guardian*, 13 February 2013, http://www.guardian.co.uk/commentisfree/2013/feb/13/john-ofarrell-why-standing-eastleigh-labour [accessed 12 April 2013].

supposed terrorist sympathies.[39] In a satirical book he mocked himself for fantasizing about Mrs Thatcher's death in 1984 despite his pacifist and anti-IRA convictions. The *Mail* shamelessly sought a quote from Lord Tebbit, whose wife was injured by the IRA in the Brighton bomb, who called him an incontinently voiced moral reprobate. In another article the title asks: 'Is Ed's pal the sickest man in politics?', clearly a ruse to discredit the leader as well as eat away at their votes in the by-election.[40] John O'Farrell tweeted: 'So the *Mail* have gone for me on something I already volunteered about myself, which I said in 1984, and acknowledged was wrong as I said it.' The Tory backbenchers picked it up in PMQs. O'Farrell was clearly shocked by the whole experience and decided never to stand again.

Graham Linehan (Glinner)

<u>27/02/2013 15:27</u>

Pathetic PMQ attacks on John O'Farrell perfectly illustrate how UK politics squeezes out anyone interesting so that only nonentities remain.

Graham Lineham is a television comedy writer and director

Canvassing with Labour was a relaxed affair because they knew they were going to lose. On discussing the by-election with a Labour peer, he claimed that they did not want to do too well – in fact, tactical anti-Tory voting meant that some Labour canvassers encouraged people to vote Liberal Democrat. I travelled down on the train with my own MP, Andy Slaughter and a colleague of his, a woman Labour MP. I asked them why MPs canvassed so much at by-elections. They said it was partly shortage of activists in Eastleigh, partly whips asserting their authority for the sake of it, and partly tradition. The Labour HQ was a small Victorian red-brick house with worn carpets and peeling paint. I was greeted by elderly men with Yorkshire accents and young women with brightly dyed hair offering tea. John O'Farrell appeared calm and smiley, joking with his MP minder about how well the campaign was going. I badgered Andy and his colleague to canvass rather than deliver literature, but the organizers insisted that they

---

[39] Simon Walters, 'Fury over "moral reprobate" Labour candidate who wrote of disappointment that Mrs Thatcher didn't die in the Brighton bomb', *Daily Mail*, 17 February 2013, http://www.dailymail.co.uk/news/article-2279886/My-disappointment-Mrs-Thatcher-didnt-die-Brighton-bomb--Labours-Eastleigh-candidate.html [accessed 12 April 2013].
[40] Andrew Pierce, 'Is Ed's pal the sickest man in politics', *Daily Mail*, 22 February 2013, http://www.dailymail.co.uk/debate/article-2283026/Is-Eds-pal-sickest-man-politics.html?ito=feeds-newsxml [accessed 12 April 2013].

needed to get rid of 40,000 leaflets so there wasn't time to knock on doors. As we tramped the streets of Eastleigh – getting lost, cold and footsore – they told me amusing but unrepeatable stories about their time in government, past whips and leaders. We delivered a few hundred leaflets and went home.

At a hustings, prefaced by some happy clappy hymns with local Christians on guitar and young people in the audience waving their arms in the air, the candidates of the three large parties were joined by three others: Gavin Marsh, speaking for the Trade Union and Socialist candidate, sounding indignant and solemn; Danny Stupple, championing democracy and marriage as an independent with sunny enthusiasm; Diane James (UKIP), an austere version of TV game show host Anne Robinson in a sober blue suit, protesting about the number of immigrants and the power of the EU. UKIP had a small HQ shopfront near the market with posters at eye level warning the voters that 250,000 Romanians and Bulgarians were likely to flood the country within five years. Their leaflet claimed that the EU will allow 29 million to come to the UK, an assertion that the campaign co-ordinator later justified on grounds of attracting attention.[41] They had been steadily pinching votes from LD, Conservative and Labour all week.

Mark D'Arcy (DArcyTiP)

<u>12/03/2013 11:20</u>

Eastleigh tale –
Voter: I'm UKIP, others all the same.
MP Canvasser: Fair point – all parties have dismantled ideology.
Voter: Y'what?

Mark D'Arcy is a BBC Parliamentary correspondent

On the day of the election I canvassed one last time with Simon Hughes. He took me knocking people up and gave me a crash course on election day canvassing. I was the Driver. You must take care not to wake babies, or in rural areas chickens, when you knock on doors. When they answer that they have already voted it is essential to send the information back to HQ so that they can be taken off the lists; then they will not be pestered again. In Eastleigh the LD did four sweeps on election day of the whole constituency, each time minus people who had voted as they were struck off the printouts. Meanwhile, activists

---

[41] Lisa Duffy, interviewed by journalist John Harris, in 'The Battle for Britain', *Guardian Weekend*, 18 May 2013, p. 28.

from around the country were phoning LD voters to encourage them to go to the polling booths.

I asked the Deputy Leader of the Liberal Democrats, Simon Hughes MP why other MPs, especially high-profile ones, canvass. Mainly to keep the activists going, he said, but also to get results. And the response he received on the doorstep would have been beyond belief if I hadn't seen it for myself. When voters answered the door, he fixed them with an intense gaze and the hint of a smile and said in an intimate, confiding way: 'I will be the last person to pester you tonight.' They would almost instantly tell him what they were thinking about the election, how they voted and why. As he advised Mike Thornton, the candidate, you should take care not to talk too much. You should take care with direct questions: 'Do you have children?' would be tactless to a childless couple desperate for offspring; 'How do your parents find the health services?' would upset those whose parents were dead. You should use an indirect approach by asking about local schools or the generation above. One man voted for the Conservatives, so he gently teased him and slapped him on the side of the arm quite hard. But he did not seem to mind; he looked tickled pink. While others had doors slammed in their face, or at the least complaints about the vast quantities of campaign literature from all parties, Simon Hughes connected with total strangers within 5–10 seconds. At one door he met a Labour voter: 'I'm a Labour girl, have been all my life. Normally I vote LD tactically but this time I couldn't bring myself to. Because of the coalition.'

'Do you mind me asking how you did vote?' Simon added.

'You won't believe me.'

'Try me.'

'Peace party.'

'Ohhhhh. You obviously know that is a vote for the Tory party.'

'I know, I know … I agonized.'

'At the next election will you consider voting for Mike?'

'Yes, to be honest if you had been here 30 minutes ago I might have voted for him. I will.'

We finished up back in the LD factory-like HQ. By now I was feeling an old hand at elections but rather a rat for helping three parties. I joined what was like a huge extended liberal family who had been helping each other to move house for three weeks solid – tired, bonded and relieved it was nearly over. With ten minutes to go before the polls closed, LD President Tim Farron was still phoning like crazy. They printed off the residents within five minutes' walk of polling booths and checked that they had voted. Tim Farron did it till the last minute so the other phone-canvassers kept going, he told me later, because possibly it was another few votes in the bag. At last the clock struck ten. Simon the Showman gave a rousing speech of thanks to the organizers and we rushed for the train station so that he could get up to London in time to be on the BBC election special.

At the Count – in a soulless leisure centre – the Returning Officer gave me permission to observe proceedings. The room had lines of trestle tables with people counting votes. Each party's 'election agents' double up as scrutineers, making sure that there were no mistakes being made, but also surreptitiously counting how many votes their party had received in a sample. The LDs crunched the sample vote in a laptop and came up with the result well before 1 a.m. I was talking to one of their media apparatchiks just as the news began to circulate via text around the LD Party. Mike was first and, to the surprise of almost everyone, UKIP were second. They ran around preparing the MPs, and the candidate, to be ready to talk to the press. They tried not to look euphoric. One told me the order but got the margin out by a thousand votes hours before the result was announced.

While we waited for the official result, with the delicious sensation of being ahead of the nation, I talked to Danny Stupple, the independent candidate. He said that the whole experience had made him more convinced that the party machines were undemocratic. He was chilled by the party machines sweeping up Mike Thornton and Maria Hutchings, who he knows well – telling them what to say, where to go, how to look. He thinks MPs should follow their own conscience and our democratic system needs to go back to a time pre-party. 'But then how would government and opposition work?' I asked, but he got distracted talking about what he saw as the foolishness of gay marriage.

As those party machines ran around preparing their MPs and candidates for the result, telling them what to say and how to look, I wandered away from the ordinary farm animals to mingle with the exotic and wild fringe candidates. I went up to one and asked what his policies were. He gave me a furious look and, with several colleagues looking on, he said: 'We are anti-racialist, anti-Scottish people voting on English laws, anti-European federalism, and pro-English people governing themselves.'

'What do you think about Scottish independence?'

'They can do what they like.'

'What do you think about immigration?'

'We are against mass immigration. But we are not racialist. Our opponents claim we are. Especially the Defence against Nazism League, playing their dirty tricks.'

'So you are different from, say, the English Defence League.'

'Yes! They are anti-Muslim. We have nothing against Muslims.'

'Ah, because someone told me they thought you were similar.'

'Well that might explain why we got so few votes. Looking at the count it appears that we did not get many. But if our opponents have been spreading rumours that we are the English Defence League, that explains it. The people of Eastleigh have been misled.'

'Well, it was only one person here, I don't know about the people of Eastleigh.'

He looked still more furious so I evaporated.

The Monster Raving Loony William Hill Party's Leader, Alan Hope, was a heart-warming contrast. He told me that he did not have any members in Eastleigh a month earlier so he went to the pub and got talking to people. By the end of the evening he had four members, one of whom was his new agent for the by-election. His deputy invited me to their AGM, due to be held in a pub in September, and encouraged me to come with ideas for the manifesto. Before I could find the other wild cards, including the Elvis Loves Pets Party who plan to prosecute Damien Hirst for killing butterflies, the party machines sprang back into action. Everyone knew what had to be done. The TV needed some drama, so the political parties arranged some. First came a small gaggle of Liberal Democrats waving orange 'I like Mike' banners, cheering as loudly as their exhausted beings could muster and crowding around the candidate as tightly as possible. The cameras descended on them, urgent and close up, giving the impression of a massive and spontaneous crowd. The spectators looked on with wry amusement at this tiny huddle of showy supporters providing some entertainment for the cameras, starved as they were of action and relying on talking heads in studios with nothing new to say. The others followed with their own band of supporters at five-minute intervals. Diane James for UKIP came next with supporters in purple, looking equally buoyant and noisy. A gap and then John O'Farrell breezed in with an air of weary sophistication and his Labour crew in long dark coats and red badges looking like an unionized mafia. Finally Maria Hutchings, brave but close to collapse, appeared surrounded by anxiety dressed in blue.

When the waiting was finally over, the journalists, agents and supporters crowded around the platform. Their speeches were true to form and given in the order of numbers of votes won: Mike's was solid, Diane was feisty, John was amusing and Maria was distressing. Howling Laud Hope gave a rendition of the jazzy *Mack the Knife*. But it was the 'anti-racialist' who surprised me by saying that it had come to his attention that the people of Eastleigh had muddled him up with the English Defence League, implying that his opponents had engineered this misunderstanding. 'Oh God', I thought, 'so much for political neutrality. I just gave a bit of spin to a political party that received fewer votes than "Elvis Loves Pets".' I left the Count depressed at the thought that this may be my only impact on British politics, but cheered by a revelation. Elections draw people in not just because they are the most participatory way to choose our representatives – conferring greater democratic legitimacy than any other method – but also because they are intoxicating, if you like that kind of thing. Democratic politics is like sport with ideas, I remembered an MP saying, and the analogy finally made sense to me. Some get so addicted they do it continually

– Kelvin Hopkins MP has canvassed on the doorstep at least once a week for 50 years. Then MPs get hooked on increasing their majorities and, like fishing fanatics, can't resist telling you the size of their latest triumph. It is not just the prospect of power that draws you in, I decided, it is winning people to your side that becomes addictive. Canvassing for elections entails a strange mix of order and disorder: the mechanical work of intelligence-gathering and counting, on the one hand; and theatrical performance and engaging people's attention in conversation or through cameras and mediators, on the other.

If you have lost, you have to rethink. Former MP Matthew Parris told Tory MPs at a Conservative Party meeting 'Don't forget that 95–96 per cent of people don't think about politics most of the time. They wake up a few weeks before election and then they consider which party has (a) a plan, (b) a good leader with the party united behind him, (c) the plan looks like it is working, and, very much last, (d) whether he/she is a good MP.' Bad press for a good MP can ruin a good party campaign, so the devil of negative campaigning tempts some. One Labour Party activist told me he couldn't resist pointing out to a journalist that if he took a photo of a candidate in his swimming trunks from a particular angle then it would read 'peedo'. The swimmer lost at the election. One of the most famous mud-slinging campaigns took place in Bermondsey in 1983. A Lib Dem leaflet described the election as a straight choice (misreported as '*the* straight choice').[42] Lib Dem canvassers walked around with badges saying: 'I've been kissed by x' (that is, the gay Labour candidate) and an anonymous leaflet asked: 'Which Queen Will You Vote For?', even supplying Mr x's phone number and address. Paul Flynn, too, reports skulduggery in Newport West. On the day of voting in 1987 the Liberals circulated a leaflet door to door: 'We the Liberals in Newport West believe in campaigning on the issues not the personalities. That is why we have not published the information given to us anonymously by the Conservative Party, that if published, would prove that the Labour candidate, Mr Flynn, is not fit to be an MP.'[43] It turned out that the information was the scandalous news that he had once been fined because his MOT certificate was out of date. Much more effective to leave it mysterious. The Eastleigh campaign witnessed the Tories playing on the fact that Chris Huhne had lied[44] and resorting to veiled accusations that Lib Dems are generally untrustworthy.

---

[42] For example, Andrew Grice, 'The homophobic campaign that helped win Bermondsey', *Independent*, 27 January 2006, http://www.independent.co.uk/news/uk/politics/the-homophobic-campaign-that-helped-win-bermondsey-524703.html [accessed 2 May 2013].

[43] Paul Flynn MP, *The Unusual Suspect* (London: Biteback Publishing, 2010).

[44] According to the *Guardian*, Iain Duncan Smith MP encouraged canvassers to remind voters that the outgoing Lib Dem was a liar, http://www.guardian.co.uk/politics/2013/feb/22/eastleigh-byelection-tories-chris-huhne?utm_source=twitterfeed&utm_medium=twitter [accessed 7 May 2013].

On the other hand, some MPs argue vehemently against negative tactics. When Jesse Norman MP avoided personal attacks, despite negative campaigning by his Lib Dem opponent in 2010, he gained in the long run. Three prominent local Lib Dems declared their support for him in the local newspaper. Aside from casting yourself in the role of villain, you inevitably antagonize a large section of your electorate if you slag off the other parties or candidates, Jesse Norman points out.[45]

The main three political parties have the organization, information and funding required to win a serious number of seats. But voter behaviour is changing. Gone are the days when people have reliable allegiances to parties; they consume politics, and swap loyalties in the flash of an eye, rather than belong to one tribe or another for decades, life or even generations. The local elections in May 2013 and May 2014 witnessed a huge increase for UKIP, possibly snatching some of the protest vote from the Lib Dems, but also attracting an anti-political vote. When canvassing in Eastleigh, a surprising number said to the candidates that they were sick of all the parties: 'You are all the same.' They did not necessarily mean in terms of ideology but in the sense that they are lying and venal politicians. The only route for them, as Robert Halfon MP suggests, is to recognize that 'the pure science of political campaigning will only have a limited degree of success – unless it is buttressed by a deep understanding of the most important ingredient – the building up of human relationships ... Human relationships, and a level of emotional intelligence, are a prerequisite to ensuring that voters don't see you as just another politician.'[46] Nicola Blackwood MP stole a seat from LDs by finding out the intentions and concerns of tens of thousands of voters and sending out a million pieces of literature. So here are the ingredients of modern electioneering: nurturing relationships, gathering intelligence and making promises that respond to demands in your constituency.

---

[45] Jesse Norman MP (ed.), *Lessons from the Marginals* (ConservativeHome, 2012), p. 31, http://conservativehome.blogs.com/files/4121-lesson-from-the-marginals.pdf [accessed 23 May 2013].
[46] Robert Halfon MP, in Norman, *Lessons from the Marginals*, 2012, pp. 6, 7.

If you have lost, then you have to keep trying. Betty Boothroyd is not unique in standing for 17 years in unwinnable seats before she finally got in. If you have won the election, and your hangover has worn off, then you walk into the Palace of Westminster and begin your career as an MP. You have no office, no equipment and no staff. You collect your mail and they hand you thousands of letters from constituents. So what on earth do you do next?

First days in Westminster

MPs arrive in in the Palace with their party membership, a few ideas about how to change the world and huge ambition. It is a position shot through with contradictions. The history and ambience of the Palace inspire awe in some new MPs, but confusion in others. After the giddy whirl and sleep deprivation of the election, the new MP's mood will swing between bewilderment and euphoria. Laura Moffatt MP arrived in Westminster and her eyes filled with tears.[47] For Tony Blair, becoming an MP was like an 'arrival at a new and higher level of existence'.[48] Others were horrified by the public school or Oxford college appearance and the long-standing MPs strutting around with an air of born to rule. But then again, emotion is wrapped up with whether or not your party has won; in 1992 newly elected Tessa Jowell MP was walking on air for two weeks before the bubble burst and the defeat of her party sunk in.[49]

MPs have to grapple with more diverse roles, rules, audiences and pressures than they can possibly have imagined.[28] They need to learn to deal with a hostile media, public loathing, separation from their families and political disappointments. In the old days you did not receive much guidance, particularly if you arrived in a by-election. When Austin Mitchell MP won the Great Grimsby by-election in 1977 no one told him what to do; he just followed the herd. He moved his stuff into an office in the Palace – a tiny room – but it turned out to belong to Robert Kilroy-Silk, who was furious and threw his things on the floor. So he wandered about the Norman Shaw Building until he found an empty office, where he stayed for years. Sir Malcolm Rifkind became an MP in 1974 and he was shown the cloakroom and loos and told to get on with it. He left the Commons for a spell and when he returned in 2005, he encountered the novelty of 'induction' – he was offered copious bumph, courses and far more staff. By 2010 MPs could attend courses on almost any aspect of their work in Parliament.

When they first arrive, new MPs receive a mailbag with an avalanche of perhaps 5,000 letters, no office, no staff, and little idea about how to do the job

[47] McDougall, *Westminster Women*, p. 38.
[48] Tony Blair, *A Journey* (London: Hutchinson, 2010) p. 35.
[49] McDougall, *Westminster Women*, p. 38-9.

unless you have already worked for an MP. The letters plead for help to deal with desperate crises faced by constituents – they can't be ignored because these are the very people who will decide whether or not they stay in their job. Most MPs start answering the letters sitting at a public table in Portcullis House (a parliamentary building close to the Palace) or on a bench in St James's Park, until they are allocated an office and have time to recruit some staff. The allocation of offices by the whips is the most contentious and secretive process in Parliament, revealing as it does where MPs are within the party hierarchy. Some MPs assume that loyal election campaign-workers will make effective caseworkers dealing with constituents' problems or policy advisers/researchers. A few might, but most do not, so some MPs find themselves embroiled in a HR nightmare. The adroit employ staff who know their way around Westminster or find out fast how to get advice from the network of other MPs' staff.[50]

Increasingly, new MPs receive induction courses and guidance from House officials. The Members' Centre staff could answer any query thrown at them by MPs.[51] Questions have included:

1 'Can I bring a horse through carriage gates?' (Answer: yes)

2 'Did the Race Relations Act come about because of Enoch Powell's speech about rivers of blood?' (Answer: no)

3 'Will you sew up my skirt, I have a committee meeting in 5 mins?' (Answer: no, but you can borrow my sewing kit)

For procedural advice, Clerks are holders of the sacred knowledge of rules and privilege. They are scrupulous in remaining politically impartial when giving advice. This means understanding the motivation of whoever is asking the question at that moment, but being equally prepared to do so for the next MP who approaches. So when an MP seeks guidance a Clerk will advise about how to gain advantage, but if another from the opposing side comes two minutes later to ask about how to get the better of opponents in the same debate, then the Clerk will be just as ready to sabotage his own previous advice. They don't act as if they have favourites. Although Clerks react to individuals – thinking 'Oh God, it's him or her' or 'What a pleasure to deal with x' – they are uninfluenced by the MP's party membership.

MPs meet clerkly objections if they try to fix the problem themselves in a clumsy way but get useful advice if they ask the questions intelligently. If an MP asks: 'Can I nationalize x industry by doing this and that?', some Clerks

---

[50] MPs' staff were once chronically isolated and left to their own devices, but support is improving, with parliamentary services providing more advice alongside various websites (www. w4mp.org), a union, a staff association and a guide http://viewer.zmags.com/publication/0ce1 5b66#/0ce15b66/1 [accessed 20 May 2013].

[51] This Centre was transformed into a workspace for MPs in 2014.

(and especially those they do not know well) will reply: 'This won't work for this reason and that will run into various obstacles' and stop there. If an MP asks them an open question: 'How can I nationalize x industry?', then any Clerk would be more likely to discuss the full range of possible procedural strategies and processes. When MPs and Clerks establish a strong rapport – for example, on Select Committees – then they may go even further. In one instance a Clerk was drafting a Select Committee's report on behalf of the Chair, and therefore the committee, as usual. In a particularly contentious passage he summarized the MP's views and then added a paragraph that went 100 per cent further in criticism of a particular national practice. He suggested to the Chair that he could use this over-the-top paragraph as a bargaining chip, suggesting to those on the committee that were likely to object that he could remove this if the earlier bit of the passage was kept intact. It worked a treat. They key thing to get from officials in those first weeks is not a whistle-stop tour of all procedure, which takes years to learn, but knowledge about where and how to get advice: to the Table Office for questions, to the Public Bill Office with a query about bills, and so on. Even more importantly, smart MPs establish rapport and respect among the Clerks.

Some MPs realize that Clerks can be their greatest asset; others fail to appreciate the nature of the Clerk–MP relationship and don't ask for advice at all. Those that do pop into the Table Office near the back of the Chamber, where a small team of these brainy procedural-priests are on hand to advise about the best tactics for what they wish to achieve. There is only one comfortable chair. Current legend has it that the chair was put there because Tam Dalyell MP (former Father of the House) spent so much time getting advice to hone his questions about the sinking of the *Belgrano* during the Falklands War, so that he could in turn sink Mrs Thatcher, that they thought it only polite to provide him with somewhere to sit. Sir Robert (Clerk of the House during my time there) clarifies that he personally acquired admiralty charts of the seas around the Falklands for Mr Dalyell, but adds that the chair predates him.

While Clerks advise on procedure, old hand MPs tend to give tips on performing and coping. Most advice relates to speaking: begin speeches by thanking everyone and, if you are a woman, make light remarks and flirt with your audience but don't make jokes. They recommend to new MPs to find their own authentic tone when speaking in the Chamber – whether it is aggressive and partisan or emollient and thoughful, to sound convincing and inspire respect. They suggest mentioning the constituency at least once in every speech/question and specializing on a few topics to sound knowledgeable. Others counsel them to keep Sundays free to avoid angry partners, divorce and troubled children.

I accompanied new MP Mike Thornton during his induction to Westminster. A long-standing Lib Dem MP took us on a tour, taking in the Chamber to show

Mike where to put his green card to reserve a seat, which only remains yours if you are there in time for prayers at the beginning of the day, though if you are sitting on a Select Committee then you can use a pink card and defer your entrance. The tour guide Lib Dem tried this, saying to a lurking doorkeeper: 'Defence Select Committee', but the Doorkeeper retorted: 'No, Sir, it's not sitting today.' In the voting lobbies behind the Speaker's Chair I asked about the etiquette for nobbling Ministers during a vote. 'There is no etiquette, but yes, this is when you do it. That is why I don't like electronic voting.' He said his technique is to write a letter to the Minister, sending a copy to the department and keeping another in his pocket ready to hand over when he next bumps into him in the division lobby. This worked recently with Secretary of State Eric Pickles MP. He read the letter in the car on his way to his next appointment and took action the same day.

Labour MPs told me that when their lot were in government they would put requests to Ministers on post-it notes and stick them on his or her lapel. All-night sessions were sometimes like a Greek wedding, with all Ministers' jackets fluttering with yellow messages, except David Blunkett, whose incredible memory needed no jogging. Until recently, division lobbies were strictly forbidden to anyone other than MPs or Clerks, which presents problems if you have a small baby in tow. Jenny Willott MP told me she used to hand her three-month-old baby to any MP who would take him before going in to vote; Sir Alan Beith and Harriet Harman were always happy to hold him. Another used to smuggle hers under her coat. However, in July 2014 the son of Jo Swinson and Duncan Hames, both MPs, made history by being the first baby into the division lobby.

Whips do not like new MPs being given advice by rebels. In 1997 Jeremy Corbyn MP had a cup of tea with a new Labour MP. When she got up, a whip approached her and said: 'If you're seen talking to him again, you're finished.'[52] Paul Flynn's book *How to be an MP*, one of the most frequently borrowed books in the House of Commons Library, encourages backbenchers to resist the whips and follow the Commons daily prayer: 'May they never lead the nation wrongly through love of power, desire to please, or unworthy ideals, but laying aside all private interests and prejudices keep in mind their responsibility to seek to improve the condition of all mankind.'[53]

The whips counter the implication that MPs might decide ideals for themselves with guidance about party rules and parliamentary procedures, defining correct behaviour in the Chamber – how to ask a question or intervene – but also how to be a team player and follow the instructions of the whips, or at least inform them about your plans. Since whipping is about intelligence-gathering, you must let the whips know your voting intentions. They point out that if asking a

---

[52] Interviewed by Emma Crewe, 17 May 2012.
[53] Paul Flynn, *How to be an MP* (London: Biteback Publishing, 2012), p. 252.

question of a Minister on your own side, a backbencher should warn them in advance. Whips also help you when you get into trouble. One new MP was so overwhelmed after winning a by-election that he seemed to stop functioning. After two months doorkeepers told his whips that the mail was piling up and they spent two days getting his correspondence into order. Whips discourage new MPs from hogging the limelight – getting into the national media, for example – as Ministers need it to give prominence to their party agenda. If you do find yourself unavoidably interviewed by some national journalist, then you back everything your party and leaders do. A backbencher's remit is always to get into the local paper as often as possible, plugging the party's achievements and the idiocy, incompetence and turpitude of the other side.

New MPs have also to navigate their way through various initiation rites. The oath, so dignified and individual in the House of Lords, is a scramble that MPs mutter and exit swiftly. Flynn points out that getting to the front of the queue is vital as it may ensure that decades later you are ahead of the rest in the race to be Father/Mother of the House. Ted Heath MP had to wait five extra years because he took the oath just over an hour after Bernard Braine MP.[54] The most nerve-wracking rite is the maiden speech; it makes even the most hardened public performer wobbly. In this sense the Commons hasn't changed. After the writer Hilaire Belloc MP gave his, he was sick, literally.[55] Unlike normal speeches, no one interrupts, and they always make pleasant comments of welcome after-wards, and just as one new MP told me how the kindness of other MPs made it difficult to criticize the institution in 2010, so too Aneurin Bevan MP did not care for politesse. After a forceful speech about the grievances of constituents he was horrified to hear insincere murmurs of approval in the subsequent speeches: 'The new Member crawls out of the House with feelings of deep relief at having got it over, mingled with a paralysing sense of frustration. The stone he thought he had thrown turned out to be a sponge.'[56]

While the institution has remained the same in certain ways over decades, learning the ropes is a different experience for different MPs. Men from rule-bound, old-fashioned and male-dominated institutions, such as boys' public schools or trade unions, are more likely to revel in joining the Commons. Unfazed by initiation rites, raucous talk and the intense competition, most of them thrive. MPs that are new to both politics and to hierarchical rule-bound institutions are more likely to struggle. One Conservative woman in the 2010 intake decided she had better fraternize. She went into the Smoking Room (where MPs are no longer allowed to smoke) and sat with a group of men of about her age. They were talking about what they shot during their holidays. Not

[54] Flynn, *The Unusual Suspect*, p. 3.
[55] Christopher Silvester (ed.), *Pimlico Companion to Parliament* (London: Pimlico, 1997), p. 40.
[56] Aneurin Bevan, *In Place of Fear* (London: Simon and Schuster, 1952), p. 27.

only had she never shot anything in her life, but these colleagues reminded her of inmates of a 1950s boarding school. Later she sat at a table where colleagues were discussing the intimate details of a Minister's sex life. It made her uncomfortable and seemed like another throwback. If she said she was uneasy, they would say they were only joking. But she added: 'If you don't take part in the social networks, then you don't get included in the policy discussions.'[57]

In the 2010 intake Conservative women had a rougher time from their own side than the Labour women did from theirs. To find such systematic bullying of women on the Labour benches you have to go back to pre-1997, when they arrived in larger numbers for the first time. Former MP Barbara Follett gives examples: 'Even on our side, the men would stick their hands out, so you'd sit on them. It was like stepping back in time.'[58] Of course, there are exceptions. Kate Hoey MP (Labour) loved joining the Commons. She was the 39th woman in 1989; she wore bright clothes and people paid special attention to women in those days. A Conservative woman who worked for the public sector loved it when she arrived in 2005 – she was warmly welcomed by two Labour stalwarts who wanted to shake the hand of the MP who had rid the Commons of her Lib Dem predecessor. And some recently arrived Conservative women have faced rougher treatment in other organizations – one told me the Commons wasn't nearly as bad as the financial company she joined 20 years ago, whose staff inducted her by handing her three porn videos. Furthermore, sexist abuse in the Commons was more overt for all women some years ago. Teresa Gorman related a conversation from her early years when sandwiched between two men in the Chamber. They complained she was planning to talk against her party and they shouldn't have let women in, since their place is in the home:

Male MP: 'Yes, flat on her back.'

Other male MP: 'Do you think Teresa would be any good on her back? I wonder what kind of knickers she wears.'

Teresa: 'Why don't you go somewhere else and find someone else to talk dirty to if you feel like that?'

Male MP: 'I thought you'd be enjoying it. I thought that was what you liked about this place. Plenty of men.'[59]

It is difficult to imagine such a conversation in the present, but bullying of women remains a feature of the Commons, with opponents gesturing about women's breasts or calling out 'melons', especially when they are new and apparently

---

[57] Interviewed by Emma Crewe, 14 November 2012.
[58] As quoted by Rachel Cooke, 'Oh Babe, just look at us now', *Observer*, 22 June 2007, http://www.guardian.co.uk/politics/2007/apr/22/women.labour1 [accessed 20 May 2013].
[59] As quoted by McDougall, *Westminster Women*, p. 50.

need to be put in their place.[60] The inevitable antagonism and competition between MPs can take ugly chauvinistic forms.

Public-school men do not always feel comfortable in the House. One former Labour MP I spoke to went to a public school and cut his teeth on unusually tough local politics, but hated the shift from being a big fish to a small one. He was a quivering jelly every time he tried to speak in the Chamber. He joined a clique or two, but made few friends. He could not make his way and retreated into constituency casework. Conversely, another former MP, Jack Weatherill told me that when he entered Parliament he was in the first wave of 'non-gentlemen', as called them, to join Conservative benches in 1964. He was so frightened he spent his first day mostly hiding in an office. When he summoned the courage to venture to the loo, he heard one Conservative MPs say loudly to another: 'D'you know they've even got my tailor here now.'[61] But he grew to love it.

Paul Goodman (PaulGoodmanCH)

21/10/2012 10:41

@Mike Fabricant That's the Commons, though, isn't it? There was one colleague with whom in ten years I exchanged … not a single word.

Paul Goodman is Executive Editor of *ConservativeHome* and a former Conservative MP (2001–10)

The majority try to acclimatize. Sitting in the right place helps. In the Chamber you sit with your side – government on the right of the Speaker, opposition on the left (from the Speaker's viewpoint). To get noticed it makes sense to sit in view of the cameras, near those who are planning to make a speech. Sandwiching the speaker – doughnutting, it is called – has the added benefit of making the Chamber look busy. Finding their way around the restaurants and bars is vital for networking. The Despatch Box cafe in Portcullis House is popular for those who don't mind sitting among visitors. In the Tea Room MPs organize themselves by party: there are Conservative tables, Labour and Lib Dem. But there is also a Welsh Table, which doubles up as a haven for Labour miscreants. Jeremy Corbyn MP explained that he went to the Welsh Table one day and said: 'Is it OK to sit at the Welsh Table?' So a Welsh MP asked: 'Are you Welsh?'

'No. But I had a cycling holiday in Wales once as a boy and never recovered.'

'In that case it will be perfectly alright and you are welcome.'

---

[60] http://www.bbc.co.uk/news/uk-politics-25266177 [accessed 10 May 2014].
[61] Interviewed by Emma Crewe, 26 June 2000. I have heard this story about the tailor many times and variously attributed to different MPs, but Lord Weatherill chose to leave it mysterious.

There is another called the Peter Pike Table, for another Labour clique, in the Members' Tea Room. Other eating places have morphed over time: because most MPs no longer relish a three-course lunch, the Dining Room has become less popular; one restaurant has been replaced with a crèche; while Strangers has become a gay bar, according to at least one gay MP.

Most MPs aim to learn how to be effective in the Commons, for some it is merely a route to somewhere else. For example, Jonathan Edwards MP really wants a seat in the Welsh Assembly and is only cutting his teeth in the Commons. Along the way he will advocate for more powers for Wales and resist the temptation to become co-opted or assimilated:

> I don't want to get into the drinking culture of this place and I don't want to get comfortable. I don't want to settle down, I want to settle up. You can see how in this big grand building people get moulded to serve the institution. I never forget the people who have sent me here – I am here to serve them, not this place. When I speak in the Chamber I always begin with 'Diolch Mr Speaker' for two reasons. It breaks the rule. You can only speak in English or Norman French and not in a foreign language. I keep meaning to learn Norman French to see what happens. But anyway. The second reason is to remind myself why I am here. I am not here to be seduced by power; I am down here for the people who sent me. I do not want to become a creature of Westminster. So I don't speak much to those who are.[62]

The point of telling these stories about how MPs learn the navigation of Westminster, or fail to, is to create a picture of MPs' work as a process of endless social encounters. MPs learn to converse, write letters or talk to journalists and perform in a range of rituals – all vital for doing politics through the creation and maintenance of relationships. Shaming your opponents and making political friends, and winning support for yourself and your ideas, runs through the whole of an MP's career.

In the next chapter I will describe how politics involves continual realignment of your friends and foes – or, to be more precise, allies and adversaries – with far more cross-party working than in the past and than the public realize. In Chapter 3 the role of MPs in constituencies is the focus; winning support never stops, and giving advice to citizens has become part of this for almost all MPs, but tactics for embodying constituencies vary. The fourth chapter sees what happens to MPs when they join government. The work of whips relies most heavily on the business of making allies – reinforcing the credibility of the party leaders, and both gathering intelligence on and winning round their potential

---

[62] Interviewed by Emma Crewe, 11 October 2011.

waverers. But when MPs go into departments as Ministers, this is the area where they lose their ability to apply the social skills that underlie politics. A mix of neglect of social relationships and a cult of modernization combine to create havoc in the process of managing the state. Our rulers lose touch with those they rule. But in MPs' scrutiny roles (described in Chapter 5) they re-emerge again, whether in opposition parties, Select Committees, or – in a less healthy form – in relations with the media. In general, MPs have to win support from a huge range of audiences to stay in power or even to remain in their seat.

How do these different strands interconnect? These many interwoven roles encompassed in their job increase in intensity as every year goes by. Every MP is required at Westminster every week Parliament sits, unless ill or on government business, usually between Monday and Thursday. Nearly all visit their constituency weekly or fortnightly to soothe the local party, provide citizens' advice surgeries and get involved in local campaigns. They run offices of staff, usually one in the constituency and one in Westminster. At some point most sit on Select Committees, Public Bill Committees and All-Party Parliamentary Groups, getting into the scrutiny of law, policy or administration to hold government to account. Some get into government. These often-conflicting roles throw up daily contradictions – so that MPs don't merely win support in different directions, they inevitably please some and infuriate others at the same time. In the last chapter, I explain why and how most MPs cope and a few sink when faced with these endless pressures. In this book I paint a picture of the contradictory work of MPs, suggest why MPs are so changeable, and conclude that this change-ability is necessary for our politics to work.

Table 1.2 A Tuesday in the life of Richard Graham MP (Conservative, new in 2010)

09.30–10.00	Attending a debate in Westminster Hall about apprenticeships and engineering. He intervened.
10.00–11.00	Meeting with Lebanese Druze Progressive Socialist Party Walid Jumblatt. Walid had already seen Foreign Secretary William Hague and Richard had seen him in Lebanon.
11.00–12.00	Meeting of the APPG on Occupational Pensions – they heard from an actuary. He is Chair of this (and other APPGs as well).
12.40–14.00	By tube to Blackfriars for lunch with the Worshipful Company of Spectacle Makers about skills and training and whether their guild qualification could be recognized as apprenticeships. Gloucester, his constituency, has one of the largest specs factories in the country. (He missed a meeting of the Treasury Support Team, which he also sits on.)
14.30–15.30	Meeting with a constituent in the Navy and a group of naval cadets from *HMS Gloucester*. They had a tour and then he met them for a 40-minute Q&A session.
15.30–16.30	Met with a lobby group on social care issues to discuss disability allowance.
18.00–18.45	Attended a meeting with Nazir Ali (former Bishop) in the Grand Committee Room about marriage (the debate on the Same Sex Marriage Bill was coming soon).
18.45–19.30	Met a new peer, Lord Popat, to discuss the APPG for the Commonwealth (which Richard was creating).
19.30–20.00	Oliver Letwin's Open Policy Session. This takes place regularly and is usually attended by about 15 Conservative MPs. They raise policy issues – for example, on this evening, how to make swapping to a different bank or energy supplier easier.
20.00	Dinner with Sir Jo Hotung, a philanthropist, to discuss funding for good causes.
After dinner	Did his emails.
01.00	Home to his rented flat.

2
Allies and Adversaries

Challenging the assumptions and prejudices about MPs with a defence of politicians and party politics, this is also about the tribal identity that MPs arrive with, what parties stand for, and how MPs forge both friends and enemies across the House in their bid to make their mark as national representatives.

****

There is one important problem facing representative Parliamentary government in the whole of the world where it exists. It is being asked to solve a problem, which so far it has failed to solve: that is, how to reconcile Parliamentary popularity with sound economic planning. So far, nobody on either side of this House has succeeded and it is a problem which has to be solved if we are to meet the challenge that comes to us from other parts of the world and if we are to grout and to buttress the institutions of Parliamentary government in the affections of the population.[1] (Aneurin Bevan, 1959)

In defence of politicians

Politicians are loathed. If you cherish disdain towards our rulers, this chapter may be disturbing. I portray MPs as plucky individuals and almost like the rest of us. It is about why MPs take sides, how this is not morally different from all organizational politics, and how they cross over divisions almost as much as they maintain them.

That people are disenchanted with politics and politicians is also expressed in low voter turnout and surveys; only 24 per cent of the public thinks that the system of government is working well.[2] Angela Eagle encapsulated the public view of politicians in three phrases:

---

[1] Aneurin Bevan MP, *HC Debates*, 3 Nov 1959, col. 862.
[2] Hansard Society, *Audit of Political Engagement, The 2012 Report: Part One* (London: Hansard Society, 2012).

- You're all the same.
- Nothing ever changes.
- You're all in it for yourselves.[3]

Gloria de Piero MP bravely asked why politicians are hated on Twitter with the hashtag #whydoyouhateme. People told her that 'MPs are not like us and they do not understand voters' concerns', that the abusive shouting is ridiculous and that they are self-seeking, devious and arrogant. Blogger Guido Fawkes added: 'Politicians are despised for not being truthful, making promises they don't keep and their venality.'[4] The same character assassinations can be found in most exchanges with the public on the subject.

These accusations become less convincing the closer you study MPs. For a start, they are not homogeneous. It is true that Parliament is not representative of the population: certain groups are under-represented (women, ethnicity minorities, working class) while others are over-represented (men, Etonians, political researchers), and politicians can sound samey, spouting the party line in interviews. But the differences between them are striking, partly because they go to great lengths to make an individual impression. Each MP is individuated by the problems within their constituency, the date of entering Westminster and the experience they bring with them. A gulf exists between those with specialist professional experience and those who have never done anything but politics. Social identity matters too. My interviews with MPs indicated a general pattern that many women feel ill at ease in the roughhouse of the Chamber, while conversely some men MPs are uncomfortable listening to the more painful stories of constituents in face-to-face meetings. One study claims that just under two-thirds of a sample of women MPs viewed women's style as more measured and less noisy.[5]

The cultures of the political parties give female–male dynamics an extra twist. Labour has a long history of feminism, whereas it is only the 2010 intake of Conservative MPs – both male and female – who have brought women's interests into their party discussions with vigour. Labour sees women as subordinated, so steps are needed to improve their social position. Progressive Conservatives see the need for a more 'modern' attitude and see women as individuals in need of better opportunities, but quotas are resisted. The Conservative modernizers approach difference with care, fearful of creating antagonism and sceptical of the tendency of the left to take sides. As equality and fairness is central to their

---

[3]Angela Eagle MP, *Building a Better Politics, Speech to the Hansard Society*, 24 April 2013, http://www.labour.org.uk/building-a-better-politics,2013-04-24 [accessed 2 May 2013].
[4]http://www.guardian.co.uk/politics/2012/dec/31/labour-mp-gloria-de-piero [accessed 5 June 2013] and Guido Fawkes tweet (18/09/2012, 10:12).
[5]Sarah Childs, 'A feminised style of politics? women MPs in the House of Commons', *British Journal of Politics and International Relations*, vol. 6, 2004, pp. 3–19.

philosophy, Lib Dems should be the most progressive on gender, but they have the smallest proportion of women MPs of all the main parties. Others aspects of identity, too, create a pressure for MPs to be ambassadors for their religion, ethnicity, disability or illness.

The second attack – that nothing ever changes – is more difficult to evaluate. Comparisons between party political promises and the inadequacies of government reveal a huge gap. But there is always a gap between the rhetoric or ideals and the practices of implementation within organizations, whether charities, businesses or churches, or even for individuals. And if you consider what the British state provides in the face of staggering complexity and change, then politicians' achievements and failings become even more complex to assess. More fundamentally, a distinction has to be made between government and Parliament. All politicians are blamed for government blunders, but it is only the 95 MPs with a job in government who should be held directly accountable for the failures of the state and backbenchers in the government party/parties only indirectly so. The vast majority of MPs have no executive power.

The broken promises of politicians are seen as a form of deceit that keeps politics the same. A notorious example concerns tuition fees. In 2010 many Liberal Democrat MPs pledged to vote against an increase in university tuition fees. But the party subsequently went into a coalition with the Conservatives. An increase in fees was part of the Coalition Agreement, and then LD MPs were between a rock and a hard place. If they voted for the increase, students (and their parents) in their constituencies might punish them; if they voted against it, then they were breaking the pledges in the Coalition Agreement, which had received the backing of the whole party. How did this policy get into the agreement? It was argued that, in a fair system, students who are likely to go on to earn above-average salaries should pay for the economic advantages that university education gave them. Why should the less educated subsidize the privileged? So by increasing fees paid by students, a reduction in tax spent on higher education would be possible. If cuts in public expenditure are the order of the day, this one is fairer than many, the LD leaders argued. But many supporters never forgave the party. The two bigger parties have played on the image of their unreliability relentlessly ever since and much public disappointment has been expressed. This is a letter to the *Guardian* about broken trust:

> Their broken promise not to increase university tuition fees is about to cost my son an extra £18,000 over the next three years. More fundamentally, however, the Lib Dems have robbed me of my belief in politics. I imagine I'm feeling a bit like a religious person who's lost their faith ... I cannot trust any of them. People have asked me why I don't stand for election myself. Well, I know first-hand of better people than me who, having been elected with the best of intentions and motives, were mauled and spat out by the

system, leaving them, and me, to reflect on what might have been in a different political landscape ... And to be fair, it's not just the Lib Dems, it's all of them.[6]

Such a view ignores the inevitable nature of good politics; the need for compromise in politics means that politicians have little choice but to change their minds sometimes. They state: 'We will do x', when they should say: 'With the information and circumstances we have at the moment we are inclined to do x, but things may change and we may need to do y or maybe z', which wouldn't attract many votes. When journalists harangue them for having vague policies, or not being clear about what they are offering, then another accusation of deceit comes into play: politicians hedge their bets, dissembling and flannelling. But do we really want politicians to stick to their promises rigidly even when they have new information or need to compromise when a group of citizens articulates an important view rather late in the process? We hate them for adversarial politics – sticking to a position and opposing the other side come what may – and we hate them for co-operation and compromise. And we hate them particularly if we, or those close to us, lose out. From the perspective of MPs, the public are asking for the impossible.

The third and final charge is that they are in it for themselves: for the money, status and power. When the Independent Parliamentary Standards Authority consulted about reviewing MPs' pay, the initial response was a torrent of abuse towards MPs as venal and undeserving.[7] This long-standing view of politicians seemed to be confirmed when the expenses scandal of 2008–9 exposed some ridiculous and a few criminal claims. Whips had long encouraged MPs to claim whatever they could to compensate for salaries that were kept low for political reasons. Even when independent bodies recommended a pay rise, successive governments balked at the likely public disapproval. Salaries had decreased in value and so inflated expenses claims had been a feature of Parliament for many years.

But that is all over. The Independent Parliamentary Standards Authority (IPSA) makes all claims public and confirms that MPs do not break the rules; in fact they often under-claim to avoid the press making fun of, say, the purchase of toilet paper. Most MPs subsidize the costs of running their constituency office. In fact, the caricature of greedy MPs is the least convincing of all. Most could earn more doing a different job and over half of the new MPs took a pay cut to

---

[6]Alan Bowen, Letters and emails, *Guardian*, 4 May 2013.
[7]For example, see the public responses in IPSA, *Reviewing MPs' Pay and Pensions, A First Report – January 2013* (London: Independent Parliamentary Standards Authority, 2013), pp. 74–121, http://parliamentarystandards.org.uk/payandpensions/Documents/1.%20 Reviewing%20MPs'%20Pay%20and%20Pensions%20-%20A%20First%20Report.pdf [accessed 8 May 2013].

become MPs in 2010.[8] It costs those who are not in seats targeted by the party at least £20,000 to get elected, usually out of their own pocket. They get less than MPs in Ireland, France, Italy and Germany and much less than those in Singapore.[9] The public tends to assume that MPs are paid more than they are, and when IPSA explained to focus groups that MPs earn less than GPs, head teachers and police superintendents, 69 per cent of the public admitted that MPs' salaries are fair or even niggardly.[10]

If it is not money that motivates MPs, is it status and power? As I suggested in the last chapter, if it is, then at the same time they seek the status and power to champion the interests of some wider group: their constituents, enterprise, the poor, their country, or people they identify with. If MPs were only after Ministerial office for their own ends, why do so many pour time into constituency work even when they have the benefit of an easeful majority, and why do some rebel against the whip even when constituents are indifferent and it damages their prospects for promotion? Politics is only partly about personal ambition or status; it is also about a collective process of taking sides and trying to do good or tackle evil as they see it, as I hope to show in this book.

Taking sides

Public hatred for politicians, politics and political parties is interconnected. So is the defence of these three. The late Bernard Crick wrote about democratic politics as a civilizing activity: 'It is something to be valued as a pearl beyond price in this history of the human condition, though, in fact, to overvalue it can be to destroy it utterly.'[11] Politics has to be murky, relying on compromise and deals, because different and rival interests, truths and traditions exist under a common rule. To renounce politics is to destroy the very thing that orders pluralism in non-violent ways and keeps despotism at bay.[12] As John Thurso MP (Liberal Democrat) put it, in his usual pithy way: 'MPs are all that stand between the government and tyranny.'[13] If you value democratic politics, then

---

[8] Korris, 2011, *A Year in the Life*, p. 3.
[9] IPSA, *Reviewing MPs' Pay and Pensions: A Consultation, October 2012* (London: Independent Parliamentary Standards Authority, 2012), pp. 99–100, http://parliamentarystandards.org.uk/payandpensions/Documents/2.%20Reviewing%20MPs'%20Pay%20and%20Pensions%20-%20A%20Consultation.pdf [accessed 8 May 2013].
[10] ComRes, *MPs' Pay and Pensions, A Public Verdict* (London: Independent Parliamentary Standards Authority, 2012).
[11] Bernard Crick, *In Defence of Politics* (Chicago: Chicago University Press, 1962), p. 13.
[12] Ibid., p. 21.
[13] Interviewed by Emma Crewe, 8 November 2011.

political parties should not be dismissed. Politics in our adversarial system is about picking from opposing sides and going into ideological battle so that both politicians and voters have clear choices. Politicians themselves sometimes forget this. Crick warns against the kind of Conservative who sees himself as above politics, as if Conservatism doesn't have presuppositions and theories to choose from, or prudish apolitical Liberals whose individualism becomes dogma, and anti-political socialists with their stark contrasts between good and bad which don't allow for that intrinsically political process – compromise.[14]

Compromise is the name of the game when politicians organize themselves into parties to develop a coherent and consistent set of policies that answer what they perceive to be the major questions. They put them in a manifesto before an election and, if voted into government, these guide the way they govern us. In theory, MPs pick the party that best represents their viewpoint. In practice, parties tend to contain people with wildly different views. Angela Eagle MP, Shadow Leader of the House,[15] thought it was typical for people to agree with only about 40 per cent of their party's manifesto. This is less surprising that it might sound, partly because neither voters nor MPs probably choose parties exclusively on the basis of their policies at any one time. A mixture of ingredients influences their decision. MPs are drawn to the most general ideas and cultures of a particular political party because it is a family tradition, part of their political awakening as students (more common for Lib Dems), or through friends and other social relationships. Bob Marshall-Andrews (former MP) swapped from Tory to Labour under the influence of his wife.[16] Party membership is not the result of a cold rational assessment of the rhetoric offered by Labour, Conservative or Liberal Democrat, but a far more complex mix of being drawn into one sociopolitical group in part to set oneself in opposition to the others. One Labour member told me: 'The bonds of party are not the same as family but it feels like it.' Of course, like political parties, families can be both brought together by loyalty and standing against others but also driven apart by internal conflict. Sarah Teather MP felt that the LDs were losing their commitment to social justice and liberalism, so decided to leave her parliamentary family and stand down as an MP.[17]

---

14 Bernard Crick, *In Defence of Politics*, pp. 154, 136.
15 Eagle, *Building a Better Politics*, remarks in the Q&A.
16 Bob Marshall-Andrews, *Off Message* (London: Profile, 2011) pp. 10–14.
17 http://www.theguardian.com/politics/2013/sep/07/lib-dem-sarah-teather-step-down [accessed 23 June 2014].

Table 2.1 General Election results by party 1987–2010

Party	1987	1992	1997	2001	2005	2010
Conservative	375	336	165	166	198	306
Labour	229	271	418	412	355	258
Liberal Democrat	23	20	46	52	62	57
DUP	3	3	2	5	9	8
SNP	3	3	6	5	6	6
Sinn Féin	1		2	4	5	5
Independent			1		1	1
Plaid Cymru	3	4	4	4	3	3
SDLP	3	4	3	3	3	3
Alliance						1
Green						1
UUP	9	9	10	6	1	
Respect					1	
Health Concern				1	1	
UK Unionist			1			
Ulster Popular Unionist	1	1				
Speaker			1	1	1	1
Total number of seats	650	651	659	659	646	650
Actual government majority	102	21	179	167	66	83
Turnout	75.30%	77.70%	71.30%	59.40%	61.40%	65.10%

Data: www.politicsresources.net [accessed 6 October 2014]

Most MPs arrive in Westminster as members of political gangs, as Frank Field MP calls them, with only a very few exceptions. Even Martin Bell, the white-suited former war correspondent who won the supposedly safe Tory seat of Tatton in 1997, only managed to get in as an Independent because both the Labour and Lib Dem candidates stood aside and the Conservatives were reeling under accusations of sleaze.[18] So voters support parties because they need them. But that does not mean they like them. The main parties are in

---

[18] For another example, Richard Taylor won a seat in defence of the NHS because the Lib Dems stood aside, but he lost when the LDs re-entered the race in 2010.

chronic decline. Conservative membership has dived from nearly 3 million in 1951 to under 180,000 in 2011, while Labour's figures are 880,000 to under 200,000 during the same period. Lib Dems have lost over 20,000 of their 90,000 members since 1991. The Caravan Club has more members than all the political parties put together. On the other hand, smaller parties are growing. The Greens have doubled in ten years, some say because their values appeal to young people. UKIP's rise is put down to a mix of anti-government protest and colourful candidates or touching a nerve in public opinion. Their Leader, Nigel Farage, wears bright trousers and talks not as if he has had media training but as if he is simply speaking his own mind like someone down the pub. In the local elections of 3 May 2013 they won 147 councillor seats, up from eight, and a quarter of the share of the vote. In the 2014 European elections UKIP won the popular vote and the most seats, pushing Labour into second and Conservatives into third place, the first time a party has beaten these two for over a hundred years. Even more significantly, they won their first seat in the House of Commons in October 2014. Former Conservative Douglas Carswell MP defected from the party, saying that 'I know the party is full of good people, who want the best for this country. The problem is with those at its top. They are not on our side. They are not serious about the change Britain needs.'[19] In the by-election triggered by joining UKIP he won back his Clacton seat with a majority of 12,404 votes. With a second Tory MP defector, Mark Reckless, re-winning his seat for UKIP only a few weeks later, Farage was aiming to hold the balance of power after the General Election in 2015, while the Conservatives warned that votes for UKIP will put Labour back into government. Since the 1950s the combined votes for Labour/Conservatives have declined from over 90 per cent to the mid-60 per cent mark. The Lib Dems have increased from below 10 per cent to 23 per cent in 2010, but the Coalition does not appear to have enhanced their prospects, while other parties have gone from around 1 per cent to over 10 per cent.[20] The changeability of voters' preferences is challenging the once-stable three-party landscape.

MPs are pilloried for their political tribalism. But for democracy to work, the parties need to differentiate themselves from each other and despite popular opinion insisting that they are all the same, ideological differences persist. The rough headlines of party rhetoric could be caricatured as follows: Conservatives champion the aspirations and freedom of individuals; Labour argue the state should protect the vulnerable; and the Lib Dems fight for equality and human rights. The smaller parties are partly created and kept alive by dissatisfaction

---

[19] Douglas Carswell, 'Voters have turned against politics-as-usual', *Telegraph*, 6 October 2014, http://blogs.telegraph.co.uk/news/author/douglascarswellmp/ [accessed 11 October 2014].
[20] Guy Lodge and Glenn Gottfried, *Worst of Both Worlds. Why first past the post no longer works* (London: IPPR briefing, 2011) pp. 4–5.

with a status quo that includes the larger parties. People joined Plaid Cymru not only in support of Welsh self-determination but also because they felt that New Labour had moved too far to the right. The Scottish National Party offers itself as an alternative to Labour, particularly since there is only one Conservative MP from Scotland and only 15 sitting in the Scottish Parliament. Greens protect the environment, but they are often charged with being watermelons or mangoes – green on the outside and red (Labour) or orange (Liberal Democrat) on the inside. Outside the Westminster Parliament UKIP has emerged from the nation-alist right-wing end of the spectrum; its candidates might otherwise have been Conservatives, but they have pinched disaffected Labour votes as well. But these simplifications gloss over change and complexity within parties over time and across factions; the parties are straining more than ever before in the face of internal disagreements and endless adjustment to take account of public and media reactions. To illustrate these currents, I will take the three main parties in turn.

During the twentieth century the Conservatives corralled nearly all right-of-centre votes and governed for 80 per cent of the time. Traditionally Conservatives were anti-ideology but inclined to protect national institutions, the Empire and the general welfare of the people.[21] Since the rise of Labour, their alliance with the poor has been less prominent, and Conservatives saw successful people as the ones to cultivate. Conservatives are now more specifically on the side of 'aspiration'. As Chancellor of the Exchequer, George Osborne's 2012 conference speech put it clearly, suggesting that the unemployed deserved less government attention: 'Where is the fairness, we ask, for the shift-worker, leaving home in the dark hours of the early morning, who looks up at the closed blinds of their next door neighbour sleeping off a life on benefits?... Whoever you are, wherever you come from, if you're working for a better future – we are on your side.[22]' During 2012 the Prime Minister, David Cameron MP and his Ministers all placed themselves firmly on the side of those individuals and families who work hard, strive to contribute to society and aspire to enhance their economic position.[23] Those obeying the law, or victims of crime, are also championed, while distance from offenders and prisoners is created by stressing punishment, not forgiveness.[24] When talking about someone Conservatives hold in low esteem in another party, they are inclined to say: 'He is not very nice, very party political and tribal.'

---

[21] Ian Gilmour, *The Body Politic* (London: Hutchinson, 1969), p. 85.

[22] http://www.newstatesman.com/blogs/politics/2012/10/george-osbornes-speech-conserv-ative-conference-full-text [accessed 8 May 2013].

[23] Grant Shapps MP (Conservative) said to the House: 'We are on the side of aspirant people who wish to buy the roof over their heads', *HC Debates*, 12 March 2012, col. 13.

[24] For example, http://www.bbc.co.uk/news/uk-politics-20431995 [accessed 8 May 2013].

Michael Fabricant (Mike_Fabricant)

17/04/2013 22:22

The Conservative Party came together today as a family. We are not normally 'tribal' like Labour, but today we were. Good feeling.

Michael Louis David Fabricant has been a Conservative MP since 1992 and is a frequent twitterer

---

The leaders and many of the 2010 intake are determined to modernize the 'nasty party', as Home Secretary Theresa May MP once referred to the Conservative Party. In the 2010–15 Parliament, modernizing for Tories means taking sides with those getting a hard deal, for example by allowing same-sex couples to marry. The majority of Conservative MPs and voters are against gay marriage[25] and the cost to the party has been that the dinosaurs, as the modernizers call them, felt betrayed. By May 2013 a right-inclined Tory MP, Jacob Rees-Mogg, was suggesting that UKIP was a more natural ally than the Lib Dems, not only because they share similar values, but they have mostly come from the ranks of the Conservatives.[26] So ideology within any party is never fixed; the party line is endlessly questioned and adjusted as the influence of factions and other parties oscillates.

Within the Labour Party there are still wounds from its internal battles fought bitterly during the Thatcher years between the left and right of the party. The latter won and branded themselves New Labour. Labour politicians traditionally take the side of the vulnerable, but former Prime Minister Tony Blair completely reshaped the party when he allied himself to the aspirant in society, stealing ideological ground from the Tories. He perceived a cultural gulf between Labour Party insiders, who agonized about the iniquities of Tory policies, and ordinary people who were less moved by adversarial politics. To change from the party of protest to a party of government, he retrieved what he saw as Labour's basic purpose: 'to help the individual gain opportunity, to let him or her overcome limitations ... That echoed and captured something deep within human nature: the desire to be free, to be the best you can be.'[27] Ed Miliband and most of

---

[25] Phil Cowley and Mark Stuart, 'Five things about the gay marriage vote', 2 May 2013, http://nottspolitics.org/2013/02/05/five-things-about-the-gay-marriage-vote/ [accessed 10 October 2014]; table taken from Mike Simpson [accessed 8 May 2013].

[26] As cited by Paul Goodman, 'Jacob Rees-Mogg becomes the first Tory MP to back a Conservative-UKIP pact', 8 May 2013, http://conservativehome.blogs.com/parliament/2013/05/jacob-rees-mogg-becomes-the-first-tory-mp-to-back-a-conservative-ukip-pact.html [accessed 5 June 2013].

[27] Blair, A Journey, 2010, p. 90.

his team have returned to the older tradition of expressing sympathy, and sometimes even protest, on behalf of those groups who face disadvantage. Labour may be nudging back towards a more collective understanding of both problems and solutions to the political questions, at least while in opposition.

Current Labour MPs are split just as the Conservatives are. Those who support Ed Miliband tend to speak for the vulnerable. Stella Creasy MP, for instance, has become well known for taking sides against loan sharks on behalf of their victims.[28] The left-inclined argue that it is high time Labour revived economic policies that clearly sided with the working class through investment, employment creation and workers' rights. On the other side there are those who think wistfully about how it might have been under the leadership of Ed's more right-inclined brother David Miliband, who was defeated in a leadership election in 2010, and want to keep in with achievers. One David supporter, a Labour candidate aiming to get in at the 2015 election, quoted Mandelson's conclusion that there is nothing wrong with the filthy rich as long as they pay their taxes. She added that there is a new breed of Labour politician that distances themselves from the monolithic power camps inherited from the past and celebrates difference. They hope to advance through persuasion, not division. Those on the right of the Labour Party worry that a move towards the left will reduce their chances of a win at the next General Election. Blair's former speechwriter, Phil Collins advised: 'Labour can't win if it's on Mick Philpott's side.'[29] Philpott killed his children by starting a fire, but his secondary crime, in the eyes of many, was having children to increase his benefit income. The implication is that too much sympathy for the downtrodden puts you on the side not only of the 'undeserving poor' but even cheats or criminals. However, being in opposition rather than in government takes some of the heat out of these ideological battles, as less is at stake until the election draws near.

Lib Dems try to avoid taking sides between the hard-working versus those who need help, between collective versus individualistic approaches, and between wealth creation and distribution, by aiming for all of this as well as rights, equality and fairness for all. That does not banish other tricky choices. On secret courts, the Lib Dems are divided. Most of their MPs put the security interests of the many above the human rights of a tiny few and supported the use of secret court proceedings. Activists at the Autumn 2012 Party Conference were furious, seeing the measure as a betrayal of civil liberties. One said that 'fairness runs in our veins', another that 'civil liberties is in our DNA', and a third

---

[28] http://www.workingforwalthamstow.org.uk/category/legal-loan-shark-campaign/ [accessed 8 May 2013].

[29] Philip Collins, 'Labour can't win if it's on Mick Philpott's side', *The Times*, 5 April 2013, http://www.thetimes.co.uk/tto/opinion/columnists/philipcollins/article3731420.ece [accessed 8 May 2013].

that the moral rationale for the Coalition – to make the Tory government more liberal – was demolished by the idea of secret courts. The theoretical choice of siding with Labour or Conservative at the next election also brought out tensions at fringe meetings. Most Lib Dems assume that they will agree with more Labour than Conservative policies, but they dislike Labour's more antagonistic style. The Conservatives tend to have better manners, so goes the LD stereotype, but tend to be more hostile to the idea of rights. But like the other two parties, the LDs are a broad church. In constituencies where they are fighting against a Conservative, they are more likely to lean to the right; where Labour is the adversary, LD MPs incline towards the left.

During the time I was watching MPs the government consisted of a Conservative/Lib Dem Coalition. During a frantic few days after the 2010 election the cabals around party leaders Cameron and Clegg forged some principles for working and a policy manifesto, or Coalition Agreement, as a basis for sharing power. Infuriatingly for the two largest parties, in such circumstances it is the third and smaller main party that clearly gets to choose which party to favour. Lib Dems explain that they went with Conservatives because they had more votes than Labour. But gossip revolves around a loss in confidence in Labour as well – they had been in government for 13 years and seemed tired, and their leader, Gordon Brown, was viewed by many as difficult to work with.

A positive view of the Coalition is encapsulated by a LD peer:

A Tory MP came up to me the other day and said: 'This Coalition is marvellous!' I looked at him in amazement. After years of being opponents how could he say this? The Tory clarified: 'Don't misunderstand me. I mean that we can say to our nutters that we'd like to do something about Europe, but we can't because of the Liberals.' Of course the same is true for us. To our purist orange brigade who want a perfect world we say: 'That would be nice but the Conservatives won't let us.'

For those on the Tory right and the Lib Dem left, the Coalition is frustrating. Both leaders are subjected to an onslaught of criticism, and even fury, especially from the extreme wings of both parties. Labour maintains an elevated level of indignation towards the third party. For them it seems unforgiveable that the Lib Dems, who purported at one time to be to the left of Labour, should sell out and side with the Tories. As the next election approaches, some forgiveness may be countenanced just in case Labour doesn't get an overall majority. But continual teasing persists, especially on Twitter. This story by Jamie Reed MP captures the tone:

Once upon a time, there lived a forgetful little frog called, for the sake of argument, Nick ... One day, Nick was hopping along the riverbank when he came across an evil, deceitful scorpion, called ... ooh, tricky one this, erm ... let's call the scorpion Dave. Dave had stung Nick quite badly in the past, but Nick could never remember these incidents.

'I say, Frog! Come here!' the scorpion bellowed. Dutifully, the frog hopped over.

'How can I help?' asked the little frog, who, for some ... reason, was now wearing an Elizabethan courtier's hat.

'Could you help me cross this river old boy?' asked the scorpion.

'Of course,' said the frog, 'hop on my back and we'll swim across. What could possibly go wrong?'

Halfway across the river, the scorpion ... inflicted his worst sting upon the frog, injecting him with lethal venom.

'Why did you do that?' asked Nick. 'Now we'll both die ...'

'You must have known I'd do that,' said the scorpion, 'everyone else did.'

'Do what?' asked the forgetful frog.

They were never seen again.[30]

The sides people take in politics may expand, contract and shift more rapidly than is typical in most organizations, but this social and political process of fission and fusion can be found in any community and workplace. When writing about the House of Lords, I compared this with what the British anthropologist Evans-Pritchard found among the Nuer in southern Sudan in the 1930s.[31] Within the Nuer nation, people belonged to tribes and the members of each considered themselves superior to other tribes. Each tribe was divided into clans, with a common ancestor, which were in turn composed of lineages. People normally identified most strongly with their lineage, but when a tribe was threatened by another, then lineages and clans would unify. Conversely, when disputes between clans couldn't be resolved, then the tribe might split. If the Nuer nation was in dispute with another nation, the Dinka for example, then all the Nuer's segments came together against the common enemy. A similar pattern can be found in Westminster, where identity shifts depending on who the MP is with. MPs belong to political parties when sitting in the Chamber but party factions when sitting in the bar with political allies. With endless factions and divisions, MPs no longer have two sides to choose from but a multitude. The competition is intense; one MP compared Parliament to Smithfield Market. You have two lines – one selling lamb and the other selling beef – and the lines are in competition for customers but so are the sellers in each line. It is clear that political relations are not given a pattern by a purely abstract formulation based on

[30] Jamie Reed MP, a series of tweets, between 15:02 and 15:16, 23/07/12.
[31] Crewe, *Lords of Parliament*, pp. 154–5.

opposing ideologies but a web of relationships with both networks in permanent competition as well as forms of cooperation that ignore the usual antagonisms.[32]

When the nation faces a crisis, then MPs belong to Parliament and unity across parties becomes possible. When we go to war, all parties back the country, and therefore the government, against aggressors. (There are, of course, exceptions when governments take the country into unpopular conflicts such as those in Iraq [2003] and Suez [1956].) Almost all MPs backed Adam Afriye when he was leading a debate about expenses and the need for reform of the new expenses regime.[33] All three party leaders agreed to campaign for the union of the UK and against the idea of Scottish independence in September 2014 as soon as the polls indicated that the referendum might be won by those favouring separation. When the Leader of the Scottish Nationalist Party, Alex Salmond gave a speech accepting defeat, he said: 'Let us say something which I hope unites all campaigns and all Scots. I think the process by which we have made our decision as a nation reflects enormous credit on Scotland.'[34] Belonging to a side, and the moral judgements that are associated with that side, are as changeable for MPs as they are with any social or political group.

Enemies and friends

Popular opinion assumes that MPs are rabidly tribal when they do party politics. They are in public performances and although the public despises MPs for their show of aggression, many enjoy the theatre. The most dramatic example of aggressive and competitive theatre is PMQs, led by either the PM or Deputy PM. John Thurso MP describes the Chamber as a bear pit at PMQs: 'When discussing the big issues, and at PMQs, it is like a storm, a great crash on the rocks. No other forum delivers so much adrenalin and demands so much nerve. If you can command respect in the House, you have made it.'[35] Each time there is the perception, especially voiced by sketch-writers and lobby journalists over Twitter, that one side has won by outshining or humiliating their opponent. David Cameron said that when Margaret Thatcher prepared for PMQs the whole of Whitehall went into convulsions: 'Twice a week it was as if the arms of a giant octopus shook every building in Whitehall for every analysis of every problem and every answer to every question.'[36] But a win at PMQs in the eyes

---

[32] Abélès, *Quiet Days in Burgundy*, p. 248.
[33] John Mann is one of the few MPs who has no complaints about the way that the Independent Parliamentary Standards Authority set up the new regime.
[34] http://www.scotlandnow.dailyrecord.co.uk/news/read-first-minister-alex-salmonds-4286904 [accessed 19 September 2014].
[35] Interviewed by Emma Crewe, 8 November 2011.
[36] David Cameron MP, *HC Debates*, 10 April 2013, col. 1615.

of journalists is rarely achieved by statistics or clever arguments alone but by being quick on your feet with an insult or counter-slur.

MichaelWhite (MichaelWhite)

07/11/2012 12:34

#PMQs This week's score. Clegg calm, cheerful and lucid, not brill, but Ok. Hattie skips about too much. 3-2 to NC

Michael White is a journalist and Associate Editor of the *Guardian* newspaper

---

Insults have an important place in the Chamber in general. Vince Cable managed to wound Gordon Brown painfully when he suggested that he had gone from 'Stalin to Mr Bean'.[37] The clever MPs embrace insults. Michael Foot likened Norman Tebbit to a semi-housetrained polecat and when the polecat joined the Lords he put the animal in his coat-of-arms. Dennis Skinner does not seem to mind being the 'Beast of Bolsover'.[38] Ann Widdecombe gained the nickname 'Doris' (Karloff) with her black dresses and crucifixes and liked it so much she answered the phone with 'Karloff here'.[39] But most famous of all, Margaret Thatcher did more than tolerate 'The Iron Lady' as a title; she revelled in it. The latest favourite arena for insults is Twitter, where opponent MPs get into both amicable and abusive spats, as Jamie Reed reveals: 'Very nice series of DMs from normal Tory tweeters. Good folk.' 'However, my Tory trolls remind me of Smurfs. Small, blue, intellectually challenged, last popular in the 1980s.'[40]

Zac Goldsmith (ZacGoldsmith)

Conservative & Labour and MPs will always disagree, but whenever Lib Dems speak about principle, both sides of the House rock with laughter.

Zac Goldsmith is a journalist, former Editor of *The Ecologist* magazine and has been a Conservative MP since 2010

---

[37] Paul Flynn, *How to be an MP* (London: Biteback Publishing, 2012), p. 193.
[38] Chris Moncrieff, *Wine, Women and Westminster: Behind-the-scenes true stories of MPs at play over 50 years* (London: JR Books, 2008), p. 80.
[39] Flynn, *The Unusual Suspect*, p. 190.
[40] Jamie Reed MP, tweets, 20:20 and 20:21, 15/08/12.

The main form of political insult does not hit individuals – although leaders and Ministers in particular are always a target – but another party. Political journalists get press releases into their inboxes from all parties full of allegations about opponents and attacking their motives and integrity.[41] Each party has its own long-standing vulnerable underbelly with a layer of time-specific sensitivities at any one time. The Tories have been under attack as the 'nasty party' for some decades, dominated by arrogant rich white men, especially those educated at Eton and too cosy with players from global corporates, so goes the stereotype. Since Cameron and his modernizers took over the party they have been counter-acting this by encouraging more women and black MPs to stand, passing a bill to allow gay marriage and talking about help for the poorest despite austerity. So as time marches on, and expectations of the Coalition increase, the opposition have resorted to attacking their record in government alongside their motives or character. Any mistakes, U-turns or bad news about the management of the country is jumped on with glee. Of course under the Coalition this is not a line of attack available to the Lib Dems, so during by-elections and party conferences they remind their own side that they are distinct from Tories because the latter are illiberal, intolerant and less democratic.

cathy jamieson mp (cathyjamieson)

17/01/2013 14:57

RT@pamela_nash:What an arrogant ministerial response we are hearing in the House of Commons #ATOSDebatehe has no idea and no compassion

Cathy Jamieson was an MSP and has been a Labour MP since 2010

The hangover from the internal Labour battles in the 1980s–90s still supplies fodder for attack by other parties, renewed under the leadership of Ed Miliband, who is to the left of Blair, in the dual charge of class envy and naivety. For the first few years of government the Coalition MPs railed at Labour for the mess they left the country in before the 2010 General Election. Accusations of incompetence and profligacy, and demands for an apology, are their counter-charge to attacks by Labour. The Coalition claim that Labour is in the thrall of the unions, recklessly championing common causes at the cost of individual freedom.

[41]Emine Saner, 'Why don't we trust politicians', *Guardian*, 19 October 2012, http://www.guardian.co.uk/commentisfree/2012/oct/19/why-public-dont-trust-politicians [accessed 6 June 2013].

Douglas Carswell MP (DouglasCarswell)

30/01/2013 15:45

Amazing how tribal so many MPs are. 'But YOUR party did blah blah in 1980-something.' 'YOURS said fishcakes in 1990-whenever.'

Douglas Carswell was a Conservative MP (2005–14) and resigned when he joined UKIP. He was elected as the first UKIP MP in October 2014.

The attacks on Liberal Democrats have shifted more dramatically as their fortunes have changed. They were once depicted as hopeless, unrealistic and lily-livered, out of touch with popular opinion. The two main parties told voters that a vote for LD was a waste, because they were never going to be the party of government. However, since the LDs have been in government attacks have flipped to the charge of unreliability. According to Labour/Conservatives, Lib Dems are two-faced and changeable. During elections their morality is called into question more profoundly – their tactics are seen as shoddy, ruthless and even dishonest. The party that champions fairness doesn't play fair. Meanwhile, Deputy Prime Minister Nick Clegg MP explains this response:

> People in politics divide the world into good and bad, sacred and profane –
> they wrap things up in opposites. British politics was dominated by two parties
> and with a pendulum that swung between them. Then along comes the
> interloper – Lib Dems – and messes it up and confuses the neat categories. It
> doesn't make any sense to the two main parties. What was an eccentric irrel-
> evance suddenly is in a position of power. The right wing think power is their
> birthright and the Labour Party see the Lib Dems going with Conservatives
> as an act of betrayal – both together they constitute the British political estab-
> lishment. The LD are a newcomer so of course they are not welcome.[42]

Alastair Campbell (campbellclaret)

14/03/2013 10:56

worth switching to Parliament channel to see a minister floundering because of Cameron's weakness re alcohol abuse

Alastair Campbell is a journalist and was Director of Communications and Strategy for the Labour Party under Tony Blair 1997–2003

---

[42] Interview held by Emma Crewe, on the telephone, 16 July 2013.

These are the currents of hostility, often voiced by party leaders for the benefit of their own side – to rally the troops, maintain loyalty and remind everyone whose side they are on – and to discredit the other side in the eyes of the voters. Backbenchers do not usually speak to such large audiences, but they are encouraged to follow suit on Twitter.

Paul Flynn advises backbenchers to cultivate enemies, because the competition they engender increases your knowledge and understanding of a wide range of subjects. More often MPs are encouraged by the whips to maintain hostility (or the appearance of it) between the gangs to make their side look dominant. The whips assume it is essential for governing or opposing effectively within Parliament. Since the government always has a majority, and can therefore win nearly every division, both debate and votes are often ritualized show and few alterations to legislation are accepted. This works because, on the whole, MPs obey the whip, although less so each Parliament, and inspiring loyalty by cultivating animosity towards the other side is an important aim of what MPs refer to as tribalism. The government can be defeated in the Commons but it is a rare event, because party politics still works.

Alongside the hostility, and unbeknown to the public, MPs across parties co-operate in private. In the House of Lords, where no one party holds a majority, the party leaders, or usual channels, make deals behind the scenes. Even in the Commons, cross-party conversations take place in the tearoom or lobby, in Select Committees, MPs' offices or on the phone and constitute the performance of a different kind of politics from what the public sees on the TV and web – an everyday pragmatic politics that brokers agreements and compromises that blend abstract ideals with morality and realism in context. While the public face of politics is fractious, in private one of the well-kept secrets of MPs' world is that alliances across parties are common and becoming more so. In the past, cross-party co-operation was more about friendship despite opposition. In the 1830s Mr Hughes Hughes, MP for Oxford, attacked Mr O'Connell with verbal violence for painting death's heads and crossbones on those houses that would not vote for his nominee. Mr O'Connell retaliated with equal force. Some nights later they were spotted walking arm-in-arm up Parliament Street. After Macmillan and Wilson savaged each other in the House they would often meet for a drink. In the club-like atmosphere when the Commons used to sit in the evenings, and alcohol used to flow more freely, MPs of all parties were amicable in the smoking room. In the words of a member of the Press Gallery in 1967: 'Here we have 630 men and women, friendly – except for normal human antipathies – in private, and fighting like Kilkenny cats in public.'[43]

---

[43] Silvester, *Pimlico Companion to Parliament*, pp. 531, 542, 528.

Recent political biographies are peppered with amiable relationships across the divide often created by pairing. Up until the late 1990s Conservatives and Labour arranged themselves into pairs (see chapter 4 for the current practices on pairing). The whips issued instructions about when MPs were required to be in the House to vote. A one-line whip meant be present if possible, a two-line whip meant be present or make an arrangement with your pair, and a three-line demanded your presence (unless the whip excused you for exceptional circumstances). If the pair both agreed to be absent, then their absence would not affect the outcome of the vote. To work out when they may absent themselves, pairs would talk about the following week – inevitably revealing what their side was planning. They would gossip and often become close friends.

Other MPs across parties shared common political interests. Labour's Bob Marshall-Andrews describes Conservative's David Davis MP as a valued ally in endless battles over the years.[44] Their alliance was based on a shared love of rugby football, wine and civil liberties. They shared an aversion to Labour's Home Secretaries and their casual approach to constitutional freedoms. Bob even campaigned for David when he stood for re-election, even though the Chief Whip threatened to expel him from the party if he did. Others just got along; as John Major said of John Smith: 'We frequently clashed in public and in the House, yet afterwards, in private, we met often and amiably, again, no bruises ... Political differences are not the be-all and end-all of relationships for members of the House.'[45] One ambitious Tory MP always turns to Labour women to get an honest assessment on a speech he has made, claiming that you can't really trust someone from your own side to give a candid opinion.

The introduction of elections to the Select Committees in 2010, overturning the old system of appointment by whips, has brought with it plenty of cross-party canvassing for the position of Committee Chair. Pinning down the voting intentions of MPs is a slippery business, as Christopher Chope explains:

> Just as a matter of history, my election was contested. There were four of us seeking support, and we got together and added up the number of promises that we had each received and it came to over 2,000. Fascinating, given that there are only 650 Members. So what they tell you is not necessarily what they do if they have that privacy.[46]

He reveals the intensity of interaction between MPs inspired by committee elections. But the fact remains that an incentive to gather cross-party support

---

[44] Marshall-Andrews, *Off Message*, p. 33.
[45] John Major, *The Autobiography* (London: HarperCollins, 1999), p. 591.
[46] http://www.publications.parliament.uk/pa/cm201314/cmselect/cmpolcon/82/82.pdf [accessed 30 May 2014].

has been created, to the frustration of the whips. Voting for Committee Chairs reveals another long-established loyalty between MPs that cuts across and within parties – the affinity created within one intake. When Sarah Wollaston and Rory Stewart were elected to be Select Committee Chairs their experience in the subject area, and their readiness to speak out against their own Conservative government, may have been reasons to vote for them. But it is significant that they wouldn't have got in without the votes of fellow newcomers being prepared to ignore the tradition that Chairs are usually old hands in Westminster. This loyalty to your intake doesn't go away. MPs always remember other new girls and boys who arrived in Westminster at the same election.

The most exciting story about a cross-party alliance hinged on one conversation in 1979, which went the way it did because of a friendship between a Tory and a Labour whip. On 28 March, so Lord Weatherill told me many years later,[47] a vote of no confidence in the government loomed. Weatherill, the Tory Deputy Chief Whip, sized up the situation during the fateful day, knowing that there were two jokers on the other side: Sir Alfred Broughton MP (Labour) and the Independent republican Frank Maguire MP. Broughton, despite terminal illness, was due to travel down from the north by train. Tory activists were watching his house and the stationmaster was on the lookout to see if the ailing MP boarded the train. By 5 p.m. they knew he had missed it. Maguire flew over from Ireland and in the early evening he was still drinking in the bar with a couple of Labour whips. It looked as if he might support the Labour government so fellow Irish MP Gerry Fitt (SDLP), who felt betrayed by Labour, said to the Chamber soon after 6.30 p.m.:

> There is a rumour circulating today, and if it is true it is despicable, that the hon. Member is somewhere within the building talking to someone from the Government Whips' office. He cannot talk to me in case I persuade him to do as I am doing tonight. I shall be watching very carefully, and if the hon. Member goes through the Government Lobby tonight it will be in opposition to everything that his constituents sent him here to do.[48]

Maguire's wife appeared in the bar and dragged him off home, apparently unhappy with the idea of her husband saving the government or worried by the possible repercussions. According to Roy Hattersley, two Irish 'heavies' assisted Mrs Maguire. Weatherill went to see Walter Harrison MP, Deputy Chief Whip for

---

[47] Interviewed by Emma Crewe, 26 June 2000. This story can also be found in Crewe, *Lords of Parliament*, p. 178, and has also been told in a play by James Graham, *The House*, based on interviews held by BBC journalist Mark D'Arcy.
[48] Gerald Fitt MP, *HC Debates*, 29 March 1979, col. 521.

the Labour Government: 'Walter, you are going to lose.' I asked Weatherill why he pointed that out to his opponent. 'Because we were friends', he told me. The conversation continued:

Harrison: 'I'm having Broughton brought down by ambulance. If he doesn't make it in time, what about we abide by our usual agreement and pair him with someone who is sick?'

Weatherill: 'Unfortunately I do not have anyone who is ill. But since we do have such an agreement, I will personally stand out.'

Harrison: 'Jack, I couldn't allow you to do that'.

Harrison knew that Weatherill would get into terrible trouble; it might be the end of his political career. Harrison felt that he owed him for not making a fuss about catching a Labour whip reneging on a deal a few weeks earlier. Weatherill added with feeling: 'Honour among whips is precious.' Harrison did not bring Sir Alfred down by ambulance. At 1.20 p.m. he had already decided, against the wishes of some in the party, not to risk jeopardizing his health with a long journey. Roy Hattersley explains what happened next:

At a couple of minutes before 10 o'clock ... There was a sudden hush as Jimmy Hamilton, a government whip, pushed his way to the clerks' table. When he paused in front of the mace and gave the prime minister what looked like a thumbs up sign, the silence was broken by a gasp of disbelief. A Tory whip, a couple of paces behind, passed a piece of paper along the Opposition frontbench. If I read her lips correctly, when it reached Margaret Thatcher, she hissed – in anger only slightly mitigated by doubt – 'I don't believe it.' The message that the government had won was a mistake. The rough calculation, which had been made to soothe the party leaders' nerves, had not included the Tory tellers who had counted the votes.[49]

The Tories won the vote of no confidence in the government by one vote. The Tories waved their order papers and cheered, Labour MPs sung *The Red Flag*. Sir Alfred Broughton died five days later. Harrison's two honourable decisions on that day spelt the end of Labour's 18-year term in office and the end of his own career. John Dunn's point about co-operation in politics rings true for the House of Commons in both its present and past guises:

---

[49] Roy Hattersley, 'The Party's Over', *Observer*, 22 March 2009, http://www.guardian.co.uk/politics/2009/mar/22/james-callaghan-labour-1979-thatcher [accessed 23 May 2013].

Seen in this way, politics at its best is an intricate field of cooperative agency, linking a multiplicity of free agents, none of whom can know each other's future actions but all of whom must in some measure rely upon each other's future actions.[50]

Disloyalty

Party tribalism does not prevent friendship *across* parties nor acrimony *within* parties. Parties are coalitions of like-minded people, but that doesn't necessarily mean Members either like or want to help each other. MPs often say, for those on the way up, your opponents sit on the beaches opposite and your enemies are all around you. Bob Marshall-Andrews writes that personal vitriol is more commonly thrown at supposed colleagues.[51] (On reading this draft one informant commented: 'He would know.') Public criticism of those in your own party infuriates those who see discretion as an indispensable part of loyalty. Chris Mullin reports that Dennis Skinner gave a colleague a bollocking for taking his complaint 'outside the family'.[52] But that has not stopped public criticism within parties becoming an epidemic. Personal attack sometimes melds with factional bickering. In the 2013 autumn reshuffle Nadine Dorries tweeted rudely about a fellow Conservative: 'Very sad to see Kris Hopkins promoted. One of parliaments slimiest, nastiest MPs. Really. Awful. Decision.'[53] When challenged, she referred them to Hopkins's own rudeness. He said of Philip Davies for dismissing the need for overseas aid: 'he's only interested in promoting his little England, hang em and flog em world.'[54]

Therese Coffey (theresecoffey)

07/10/2013 21:49

@NadineDorriesMP that's not the @khopkinsmp that I recognise. May be on other wing of Party but authentic and brave

Therese Coffey has been a chemist and accountant and a Conservative MP since 2010

---

[50] http://citeseerx.ist.psu.edu/viewdoc/download?doi=10.1.1.22.5232&rep=rep1&type=pdf p. 83 [accessed 30 May 2014].
[51] Marshall-Andrews, *Off Message*, p. 35.
[52] Chris Mullin, *Decline and Fall, Diaries 2005-2010* (London: Profile, 2011), p. 88.
[53] Hayley Dixon, 'Nadine Dorries attacks newly promoted colleague on Twitter', *Telegraph*, 8 October 2013, http://www.telegraph.co.uk/news/politics/conservative/10362614/Nadine-Dorries-attacks-newly-promoted-colleague-on-Twitter.html [accessed 9 October 2013].
[54] Guido Fawkes blog http://order-order.com/2013/09/03/tory-twitter-bitch-fight-philip-davies-v-kris-hopkins/ [accessed 9 October 2013].

Increasingly such bitching reaches the public in record time, as Twitter allows MPs to indulge in quick and direct gossip, leaks become more common – and especially to the ConservativeHome website – and journalists betray confidences. Sir Nicholas Soames MP talked about how tension between the old and new guard was always a feature of Commons life, but when it was played out in the backbenchers' 1922 Committee in the past 'it used to be like a padlock – nothing got out'. As his party swung to the right under Thatcher he and other 'wets' met as the Lollard Group and they tried to get their Members onto the 1922 Committee, but it was all done strictly privately. When the modernizers, well represented in the 2010 intake, became impatient for change, one of their groups devised a slate for the 1922 Committee elections to oust some of the 'dinosaurs'.[55] Sir Nicholas and others despaired when their plans and even their nominations were revealed all over the internet.[56]

Tim Montgomerie: My fellow #MUFC fan @GrahamEvansMP is not happy Tory MPs were giving @ConHome live updates from yestday's #1922 meeting huff.to/Nqx6mL

Therese Coffey: @TimMontgomerie @GrahamEvansMP come off it Tim, you were tweeting while we were still in the meeting

Tim Montgomerie: @theresecoffey @GrahamEvansMP The meetings always leak. It's whether it takes minutes or hours.[57]

Tim Montgomerie is a Conservative blogger, founder of ConservativeHome, and was comment editor of *The Times*

It is not just the machinations of backbench politics that get leaked; even government policy is criticized by their own side in public. Ministers can't confide in backbenchers because if any don't like the plan then it will be on the internet within 20 minutes. So it has become extremely difficult for Ministers to consult with their own party, which in turn makes discontent and rebellion on the backbenches more likely.

It has always been the case that acrimony is directed towards a faltering Leader. Geoffrey Howe delivered the most famous critique when he resigned

---

[55] The 301 group is so called because that is the number of MPs needed to get an overall majority in Parliament in 2015. To make the Conservatives electable, the 301 group aims to nudge the party towards a kinder image.

[56] Paul Goodman, 2012, 'Tomorrow's 1922 Committee Elections – nominations in full', http://conservativehome.blogs.com/parliament/2012/05/tomorrows-1922-committee-elections-nominations-in-full.html [accessed 30 May 2013].

[57] Tweets: 12/07/2012 12:39, 12/07/2012 12:58, 12/07/2012 12:51.

as Leader of the Commons. In her final years Margaret Thatcher, according to Lord Howe, perceived no distinction between herself, government, party and the nation; to criticize her was an unpatriotic act.[58] On 1 November 1990, while he waited to give his resignation speech in the House, a backbencher passed him a note pleading with him not to damage the PM, threatening that he would hurt England and himself too. He ignored it and although he began with a few jokes, as he began to criticize the Prime Minister those around him breathed in sharply. She undermined her own side, he told them: 'It is rather like sending your opening batsmen to the crease, only for them to find, as the first balls are being bowled, that their bats have been broken before the game by the team captain.' Nervous laughter followed. By the last passage the House was gasping at almost every half-sentence:

> The conflict of loyalty, of loyalty to my Right Honourable friend the Prime Minister – and, after all, in two decades together that instinct of loyalty is still very real – and of loyalty to what I perceive to be the true interests of the nation, has become all too great. I no longer believe it possible to resolve that conflict from within this government.

The colour went from Mrs Thatcher's face. After he sat down the bemused silence was replaced by a babel of noise and MPs speculated what might happen next. It was clear that the PM was on Death Row.[59] For those who still revered her, it was a betrayal, but for many, she had become too difficult to work for.[60]

This was mild compared to the venom that John Major MP had to contend with as Prime Minister. He implies in his autobiography that some of the hostility was personal, but the fury of his critics was mainly directed at Europe and particularly the single European currency. In 1994 eight Euro-sceptic backbenchers had the whip (and therefore party membership) withdrawn – the ultimate sanction of the Chief Whip – for voting against the party at a critical vote and another joined them in protest. When it was later restored, on the assumption that they would show more loyalty, their public denunciations continued. Anti-Europe MPs briefed, leaked and carped. Even Margaret Thatcher publicly attacked the new PM. Although there was a large section of the party that was pro-European, Major asked them not to speak out: 'one wing of the party up in arms was sufficient. Two would have been cataclysmic if I was to keep the party in one piece. For me, the strain and frustration of trying to maintain a balance between the

[58] Geoffrey Howe, *Conflict of Loyalty* (London: Macmillan, 1994), pp. 664–8.
[59] Moncrieff, *Wine, Women and Westminster*, p. 234.
[60] Sir Robin Butler, then Cabinet Secretary, reflects on this period and why Thatcher's Cabinet colleagues turned against her: http://www.cabinetsecretaries.com/ [accessed 29 May 2013].

two sides was immense.'[61] He told the German Chancellor Helmut Kohl: 'I am in a coalition government of my own.' The hostility got so bad that Major called a leadership election, telling his opponents to put up or shut up, and he won fairly easily – but far from shutting them up, the fights over Europe raged on and contributed to a lost election in 1997.

The antagonism towards the next Prime Minister, Tony Blair, was rooted in completely different conflicts. A large proportion of his backbenchers were disappointed almost as soon as he got started. Those on the left found privatization and pro-business policies unpalatable, Labour's social liberals disliked the anti-terrorism legislation, and the Iraq War upset almost everyone. As early as 2002 one of his own side asked:

Mr McWalter: ... Will he provide the House with a brief characterisation of the political philosophy that he espouses and which underlies his policies?

Hon. Members: Hear, hear.

The Prime Minister: ... The best example that I can give is the rebuilding of the national health service today under this Government – extra investment. For example, there is the appointment today of Sir Magdi Yacoub to head up the fellowship scheme ...[62]

Political philosophy wasn't his strong point.

But the most famous, ferocious and damaging antagonism in recent times was between Blair and his Chancellor of the Exchequer, Gordon Brown. When Labour leader John Smith died it looked as if Brown would be elected to replace him. However, Blair decided that he would be a better leader, so he wooed his close friend: 'We were as close as two people ever are in politics. It was not simply a professional relationship, it was a friendship. Later when things became difficult, then fraught, and finally dangerous, the wrench was all the harder because the intimacy had been so real ...'[63] Blair felt that the polls gave him the advantage and he eventually persuaded Brown that if he would support him first, then Blair would reciprocate later. But over time, hostility seized their relationship and their respective cabals, and their view of each other soured.[64]

While Brown has been portrayed by his own colleagues as substantial

---

[61] Major, *The Autobiography*, pp. 616–17.
[62] Tony McWalter and Tony Blair, *HC Debates*, 27 February 2002, col. 698.
[63] Blair, *The Journey*, pp. 68–71.
[64] For criticism of Brown see Blair, ibid, p. 616, and for what has been called retaliation by Brown see Jonathan Wynne-Jones, 'Gordon Brown launches thinly-veiled attack on Tony Blair', *Telegraph*, 19 February 2011, http://www.telegraph.co.uk/news/politics/8335843/Gordon-Brown-launches-thinly-veiled-attack-on-Tony-Blair.html [accessed 9 October 2014].

but character-flawed, Blair and Cameron have faced accusations of lacking substance. Tory backbench critics complain that Cameron's attempts to woo the public by de-toxifying the party image will backfire. Gay marriage is perceived as an attack on marriage by traditionalists and has infuriated many on his own side. Together with Euro-scepticism re-emerging with force, by May 2013 the pundits and twitterati were murmuring about how treatment of Cameron was reminiscent of the Major years. Hostilities were further inflamed when journalists claimed that a senior Conservative close to Cameron referred to their own activists as 'mad swivel-eyed loons'.[65] When the BBC political editor, Nick Robinson, says that dozens of Tories are dreaming about replacing their leader, it doesn't really matter whether it is true or not. Mere speculation becomes a form of reality. Cameron got so rattled he issued this email to all his party's Members, stressing his friendship with them:

I have met thousands and thousands of party members. We've pounded pavements together, canvassed together and sat in make-shift campaign headquarters together, from village halls to front rooms. We have been together through good times and bad. This is more than a working relationship; it is a deep and lasting friendship … I would never have around me those who sneered or thought otherwise. We are a team, from the parish council to the local association to Parliament, and I never forget it.[66]

The party leaders are not the only targets. The big beasts in any Cabinet and their followers jostle for position. They scheme and undermine each other in private discussions, Cabinet meetings or, increasingly, in the media; but they have to try and look as if they are not. In the Autumn 2012 reshuffle David Cameron sacked the Children's Minister Tim Loughton MP despite his close relationships with children's organizations. Loughton contained his fury for some months but in January 2013, when asked to give evidence to the Education Select Committee, he compared the then Secretary of State for Education, Michael Gove MP, to Young Mr Grace from the British TV sitcom *Are You Being Served?*, saying that he hardly listened to other Ministers and was too fond of making soliloquies. A 'senior Department of Education source' retaliated with blistering ferocity about Loughton:

His approach to child protection as a political issue was disgraceful. Loughton spent his time pandering to pressure groups so they would

[65] http://www.independent.co.uk/news/uk/politics/jeremy-paxman-reveals-he-has-heard-senior-tories-calling-activists-swiveleyed-loons-8625324.html [accessed 29 May 2013].
[66] http://blogs.telegraph.co.uk/news/willheaven/100217916/david-camerons-personal-message-to-tory-members-in-full/ [accessed 20 May 2013].

praise him on Twitter. Loughton wouldn't focus on child sex abuse unless it was all over TV and the DfE now has to pick up the pieces. Loughton was a lazy incompetent narcissist obsessed only with self-promotion. Journalists should consider his actual behaviour when he calls for inquiries and attacks us for not taking issues seriously that he refused to handle professionally.[67]

Loughton defended his record to journalists and on Twitter:

Tim Loughton MP (timloughton)

17/01/2013 20:17

tinyurl.com/bya4qcj My record speaks 4 itself so no need 2 comment further but this sort of poison brings politics into disrepute

Tim Loughton has been a Conservative MP since 1997 and was Minister for Children and Families 2010–12

This public spat with Loughton was unusually bloody. But rows within government are not infrequent and when too public, can influence reshuffles. Gove's argument with fellow Cabinet member Theresa May MP came only one month before he was demoted from Secretary of State for Education to Chief Whip and although it may have been a coincidence, it appeared linked, according to journalists.[68] A more typical form of criticism between heavyweights is a swipe in the form of advice. Peter Hain provides an example of this when he suggests that the Shadow Chancellor, Ed Balls would do well to show clearer support for his leader.[69] Perhaps all these protagonists justify these public displays of enmity to themselves with thoughts about advancing their cause – education, child protection, Labour's election prospects or whatever – but at the same time they are making friends and enemies. That is what people do in politics, not only for a purpose but because it is inevitable.

---

[67] James Forsyth, 'Tim Loughton vs the Department for Education', *Spectator*, 17 January 2013, http://blogs.spectator.co.uk/coffeehouse/2013/01/loughton-vs-dfe/ [accessed 30 May 2013].
[68] For example, http://www.theguardian.com/politics/2014/jul/15/michael-gove-chief-whip-david-cameron-reshuffle-cabinet [accessed 1 September 2014].
[69] Peter Hain, 'We need to up our game', *Progress On-line*, 8 May 2013, http://www.progress-sonline.org.uk/2013/05/08/we-need-to-up-our-game/ [accessed 30 May 2013].

Social life under politics

Social relations, cultural meaning and emotion are found interwoven with politics in all societies, institutions and work environments. As Nick Clegg MP put it to me: 'We are defined and fuelled by relationships at work, in politics no less than anywhere else.'[70] People navigate power hierarchies, compete for resources and aspire for both collective and individual good.

Social relations are always governed, but not determined, by rules. Some appear rather trivial. MPs don't shake hands with one another until they have retired or lost their seat. If you do so, it means – somewhat randomly – that you want them to lose their seat, so it is considered rude. Others have profound political consequences. For example, when you address the Chamber you do so through the Speaker and when referring to another MP you say 'the Honourable Member for X' if in a different party, 'my Honourable Friend for X' if on your side, and 'the Right Honourable' if they are in the Privy Council. There are at least four important political messages in this form of address. X is always your constituency, so every remark emphasizes why MPs are there – as representatives of a particular part of the country. MPs speak to each other through the Speaker to emphasis her/his role as the mediator but also to depersonalize attacks; 'you' is not allowed, so the sting is taken out of insults. The use of 'friend' is obvious and the word 'honourable' forces an appearance of respect.

Politicians do politics partly by forging social relationships of various kinds: friendly, hostile, or both. The parties are at their most hostile when talking about money. The economy provokes profound disagreement between parties, and between the Coalition and Opposition during 2010–15, but even then, ways to mediate conflict have to be found. To take as an example: the two sides responded differently to the 'banking crisis', with the government proposing a parliamentary inquiry and Labour arguing for a judge-led one. A bad-tempered debate, punctuated by frequent furious tweets from both sides accusing opponents of low behaviour, came to an end with the government winning the vote. Osborne had accused Balls of involvement in fixing bank rates, and Balls threw back charges of cheap and partisan behaviour. But since the vote meant a parliamentary committee had to be set up, and the media would not forgive Labour for obstructing, co-operation was the only choice. Different sides were needed: Parliament against the bankers. How could Ed Balls achieve this without looking weak? Immediately he announced that Labour would support the way forward: 'The government has won its vote. We respect Andrew Tyrie

---

[70] Interview held by Emma Crewe, on the telephone, 16 July 2013. Nick Clegg studied anthropology at Cambridge University.

– he will now chair a narrow inquiry & we will work with him.'[71] So by backing this senior backbench Conservative, whose influence was rooted in the non-partisan Select Committees as Chair of the influential Treasury Select Committee, Balls sidestepped his ongoing war with Osborne. Andrew Tyrie MP had even smoothed the way by saying he would only agree to chair the Committee if he had the support of the whole House and by referring to the Conservative Party destroying an inquiry 100 years earlier. John Thurso MP, also on his Committee, joined him in raising the tone with an anti-partisan speech. Before the debate concluded Tyrie spoke privately to Ed Balls, and then to George Osborne, presumably to ensure that a face-saving form of words could be found for all so that the sides could be rearranged.

If money provokes predictable right/left hostility, debates concerned with what MPs call issues of 'moral conscience' throw up different configurations of allies. These debates are often unwhipped, so MPs are free to disagree on non-party lines. A discussion of assisted dying, for example, inspired two sides irrespective of party – those in favour of relaxing the law so that people can help others to die, and those against it.[72] Unionist Ian Paisley (junior) said that 'this House is not God' to decide who lives and dies, Labour Frank Field MP warned that vulnerable people would be persuaded to die early, and Conservative Edward Leigh MP spoke against any kind of killing. Others sat on the other side of the argument, speaking about the agony that some face in trying to protect their relatives. Labour Paul Blomfield MP spoke about how his father took his life in a monoxide-filled garage rather than peacefully with his family around him. Conservative Guy Opperman MP had thought hard about the subject, as he'd had a brain tumour the year before; he concluded that an individual's life is their own, so if they decide to end it with the help of others, it is up to them. So the sides that are normally created by party can disappear when the whips are not whipping their Members.

Such backbench debates have been revitalized by the new Backbench Business Committee created in 2010. This new Select Committee was part of a package of reforms designed to restore the reputation of Parliament after the expenses scandal of 2009. The way it was formed by the Chair, Natascha Engel MP and her Members on the committee with the guidance of its first Clerk, Andrew Kennon created a culture of transparency and cross-party collaboration. They invited MPs to pitch for time slots for their debates in public and gave preference to those with cross-party support. Natascha was amazed when she first heard backbenchers referring to MPs in other parties as their friend:

> One of the most shocking events I encountered while chairing the Backbench Business Committee – I do not know whether other hon. Members felt the

---

[71] Ed Balls, tweet, 20:41, 05/07/2012.
[72] HC debates, 27 March 2012, col. 1393–4, 1398–1400, 1402–4, 1401–2, 1431–3.

same – was the first time I ever heard a Conservative Member call a Labour
Member his honourable friend.[73]

Individuals too defy the image of tribal politics by making friendships across
parties alongside political alliances. MPs are drawn to those with constituencies
in the same region to campaign for better defences against flooding or against
airport expansion. When Zac Goldsmith MP organized a rally to protest against
plans to build more runways in Heathrow he invited all the political parties. Some
join cross-party campaigns on issues they have a personal interest in. When
Chris Bryant MP (Labour) spoke in a debate about hacking, referring to Zac
Goldsmith MP (Conservative) as a friend in these matters, Zac in turn tweeted
compliments about his speech. When the Backbench Business Committee
debates take place, at least some MPs from both sides of the House have
to support the debate. For example, in January 2012 backbenchers from all
parties took up the cause of pubs, a feature of so many villages and towns in
every constituency, arguing that government intervention was needed to force
the large brewery companies to be more generous. The government realized
that if the motion was put to the vote they would probably lose, so they let it
through. There are MPs of every party who are drawn into discussion about the
same topics, whether health, education or Europe, and for whom friendships
grow along the way. One Conservative MP explained that he makes allies in
the Labour Party because in the jungle of politics, relationships are everything. If
he ever faces a scandal he knows the other side will hold back a little if he has
made a connection with them. The lone wolves in the political world struggle
harder to make an impression.

   Disentangling the social from the political is not easy. Jeremy Corbyn MP
suggests that 'If you are very tribal then you will not be taken seriously by the
other side. You won't have a long shelf life.'[74] Tribal means a mix of party loyalty
and style of interaction. It can refer specifically to an excess of rivalry between
the political parties expressed through aggressive partisan attacks. At times
it has its place, MPs often say, most particularly during Question Time. But
an abrupt launch into tribal bile at the wrong moment – during a backbench
debate, for example – can antagonize your opponents and even your allies.
Such aggression can only be forgiven if accompanied by wit, self-deprecation
and warmth. Failure to be socially courteous in the corridor or tearoom is also
seen as tribal.

   Formal and informal rules governing relationships, mostly played out in
ritualized encounters, are where culture meets politics in Parliament. The most
important ritual of all for the Commons is the General Election that brings

---

[73] Natascha Engel MP, *HC Debates*, 26 April 2012, col. 331WH.
[74] Interviewed by Emma Crewe, 17 May 2012.

MPs into Parliament and can toss them out again. The terrible bind that political leaders find themselves in is that political tribalism is useful for keeping backbenchers onside and getting them to vote for you in the division lobbies, but it is unattractive to the public. The public may like the theatre of PMQs, but when politicians are trying to get things done they prefer a co-operative attitude. Pollsters and spin doctors all resort to the same refrain as an election approaches: 'move to the centre', and the leaders are more than ready to embrace this. Blair did this so comprehensively that Roy Hattersley was on the right of the party in the 1990s and ended up on the left by the time Labour lost the election in 2010.

Both MPs of all the main parties and voters are more cautious than party activists. But are they necessarily nearer the centre in the minds of the public? When Louise Mensch tweeted: 'Blair made Lab electable by tacking right, Cameron made Tories electable by tacking left', Tim Montgomerie, a former *Times* and ConHome journalist, replied: 'Wrong, as Keith Joseph argued in the 1970s. They're won on the common ground ...'[75] In 1970 Keith Joseph (former MP) had argued that the Tories should not be defined by the ideas of the left but should search for the *middle* ground between Labour and Conservative by finding the *common* ground between politicians and the public:

> The middle ground turned out to be like the will-o'-the-wisp, the light which flickers over marshlands by night beguiling the weary traveller; as he moves towards it, the currents of aid he sets up by his movement send it dancing away from him, and he goes on following, stumbling deeper and deeper into the mire.[76]

Of course, the common ground between the public and politicians will be different for each party. But the despairing cry of the public is: 'You are all the same.' They say this, surely, not because they deem MPs' policies or ideas to be identical, but because they distrust all politicians equally – not because they disagree with their policies, but because they don't believe them when they say: 'We are on your side.' Distrust is the problem, not disagreement. It is a moral, and therefore social, reaction as much as an ideological or political one.

The consequence of this collapse in support for MPs and their parties is dire for democracy. It means that there are far fewer volunteers to make party politics work and those who remain have to work far harder. At election time the number of party members willing to knock on doors and encourage people to take sides

---

[75] Louise Mensch, 04/05/2013, 17:32 and Tim Montgomerie 04/05/2013, 17:34.
[76] Keith Joseph, *Stranded on the Middle Ground, Reflections on Circumstances and Policies* (London: Centre for Policy Studies, 1970) p. 25, http://www.cps.org.uk/files/cps/Keith_Joseph_files/634_ProductPreviewFile.pdf [accessed 9 May 2013].

and vote is shrinking. The potential pool from which to recruit MPs is also then smaller. Increasingly a large number of MPs only join political parties once they have already decided that they want to fight to get into Parliament. So candidates' loyalty to their party can be rather sudden and shallow. It is not surprising, therefore, that each Parliament witnesses bigger rebellions against the whips, with MPs under pressure to follow their faction, conscience or electorate's demands rather than their party line. To what extent do MPs succumb to the demands of those they represent? The political cohesion of political parties is declining as the social networks underlying them collapse. Taking sides is a social business and politics can only be reinvigorated by addressing the need for live networks underlying the politics. Whether the old-style networking can be happily replaced by new social-media-based networks remains an open question. What is clear is that social and political change are intimately entangled.

3
Constituents' Champions

MPs represent tens of thousands of constituents within a locality, promote themselves to wildly different audiences and champion the interests of people they identify with. How do these different kinds of representation fit together – if at all?

****

Our parliamentary democracy has local representation at its heart. The perceived legitimacy of the Commons rests on the election of 650 Members by constituents defined by geography and population. MPs have representation of people living in an area at the core of everything they do, until, perhaps, they become Ministers. A typical UK MP will spend at least two days a week in their constituency while Parliament is sitting and work in the constituency for the majority of recess days. The average is probably far higher than 100 days per year in the constituency and has been growing steadily over the last 30 years.[1] However this obscures a huge variation. While London MPs might return to their constituency several times a day, at the other extreme there is a handful of MPs who only visit once a fortnight or less. But it is rare these days for MPs not to have a home and an office in their constituency that they visit at least weekly. The MPs who once claimed that constituencies should not be visited when Parliament was sitting, such as Enoch Powell MP, no longer exist (or keep quiet).

In addition to this central plank of our democracy, MPs engage in 'representation' in two other ways. First, they represent or do PR about themselves to impress those from whom they need support: up to 110,000[2] electors, journalists, the interest groups, other MPs and, if they want promotion, the Chief Whip and leader of their party. The final form of representation involves speaking on behalf of groups not confined to their constituencies that they identify with

---

[1] Fenno researched US representatives in their districts and found that political scientists greatly underestimate the time and importance of constituency work from the viewpoint of Members of Congress. During 1973, 13 of them spent an average of 83 days in their district. Richard Fenno, *Home Style, House Members in their Districts* (New York: HarperCollins, 1978) p. 32.
[2] The constituency with the largest number of voters in 2010 was the Isle of Wight.

or whose interests they even embody – for instance, by being black, female or gay. Whether in or outside their constituency or party, or located in a different country, this third layer of representation has no link with election. These three forms of representation pull MPs in different and often contradictory directions. I will look at each one in turn.

Representing constituents in Parliament

The public loathe politicians with the exception of their own MP.[3] As the Lib Dem John Thurso MP put it: 'Politicians as a group are derided whereas MPs as individuals still command high respect.'[4] In Westminster an MP is just one among 650 struggling for power and attention, while in the constituency they are still VIPs. In their own territory they are unique. Paul Flynn's constituents know everything about him, he told me, and they think: 'He is a mad bastard, but he is *our* mad bastard.'[5] He describes the relationship between MP and constituent as:

> … that of a priest and parishioners, solicitor and clients, shepherd and flock, shop steward and workers and friend of many friends. The MP should be the living embodiment of the constituency, tirelessly promoting and defending the territory with the ferocity of a mother protecting her offspring.[6]

The public often love their MP and the feeling tends to be reciprocated. Nearly every MP I spoke to was most relaxed when extolling the virtues of their constituency – its beauty, variety or warmth – or outlining its problems. Most develop an affinity with the place they represent, but it is also the safest topic to talk about. Articulating policy issues will always displease someone, but MPs can champion their locality, at least in general terms, without incurring anyone's displeasure.

Within the Palace of Westminster rituals of representation are played out in the Chamber, committee rooms, various offices and meeting rooms. A 30-minute adjournment debate is the occasion when MPs can go into greatest depth about a constituency concern or interest. Whether focusing exclusively on their constituency

---

[3]When asked by researchers whom they would seek help from if not happy with local health services, most of the people in the study would go to their GP, but as many as a quarter (the second biggest group) would seek the advice of their MP (Hansard Society, *Audit of Political Engagement*, p. 53).
[4]Interviewed by Emma Crewe, 8 November 2011.
[5]Interviewed by Emma Crewe, 8 November 2013.
[6]Flynn, *How to be an MP*, p. 138.

or relating it to wider issues as well, it is an opportunity to give publicity to potential supporters, such as Stephen Pound MP did in the following speech:

> It would be invidious to mention individuals in the context of the miracle that is occurring in north-west London, but if I were so tempted, the names of Nilesh Morjaria of the Church pharmacy, of Mahendra Gokani of Mandeville Road and of C.K. Nathwani of the Ravenor pharmacy would feature strongly, as would Usha and Dilip Shah of the Alpha pharmacy in Northolt.[7]

Usually the flattery is more general: Jacob Rees-Mogg MP referred to his Somerset constituents as the most intelligent people in the world[8]; Eric Pickles MP, Secretary of State for Communities and Local Government, on one occasion mimicked backbenchers by saying that Stockport was close to his heart, a gem and a magnificent town, Formby a wonderful place to invest, and Rochdale was the apple of his eye, all within the space of an hour.[9] Conversely, to effect change MPs must generalize issues and try not to sound too parochial. Some debates, such as one defending British pubs – which can, after all, be found in every constituency across the four nations – provide scope to champion constituents' concerns and a national problem at the same time.

Even the lesser-known rituals provide opportunities for constituency name-checking. Business Questions in particular is a weekly occasion during which the Leader of the House announces the agenda for the following week, and perhaps beyond, and the Shadow Leader then complains that there is too much or too little legislation, that the opposition have insufficient warning of statements and the government is generally incompetent. Backbenchers can then pile in with any question they choose, allowing plenty of scope for plugging constituents' demands, requests or opinions. Although few are watching Business Questions, MPs' questions can be uploaded on their website, demonstrating tireless pursuit of constituents' interests. Even Points of Order, when an MP can ask the Speaker to take action regarding rules being broken, can be harnessed to the constituency cause. As Speaker Bercow pointed out, they are very rarely about order and more often points of frustration or points that act like a press release: 'It is part of the choreography of Parliament that this is tolerated to some extent.'[10] Alan Simpson was not even ticked off when he asked:

> **Mr. Alan Simpson** (Nottingham, South) On a point of order, Madam Deputy Speaker. As some of my constituents have told me that their employer, Asda,

---

[7]Stephen Pound MP, *HC Debates*, 15 April 2013, col. 137.
[8]Jacob Rees-Mogg MP, *HC Debates*, 8 May 2014, col. 344.
[9]Eric Pickles MP, *HC Debates*, 12 March 2013, col. 12, 15, 20.
[10]Interviewed by Emma Crewe, 19 January 2012.

has informed them that unless they are prepared to work on Easter Sunday they will be sacked … have you been informed of any Government intention to make a statement on the matter?[11]

MPs try to represent constituency interests during the various processes entailed in making law. For example, Stephen Lloyd explains that he voted against his own party's introduction of tuition fees because 'for me, the promises I made to my constituents will always come first'.[12] During budget debates MPs show an interest in the effect of a mansion tax or higher duty on beer upon their constituents. During Select Committee enquiries MPs may raise questions that affect constituents; for example, when Dame Anne Begg MP criticizes the government's welfare reforms she does so as Chair of the Work and Pensions Select Committee, but also because she is representing people in Aberdeen South who are dealing with cuts to their benefits.[13]

'Pork barrel' funding[14] of local projects is an everyday part of politics in the USA. In the UK it is rare, so MPs told me. Several informants told me that a Treasury Minister had on one occasion asked the MPs in his party whether they had any funding proposals for capital projects in their constituencies, and that at least one technical college, an A&E unit and a bridge were built as a result. This was regarded as exceptional. It is not the way things are usually done in Westminster.

In the constituency

Over the last 50 years there has been a massive increase in the volume of communication and demands from constituents, mainly due to email. Traditionally representing constituents' interests in Westminster is seen as high-status work in the eyes of MPs and observers, while work within the constituency tends to be dismissed as glorified social work by many.[15] As this work is both undervalued and neglected by MP-watchers, I will dwell on it in some detail.

---

[11] Alan Simpson MP, HC Debates, 30 March 1994, cols 1041–2.
[12] Stephen Lloyd MP website, http://stephenlloyd.org.uk/en/article/2010/453897/lloyd-votes-against-rise-in-university-tuition-fees [accessed 28 June 2013].
[13] http://annebegg.wordpress.com/westminster-work/ [accessed 2 July 2013].
[14] The utilization of government funds for projects designed to please voters or legislators and win votes (www.oxforddictionaries.com).
[15] For example, Andrew Adonis, Parliament Today (Manchester: Manchester University Press, 1993), pp. 68–70. Tony Banks would have been typical as an MP when describing being a constituency MP as tedious, 'like a high-powered social worker', http://news.bbc.co.uk/1/hi/uk/4047123.stm [accessed 17 September 2014]. Other MPs rate it more highly and these days most would claim it is important.

MPs interact with constituents in three main ways. First they have meetings with people – business leaders, charity workers, vicars, campaigners or teachers – to discuss policy issues, usually in the constituents' workplace. Secondly, they do political work such as canvassing or drumming up support within the local party. Thirdly, they meet individual constituents to discuss their problems in 'surgeries'. The division of time between these three activities varies from MP to MP. I had assumed that MPs in safe seats would visit rarely and only dabble in policy work but keep away from surgeries and do only light canvassing. However, two of the three MPs who spent the most time on this aspect of the work had majorities of over 10,000. The one MP who met every single constituent who wanted to see him and never delegated any surgery meetings to his staff had a majority of over 15,000. This was Sir George Young, MP for North West Hampshire. He enjoyed meeting constituents and making sure that their problems were dealt with properly. He liaised with councillors from his party by inviting them into the weekly meetings and handing over local issues to them when they were best placed to deal with them. Along the way he heard about what was worrying people and although he had a position in government until 2014, so couldn't speak about their concerns in the Chamber, he could get a sense of how his government's policies were affecting people in their everyday lives. This conscientious Minister shattered my expectation that the hardest-working constituency MPs would be backbenchers in marginal seats. MPs in marginal constituencies may have the next election in the back of their minds at all times but it doesn't always make them better constituency MPs. For a start, they have to spend a greater proportion of their time promoting themselves.[16]

The gender of MPs seems to influence their behaviour when meeting constituents with problems in surgeries. The extent to which MPs get involved varies from substantial to not at all. At one end of the continuum staff do everything and at the other extreme MPs do everything. Both extremes are rare. It appears that as a rule, and with exceptions, women are inclined to be more involved in casework than men. The only MPs I met or heard about who do not personally deal with constituents' problems are male. The men who don't do casework articulated their priorities as scrutiny or getting a government job, while some felt that councillors should handle case work entirely or that their staff were more skilled at giving advice. (This difference is not just a reflection of women being newer to Parliament, because some of the MPs who rarely meet constituents are men in the 2010 intake.) There was a difference among staff as well. While

---

[16] Fenno points out that it is not the representatives in the safest seats that necessarily visit their constituencies least often in the USA (Home Style, pp. 36–9). They feel far more uncertain and insecure about their election prospects than he expected when looking at the statistics, but also they have other reasons for visiting and investing in their districts. For example, those with families in their constituencies unsurprisingly visit more often.

male policy researchers working for MPs were in the majority, constituency caseworkers tend to be women.

Of the four women and three men MPs I observed in their constituencies, all the women and only one of the men seemed entirely comfortable talking to constituents about emotional and painful personal issues. At the end of one interview a woman MP had with a particularly impressive and proud businessman who had a financial problem, he added with some emotion that he was worried about what people were saying about him at his mosque. He was collected, but concluded: 'I may seem calm but this will make me penniless. My life will fall apart.' I asked the MP whether she thought he would have been equally likely to raise that with other MPs, including men for example. She replied: 'Not in a million years. He is absolutely not the sort of person to talk about that kind of thing.' On the other hand, when a bereaved woman started crying, a male MP of a certain age was utterly unfazed. He held her hand and suggested they take a pause. She immediately looked much calmer and continued with her explanation. But he may be a little unusual. Although this man was clearly able to soothe in the face of distress, other male MPs told me that their caseworkers are better at dealing with such encounters. MPs' closer involvement does not necessarily lead to better outcomes for the constituents, because caseworkers can be extremely effective and write as if from MPs in any case, but it may mean that from the viewpoint of citizens with problems, women MPs are more accessible and sympathetic than their male counterparts. Whether this makes women more electable but distracts them from achieving political power at Westminster, or creates more stress for women MPs grappling with heartbreaking stories, is unknown. My sample was small so only tentative conclusions can be drawn and this relationship deserves both broader and closer observation.

There is a widespread assumption that what MPs do in constituencies is aimed to please and win votes. This is misplaced. In one constituency the vast majority of visits were from people who did not even have a vote, as they were not UK citizens, but the MP dealt with them with the same thoroughness as with voters. MPs still carry out surgeries in seats that are thought to be rock-solid safe. Constituents expect it; MPs feel it is their duty. Clearly there are other reasons, too, for meeting constituents with problems. Former MP Alf (now Lord) Dubs talked about how listening to constituency cases could be so serious that they stop life in its tracks, so that you can see the impact of your party's policies on real people when you are in government and make corrections, or of the other party's policies when in opposition and oppose more effectively. He added: 'The constituency system creates a balance, an early warning system.'[17]

---

[17] Interviewed by Emma Crewe, 10 November 1999.

I did not appreciate how complex it is for MPs to find out what constituents think about policy issues until I heard for myself their conversations with constituents. Citizens change their minds and hold contradictory views. On allowing same-sex marriage, for example, many MPs received as many letters in favour as against. In response to this 'free vote', should an MP go with the majority, or the most up-to-date attitude, or use their own best judgement? There is no formula. MPs pointed to endless difficulties in translating constituents' views into actions. Those towards the left tended to feel that it is the more affluent, middle-class and educated constituents who communicated their policy stance, so MPs have a duty to make an effort to gather the views of their less pushy constituents. Those towards the right fumed at organizations like 38 Degrees that encouraged tens of thousands of citizens to send formulaic, anti-Tory campaign messages rather than thinking for themselves. Some Conservatives reply to mass emailing with a template or publish a reply on their website.

Jeremy Hunt (Jeremy_Hunt)

30/05/2013 03:05

In case being misled by 'neutral 38Degrees e-petition, it IS NOT and WAS NEVER going to be Conservative policy to limit GP appointments.

Constituents wrote and spoke about policy issues far less than they communicated concerns that directly and immediately affected their lives. Of 12,357 enquiries Stephen Lloyd received during 2012, only 2,604 related to government policy and the rest were local issues or individuals' problems.[18] On the other hand, MPs also spend a considerable amount of time meeting local organizations and party members to talk 'policy' while their staff respond to problems. I watched two MPs withstand high-pressure advocacy on same-sex marriage policy. A Labour MP met a vicar and his colleague in a church to hear their concerns. The MP explained that same-sex marriage was not high on his priorities for legislation, and he felt that the Conservatives were merely aiming to detoxify their brand, but he wouldn't vote against it. The vicar threatened that he would lose votes with his Christian and Muslim constituents. The MP retorted that socially conservative black pastors still vote for Obama despite his sympathy for gay marriage. He felt strongly about this issue, so numbers of letters from constituents would not change his mind, but in any case he had

---

[18]Stephen Lloyd MP, http://gallery.mailchimp.com/cdaa010d3f3b37bc5da7e5592/files/Casework_Summary_2_.pdf [accessed 28 June 2013].

in fact received far more letters in favour. The vicar and his colleague looked furious, but the MP was polite and attentive; he gave them at least 20 minutes. As we walked away, I mused to him on the tact required by politicians. 'But actually, did you notice my barbed comment when he tried to pull a fast one about me losing the Muslim vote?' he replied. 'But I have good support from the Muslim community. That is why I told the Obama story.'

Some months later I was with a Coalition MP when he met an activist and former parliamentary candidate from his own party in Portcullis House. The activist knew that the MP was thinking of voting against same-sex marriage and wanted to change his mind. As an insider, his arguments were far more deadly. Tiny flaws could be eradicated by amendments, he said, and the change in law will happen some time soon in any case. He went on: the Quakers might take the government to court if it doesn't introduce the Bill and the MP would lose the young vote in his constituency with his stance. The activist handed over a short document written by an MP who had decided to vote in favour. The MP agreed to read it and looked rather unmoved. He announced that his local party and letters from constituents were all anti-same-sex marriage, rather as if he was fending off a salesman's offer. But then the activist's points became more threatening. Those who had voted against equalizing the age of consent for homosexual sex, he said, had lost the respect of the party and never quite recovered. 'I don't mind what people think of me', retorted the MP. More devastating still, his three staff would be upset and one had talked about resigning. The MP looked shaken but resolute – he did not like being blackmailed into voting against his conscience. The threats of withdrawal of support, and the MP's determination to ignore them, reveal emotion on both sides. It is much easier to be swayed to represent people you are bound to by shared experience.

Michael Fabricant (Mike_Fabricant)

21/05/2013 08:30

It is telling that emails from those anti gay marriage are the most virulent and unpleasant. No Christian virtues of tolerance there then.

Michael Fabricant has been a Conservative MP since 1992

If this gives the impression that policy meetings are antagonistic and emotional, they can be. You tend to ask to meet your MP on a policy issue only if you want to change their mind or get them to do something they were not planning to do. Legalizing gay marriage seems to provoke more intemperate emails than usual. Angie Bray MP (Conservative) told a journalist: 'You get emails from one side saying you're morally deficient if you vote no and emails threatening hell fire and brimstone if you vote yes. It has frankly been an ill-tempered debate on both sides.'[19] But I also watched meetings that were collaborative and calm. One was with the MD of a business who was interested in advice from the MP, who happened to know about trading in Asia. Another MP met the Vice-Chancellor of a university in her constituency to ask him to tell her about problems facing students. The underlying assumption in both meetings was that they were all working towards a shared goal.

The nature of this strand of constituency work – discussing problems and solutions with a huge range of people – is completely differently from the advice MPs dispense in surgeries. According to a survey by Sunday Politics, on average each London MP held 48 surgeries in 2011, seeing a total of 720 constituents. Stephen Timms MP (Labour), who was stabbed by a constituent in 2010, saw as many as 2,300 in one year.[20] I sat in on 32 'surgery' meetings in six constituency offices, mostly with MPs but in two constituencies with a senior caseworker as well.[21] Only three were about policy issues. In the first two, about boycotting Israel and GCSEs being badly marked, the MP agreed and promised to take action. In the last case an elderly man – let's call him Mr Frost – complained about government policy to a Conservative MP. He criticized it for taking a weak stance on immigration, especially those who can't speak English; shutting down hospitals but giving funds to overseas aid; deporting terrorists too slowly; being in the thrall of the EU; and allowing too many foreigners to claim benefits. The MP suggested he should distinguish between those born in the UK, whether Afro-Caribbean or whatever, and those who were not. So Mr Frost replied: 'I have no problem with the Afro-Caribbeans, it those Romanians and Algerians. They don't even speak the language.' The MP had a note of exasperation in his voice from this point but said they had introduced a language test. He made an eloquent case for overseas aid, but Mr Frost continued: 'I think we should look after our own.'

'Well I don't. We are all human', replied the Tory MP.

'But it all goes to corrupt governments in Africa anyway.'

Afterward the MP mused sadly that he did not suppose he would get his vote. He had spoken his mind, not bending at all to what the man might want to hear. And though he was thinking of the next election, and especially the worrying threat of UKIP pinching votes from the Tories, his response to this voter did not stretch anywhere near to deceit. The discussion made me realize that most MPs in any party face such a huge spectrum of views within their constituency that to

---

[19] http://www.independent.co.uk/news/uk/politics/some-of-the-emails-ive-had-are-simply-appalling-mps-complain-of-vitriolic-lobbying-ahead-of-historic-vote-8481240.html   [accessed 30 May 2014].

[20] http://www.bbc.co.uk/news/uk-england-london-20366342 [accessed 10 July 2013].

[21] In one constituency I did not get permission to sit in on surgery meetings.

please all of them is an impossibility. On reading a number of MPs' emails and letters, it became obvious that MPs do not react by echoing their constituents' views. Sometimes they agree, often they disagree, or occasionally they may reply that they see both sides of the argument but haven't decided which one to plump for as yet.

The other 29 of the 32 'surgery' meetings concerned problems facing individuals or families. Some MPs had as few as three appointments in a morning while others in my sample had far more, especially those in inner city constituencies – the record being 60 seen by one MP and three staff on a first-come-first-served basis in one morning. The process of finding out the nature of the problem was often more complex than the response. The person would generally sit down, take a deep breath and tell a story – usually a desperately sad one – about struggling with a terrible mixture of trials. I had made the mistake of assuming that most of these would be relatively trivial. They were heartbreaking and the depth of emotion was such that they hardly noticed the presence of an observer.[22]

David Ward (DavidWardMP)

06/01/2013 18:51

Surgery yestday. Insurance fraud, death of child, planning issue, child sexual abuse, visa problem – tmorra? 5.30am start back to HofC #fb

David Ward was a university lecturer and has been a Lib Dem MP since 2010

The emotion, and sometimes mental strain or illness, usually made it difficult for the constituent to explain the details of their problem calmly and concisely. I roughly ranked the 29 cases into 'urgent', 'medium' and 'not urgent'. Seven were not urgent and eight were medium. However, in 14 cases the person – or their relative – was destitute or about to lose their income, house, sanity or right to stay in the UK. Severe difficulties often seemed to involve several people and interlaced problems. Some examples will illustrate the urgency and complexity within this more desperate group. I observed the first three cases and heard about the other two during interviews with caseworkers:

1 A woman is trying to cope with a grown-up son who has ADHD, Tourette's

---

[22] In all cases the MP or staff sought the permission of constituents to allow me to sit in before I entered the room and not one refused.

and autism, is violent and was recently imprisoned on the word of a young woman who claims he fathered her child. The son's father has died, as have the rest of her family, and her marriage to his stepfather is under strain. As she told this terrible story, the caseworker listened with such respect and patience that the strain on this woman's face visibly softened. The caseworker promised to write to Adult Services and the First Minister in Scotland but the woman said that merely having someone to tell was as important.

2 In another case, a young woman lives in a one-bed housing association flat with her partner and 19-year-old disabled brother. The couple sleep on the sofa and take it in turns to look after the brother while the other works. They have been promised sheltered accommodation for him by the council but have been waiting for 18 months. The MP handed this case to a councillor who will follow up with the District Council.

3 A family of seven were in temporary accommodation, waiting for a council flat, because the mother was ill and needed looking after while the father was unemployed. Just before the benefits cap was due to come into effect, the council warned the family that they could be evicted because their rent was too high. They were under the impression that they might be moved out of the borough, which would mean their five children would have had to change school. The MP wrote to the council and received a detailed explanation from the housing department. The family was be moved up from a less serious category to the most urgent one, ensuring that they would be allocated a council house before either becoming homeless or being forced to leave the area.

4 A young couple had a baby taken into care. The MP's caseworker felt that Social Services were discounting their innocent explanation about bruising because they were unemployed, inarticulate and had been in trouble with the law. The caseworker represented them at a key hearing, pointed out how social workers had broken 26 rules under their own policies, and it was decided that the baby could return home.

5 Finally, another case was described to me by a woman who visited the surgery to thank the MP with a present of spring rolls. Her husband was an alcoholic who lost his job and house and was institutionalized when he injured his head. His wife struggled with the forms to get him out of the institution. The MP helped and made sure they were allocated the right benefits and housing so that the husband could return home.

These stories, even more complex in detail than they may appear, took time to explain, but once grasped, both MPs and caseworkers identified a course of action with confidence and speed. In the 29 cases they worked out almost instantly that the complaints primarily concerned the UK Border Agency (8 cases), the Department of Work and Pensions (4), the housing department of the local council (4), another government department/authority (4), a private company (3), Social Services (2), a housing association (2), HMRC (1), or private landlord (1). All MPs reported high levels of cases dealing with benefits and housing. Donald Searing points out that this role as local ombudsperson redressing grievances amounts to the revival of a very old role for MPs caused by the demands of the Welfare State.[23] Working out who was to blame, or at least responsible for delay, errors or inaction, defined which institution they would write to or phone up to request action or information. More often than not the MP or caseworker knew the specific person to write to if it was a government department. In several cases they wrote to different agencies for the same case. After years of dealing with people's problems, which may be multifaceted but often have similar patterns, they had an in-depth knowledge of the characters, rules, resources and latest changes: a sociopolitical, institutional and economic ethnography of the local welfare state, no less. The weekly ritual of these surgeries gave them listening skills and – in many, at least – empathy. It shows an underappreciated side of MPs that so many of them learn to do this so effectively. Although much of the rest of their work impels them to talk at people, to be thick-skinned and to appear oblivious to the feelings of opponents, in the privacy of the surgeries the majority of MPs become patient, sympathetic, but also attentive listeners.

MPs and caseworkers receive words of gratitude at the end of almost every interview that I observed. Often being listening to with patience seemed to be as important to constituents as achieving an outcome. They had been invariably upset by the abruptness or even brutality of bureaucrats – usually in local government but also in private companies or central government – and it was a change to be treated with respect. They gave the impression of having their dignity restored by their interaction with someone important. One constituent told the caseworker, with me listening, that the DWP 'were rude and never apologised. They don't have any standard of courtesy. I have never had a pleasant reply. We pay our taxes. Why can't they be more receptive?' The caseworker agreed. She said that you always get a far more polite and respectful service from the parliamentary helpline than from the public helpline: 'It is not right. The two should be equally respectful.'

MPs and staff treat all constituents, irrespective of whether they are supporters or even voters, as equal in the sense of giving them time and responding to all enquiries. They take scrupulous care to respect confidentiality and avoid assessing the merits of the case explicitly in their conversation with the constituent. On the whole, MPs and their staff listen without judging, or at least expressing moral judgement to the constituent's face. Refusing to take any action

[23] D. Searing, *Westminster's World, understanding political worlds* (Harvard University Press, Cambridge, Massachusetts, 1994), pp. 122–3.

is extremely rare. But, at the same time, the MP and their office are locked into a web of relationships within their area with contacts in the council, businesses and voluntary organizations. When they write on behalf of a constituent the experienced MP will give hints about the urgency and severity of the case. They would destroy the goodwill of these government and voluntary agency contacts if they gave the impression that fast and time-consuming responses had to be made in all cases. So it would be unwise of MPs to push too hard on problems that they don't believe have much urgency – or worse, validity at all – so some judgement about the merit is inevitable. A debt advice expert told me how much he appreciated the local MP's approach because although he was in a different political party, they shared a commitment to providing an excellent service to citizens. He sends people in genuine need to the MP knowing they will be treated fairly, and responds when people are referred to him by the MP (or staff), because the MP's office never sends over 'time-wasters'.

The subtlety of MPs' judgements were sometimes Solomonic. In one case an MP and I heard from an asylum-seeker about how his application to remain in the UK had been refused and he was being asked to leave his temporary housing. He planned to apply for the third time but wanted the MP's help with housing. The MP studied his papers carefully and explained in some detail the rules about applications for asylum and rights to housing. The asylum-seeker feigned ignorance. His pretence was exposed later when it became obvious that he knew the system inside out. The MP told me afterwards that it was impossible that he could remain in ignorance after years of appeals. But she explained all these rules, knowing he knew them, so that he would know that she knew the system inside out too. Unusually she declined to take action on his behalf, for example by offering to write to someone for him, and recommended various places to go – a good lawyer, the Refugee Council, homeless charities – suggesting that he should keep her informed and return to meet her whenever he wished. After he left, angry and sullen, I asked why in this one and only case she was not taking any action herself even though she was generally sympathetic to refugees.

'Because he was not telling us the truth.'

'Gosh really, how do you know?'

'He pretended not to know about section 4 – every asylum-seeker I have met knows about section 4. But also I could see from the papers that there were many claims and court appearances he wasn't telling us about. Mr Sorabji* will help almost anyone, as will the Refugee Council, so if they're not helping then it rings alarm bells.' (*Mr Sorabji is a local lawyer well known to her.)

This MP made it clear to me that she partly withheld her help – as others did too in similar situations – because she did not want to abuse her relationships with those who might give time to this man by demanding they focus on a case with little merit.

This process of making judgements is further complicated by having to take account of the common problem of mental illness. It makes it even more significant that MPs provide a service to people who are struggling to navigate anonymous and unfriendly bureaucracies. Even if a disabling illness is not the main problem, most constituents I met visit their MP when they have reached the end of their tether so are, at the least, anxious, if not in a state of despair.

Each MP organizes this surgery work differently. More established ones have a huge 'bible' of useful services, contacts and resources, while newer MPs may not. Some try and meet *all* those who seek help, to get the full story and assess its merits, whereas others encourage communication by letters, email or phone and only meet a few. Some MPs or staff feel that the aim is to empower people to sort out their lives, rather than doing everything for them, whereas others will do almost anything to help. The political position of the MP will make a difference. In some ways, it can be hard for an MP backbencher whose party is in government to please constituents in trouble. They can't blame government for their problems and if their party controls the council, then they have to defend their record. On the other hand, if their party governs either locally or nationally, then you have the advantage of better access to decision-makers who can make something happen. Government backbenchers can sometimes persuade a frontbench colleague to intervene on behalf of a constituent.

Within each constituency there is an amazing range of cultures, local economies, family structures and occupations. MPs make the mistake, according to Paul Flynn MP, of thinking they can represent this diversity but they don't; on health issues they are more likely to listen to the chair of an NHS Trust than to a hospital cleaner.[24] But some are at least aware of the quieter and silent voices. Their own identity influences whom they listen to most closely. One British Asian MP was particularly articulate about how his identity affected his work. His 30-year involvement in his constituency, and in its Borough Council, meant that everyone knew him. It also gave him a good knowledge not only of the sizes of the different communities in his constituency – white, Indian, Pakistani, Tamil, Afghan, Somali, Eastern European and so on – but what they minded about. Although some Asians trust him, others disapprove of him because he speaks out against caste and domestic violence, infuriating traditionalists who think he has been too influenced by Western thinking. Finally, he grew up with politics. His father was a politician and was even imprisoned during the fight for independence by the very Parliament that his son ended up sitting in. His way of doing politics arises in part out of this complex history and identity. From the moment he wakes until he sleeps, he is on call. He has three offices, including one at home staffed by relatives,

[24] Flynn, *How to be an MP*, p. 146.

and each accumulates invitations, requests and obligations. If they offer an opportunity to speak and exchange views, he will not refuse. He goes to a disproportionately high number of Asian functions, perhaps three or four weddings each weekend, because if he turns them down they will not forgive him, whereas a white person will assume he is just too busy and will not take it personally.

Being one of the 27 MPs with a black or Asian background adds a complex layer to this man's identity. But all MPs, and everyone else for that matter, have layers of identity with race, age, gender, nationality and class influencing simultaneously and with one or two or even more of these being pushed or pulled to the fore at given moments. MPs bring with them their own histories, world views and identities that are always multifaceted and changeable. Charles Walker MP has become the go-to MP for those suffering mental health problems or depression following his legendary speech on the subject. He began: 'I am delighted to say that I have been a practising fruitcake for 31 years. It was 31 years ago at St John's Wood tube station – I remember it vividly – that I was visited by obsessive compulsive disorder.'[25]

Dame Anne Begg, an MP who uses a wheelchair, did not want to be pigeon-holed as a disability activist but as she became well established as an effective MP at home and in Westminster, her confidence and campaigning for disabled people grew. She thought of following David Blunkett MP's example by championing the interests of groups of disabled people, but soon realized that she was better off doing her own thing. She knew about different kinds of disability; after all, being blind, as David Blunkett is, creates completely different situations to being in a wheelchair. But also, rather than working on disability as a separate issue isolated from context, she considers the interests of disabled people in the course of all her work – for example, as Chair of the Work and Pensions Select Committee, seeing how disability is related to pay, pensions, benefits, or whatever comes up.[26]

The most well-worn debates on the representation of interests revolve around class and gender. It is well known that identifying with women or a particular class does not mean that representing their interests is straightforward. Some MPs continue to assume that only working-class representatives can understand working-class issues and only women can represent women's interests – following in the traditions of Marxism and Feminism – so that increasing their number in Parliament is, therefore, urgent for better representation. Most question such neat equations these days. Given that such huge categories of people have diverse and changing interests, it makes it difficult to identify and generalize about them. In any case, such representatives are constrained by

---

[25] Charles Walker MP, *HC Debates*, 14 June 2012, col. 517.
[26] Interviewed by Emma Crewe, 4 May 2012.

the institutional structures of party and Parliament and will only make headway with challenging class or gender inequality if strong coalitions are made with movements outside Parliament.[27] All that can be said with confidence is that some women, for example, promote women's interests – however they define them – some of the time, but there is nothing inevitable about it. Childs and Krook point out the belief in the magic of critical mass theory – which assumes that when 30 per cent of parliamentary seats are held by women it creates a tipping point over which women's representation leads to better outcomes – is unlikely to be abandoned by activists any time soon, even though the evidence is flimsy.[28] The question of whether or not people are best represented by those with a shared identity becomes even trickier when you consider that there can only be overlapping, interwoven or polarized identities, never identical ones. So while a Parliament should be representative of the wider population, and one with less than one-quarter female membership is woefully inadequate, diverse representation is not a neat and tidy issue with simple solutions.

The nature of work involved in representation is changing. Rather than roughly guessing what constituents think and want, and visiting their constituency very occasionally, most MPs engage in a continual series of meetings and other types of communication with constituents every week. New communications technologies are a game-changer; one MP told me a constituent emailed at 2.30 a.m. complaining about a neighbour and then emailed again at 6.30 a.m. saying: 'Why haven't you replied to my email? You are paid with our taxes.' According to his staff, he is nearly always polite, but on receiving an email in the middle of the night saying 'Bog off', he has been known to reply: 'Bog off yourself.' Another responded immoderately to a patronising tweet thanking him for voting for same-sex marriage by calling the constituent a 'disingenuous, manipulative, illiberal little shit'. As technology proliferates, tempers fray.

Representing themselves

Interwoven with the representation *of* their constituents, the MP is in the business of self-presentation *to* constituents and others. In 1989, during the first televised speech to Parliament, in the days when the massaging of image was new, Ian Gow MP told the Commons about a letter he received from a PR company. It contained the 'following preposterous assertion: The impression you make on television depends mainly on your image (55 per cent) with your

---

[27] Emma Crewe and Richard Axelby, *Anthropology and Development, Culture, Morality and Politics in a Globalised World* (Cambridge: Cambridge University Press, 2013), pp. 105–6.
[28] Sarah Childs and Mona Lena Krook, 'Critical Mass Theory and women's political representation', *Political Studies*, vol. 56, 2008, pp. 731, 734.

voice and body language accounting for 38 per cent of your impact. Only 7 per cent depends on what you are actually saying.'[29] This provoked laughter, especially when the almost completely bald Mr Gow was offered advice about hairstyling. These days no MP ignores her/his image or appearance. Photos and reports on how MPs have raised constituency issues bloom all over MPs' websites, their campaign literature, in the local press and on Twitter. As Tony Wright told me, as soon as MPs ask a question in the Chamber, they then rush back to their office and instruct their staff to put out a press release or call the local paper.[30] Paul Flynn advises:

> Be ubiquitous and ever present in the constituency. The drip feed of blog, tweets, early morning radio interviews that are repeated throughout the day, widely advertised surgeries, and attendance in the Chamber in a camera-exposed position, all propagate the message 'Busy MP'.[31]

When I followed MPs around to meetings in public places – churches, community centres, a university, a business park, a housing association, cafés, a green, a school – they took photographs, or asked me to, and emailed them to their staff or put them on Twitter themselves. They do this, of course, in part to win support with the next election in mind. It merges with more regular canvassing for most MPs. Many spend at least a few hours every weekend knocking on doors. They are becoming increasingly sophisticated in their election tactics. Stephen Pound, MP for Ealing North, calls on every single newcomer to the constituency. All the estate agents let him know which houses have new residents, even if they can't provide the names. He introduces himself and says: 'By the way, the library is over there ...' and conveys other useful local information. He also sends letters to all his constituents, both old and new, and delivers them by hand – 150–200 a month – reaching all of them at least once between elections.

The US political scientist Richard Fenno writes of US representatives that trust is the magic ingredient. 'If people like you and trust you as an individual, they will vote for you', Members told him.[32] So a lot of conversation between politicians and their constituents is not so much about politics but about the representative and whether they can be trusted. It takes time to win the moral approval contained within trust and it means getting close to people or giving the illusion of closeness. One US representative told Fenno that no one will vote against you if you are on first-names basis and if you chew their tobacco, then they will even fight for you. Another representative put it:

---

[29] Ian Gow MP, *HC Debates*, 29 November 1989, col. 7.
[30] Interviewed by Emma Crewe, 15 December 2013.
[31] Paul Flynn, *How to be an MP*, p. 142.
[32] Fenno, *Home Style*, p. 56.

The best way to win a vote is to shake hands with someone. You don't win votes by the thousands with a speech. You win votes by looking individuals in the eye, one at a time, and asking them. Very rarely will anyone ask you about how you stand on anything.[33]

So it is not policy agreement that voters demand, according to US Members of Congress, it is a feeling of belonging to one another. They continually talk about the shared streets, the characters and the churches, stressing their commonality and understanding. US politicians vary their presentation to different groups within the constituency. When voters do see the Member as the same as them, perhaps if their identity overlaps, then he or she becomes a symbolic represent-ative – for example: 'Almost anything I do makes them feel proud. They know I'm a black man standing up for the black man.'[34] So, communication is not so much about finding out what constituents think so they can represent (or change) their views, but a more subtle process whereby US politicians spend time in their districts to measure and enhance their voting leeway. Representatives know that they will be required sometimes to vote against the wishes of their constituents. To do this without losing too many votes they have to be trusted; the more a politician is trusted, therefore, the more leeway she has.[35]

To what extent is this similar in the UK? The winning of support is equally vital to British politicians and they too believe there is no alternative to pressing flesh and looking people in the eye. I watched Simon Hughes during his canvassing in Eastleigh. His skill was in establishing the impression of intimacy with total strangers in a few minutes without offending them. Many might have recoiled from a less charismatic person. In face-to-face encounters he may have more of a gift than most, but all politicians seek personal connections and shared experiences with people and stress their local knowledge. A party worker told me that Stephen Lloyd wins elections because his focus on the constituency is total, whatever he is doing – in Westminster or the constituency – and when gathering community and business leaders for monthly meetings he even asks local politicians from other parties to join them. This is more than a mere appearance of being busy and that kind of dedication translates into votes. As Paul Flynn counsels: 'The local party must be subjected to relentless wooing between elections.'[36] Then again, it is not just electioneering. Motives are never singular and the drivers for winning support are multiple and inter-woven. Another incentive is to counter the poisonous popular view that MPs are lazy.

---

[33] Fenno, *Home Style*, pp. 64, 85.
[34] Fenno, *Home Style*, p. 120.
[35] Fenno, *Home Style*, pp. 140–51.
[36] Flynn, *Home Style*, p. 157.

Like anyone else, MPs mind about their relationships and crave some job satisfaction at the same time. In a highly marginal seat I was told that an MP had done voluntary work in two hospitals. It was an effective way to meet a huge number of staff and patients and hear their concerns as well as perhaps win a few votes. During a debate between the staff and the same MP they discussed plans for the future. When deciding whether or not more job fairs would be the best use of their time, potential votes were never mentioned – just a hard look at whether or not they had generated jobs, especially for youth. They also talked about whether they should arrange more school visits and, as an afterthought, the MP said: 'We could get political here. Why not target 15–17-year-olds as they will vote in 2015?' In the overall planning, votes had a bearing, but plans were not shaped by them; useful experiences and achieving outcomes were more important. Repeatedly when I asked which part of the backbench job MPs enjoyed, they brought their constituencies into the conversation as a place you can knock heads together, or convene critical meetings, and hurry along the progress of development.[37] It brings with it a huge sense of satisfaction, a feeling that you are a person who can cheer people up or even sometimes totally transform their lives.

Caroline Lucas (CarolineLucas)

01/02/2013 17:20

RT @ExeterStHall: Breaking News! We've done it!! Exeter Street Hall saved for the community. You are all AMAZING!! ow.ly/hjw1l

Caroline Lucas has worked for voluntary organizations, as an MEP, Leader of the Green Party and joined Parliament in 2010 as the Green Party's first MP

Even websites seem to be far more than just electioneering tools. If they were no more than that, then we might find that the more marginal the seat is, the harder MPs work on them. This is not the case. Of the 650 MPs sitting in 2013, only 42 had no personal website geared to explaining what they are up to for the benefit of their constituents. The five Sinn Féin MPs have their own reasons for refusing to participate in Parliament. That leaves 37 MPs with no website. Most of those MPs without websites have large majorities, but probably more significant is the high average age – 63 years old, rather than the overall average of 50 in 2010. Only two under 50, and none under 40, have avoided websites; it is a younger person's game.

All MPs aspire for a decent local profile; only a few go for national or even global celebrity. New MPs in the 2010 intake were told by their whips to stay

---

[37] Interviewed by Emma Crewe, 4 April 2012.

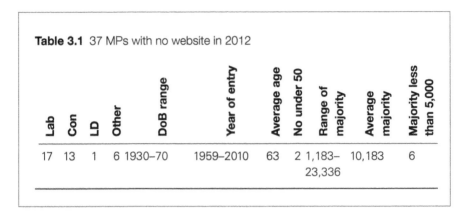

Table 3.1 37 MPs with no website in 2012

Lab	Con	LD	Other	DoB range	Year of entry	Average age	No under 50	Range of majority	Average majority	Majority less than 5,000
17	13	1	6	1930–70	1959–2010	63	2	1,183–23,336	10,183	6

out of the national media as Ministers had more need of it than they did to promote government policy. This did not stop two women celebrity-hounds, Nadine Dorries and Louise Mensch, from exemplifying an emerging trend; the latter was already a minor celebrity, a writer of chick-lit novels who became an MP in 2010, while the former is glutton for publicity who had already achieved a certain unenviable profile when she appeared on *I'm a Celebrity Get Me Out of Here* during a parliamentary sitting. She had the whip withdrawn. Both have been criticized, as if the seriousness of politics was being contaminated by entertainment. But there is no longer a clear line between where politics ends and showbiz begins, and anyway, celebrity politics has a long tradition; Milton waded into debates about the civil war and Charlie Chaplin argued in favour of US involvement in the Second World War.[38] With the increasing focus on individual politicians it is inevitable that they have to market themselves, not just their policies, and it can have potent results for representation. Politics scholar John Street argues that new forms of political communication are needed to catch up with new realities.

Nadine Dorries MP (NadineDorriesMP)

29/11/2012 19:59

People also understood, higher profile and reach can be used to benefit of constituency #nicepeopleinampthill

Nadine Dorries was a nurse and has been a Conservative MP since 2005; she was suspended from the whip in 2012 for going AWOL to appear on a TV reality show

---

[38] John Street, 'Celebrity Politicians: Popular culture and political representation', *British Journal of Politics and International Relations*, vol. 6, pp. 435–52.

Rituals and symbols are not just used in political representation, but representation is constituted by them, Street suggests. Political representatives are themselves symbols; they are a *substitute* for voters, they are part of the symbolic construction of politics without which we could have no conception of political reality. In this view representation is about organizing the world rather than just reflecting it and 'the politician must possess the essentially aesthetic talent of being able to represent political reality in new and original ways'.[39] In a sense, all politicians are celebrities, and having fans – if being a fan means forming a relationship of intimacy with someone distant – might even be healthy for our democracy.[40] So whether or not you approve or disapprove of Nadine Dorries might, therefore, be more an aesthetic and moral judgement about her specific performances and not a generalized disdain for all things culturally popular.

What is representation?

We tend to treat representation as if it is easy to understand. I asked a fellow resident in my constituency: 'What does representation mean to you?'

'It means that our MP should stand up for what we believe in.'

'Who?'

'Us, his constituents. The problem with our system today is that they follow the whips or they know perfectly well that, for example, we don't want the Iraq War, but they go ahead anyway. Our system doesn't work.'

'But we – his constituents – all disagree with each other. So who should the MP follow?'

'Oh. Well, yes. That is a good point.'

He has a point too – our MP did vote for the Iraq War despite dissent within the constituency. 15 February 2003 witnessed the largest worldwide protest since the Vietnam War, with between six and ten million people expressing disagreement with the invasion of Iraq, according to the BBC.[41] They did not stop the war and over ten years later the violence continues. Whether politicians agree or disagree with popular opinion either stance makes us feel uncomfortable within a representative democracy.

Even in more ordinary decisions, representation is a contest. For MPs to represent a diverse group of over 50,000 people who all disagree with each other and for 650 of them to represent a nation may be an almost gravity-defying feat, only possible to achieve effectively with more deliberation and

---

[39] Street, 'Celebrity Politicians', pp. 444–5.
[40] Street, 'Celebrity Politicians', p. 448.
[41] http://news.bbc.co.uk/1/hi/world/europe/2765215.stm [accessed 15 October 2013].

debate between represented and MP than is currently the custom. MPs may be pulled by their constituents in many directions, by their local parties in another, by whips in another again, while their conscience clamours for attention as well. The philosopher and MP Edmund Burke famously listened to his constituents but then refused to be dictated by their views. Taking account of views does not necessarily mean following them. Conservative MPs regularly quote Burke when they want to make the point that obeying their constituents is not their primary duty: 'Your representative owes you, not his industry only, but his judgment; and he betrays, instead of serving you, if he sacrifices it to your opinion.'[42] On the other side, Labour MPs oppose themselves to Burke and take the views of their constituents and their party as a more solid source of inspiration.

However, as Fenno found in the USA, when people appraise their MP in glowing terms – 'She is a good MP for our area' or 'He does a really good job' – they are not usually referring to their policy positions or voting record. Most constituents don't even know how their MP votes. Our relationship with our MP is often not so much about the representation of our views as the championing of our area and the people within it, for MPs are not just women or men of actions and policies, they are living symbols of a locality.[43] In France, too, politicians stress local roots; 'a politician is above all the representative of a territory with all its traditions, a territory as it has been shaped by the presence of man … it is more or less obligatory to occupy local and national office simultaneously.'[44] Furthermore, the politicians with an advantage have associations of kinship or friendship within influential local networks. To win support, MPs in the UK highlight their belonging to the locality. 'I know every street of my constituency', MPs often told me. When I was being driven around a constituency to attend a prize-giving ceremony in an allotment – the kind of ceremonial marking of territory that also happens in France[45] – the MP joked about whether he was lost because for one brief moment he did not recognize where he was. It was funny, because to be a stranger in your constituency is the greatest sin for all MPs.

All MPs symbolize the link between local and national government, and even between political locality and nation, as most succinctly illustrated when my own MP, Andy Slaughter presided over the celebrations for the Queen's Jubilee. Residents assembled on a small green and the MP joked about how close we were to his constituency boundary. MPs should never visit another constituency in an official capacity without notifying the local MP.[46] After much discussion about the order of proceedings, it began with a parade by cadets. Two vicars

---

[42] Edmund Burke, *The Works of the Right Honourable Edmund Burke. Vol. I* (London: Henry G. Bohn, 1854), pp. 446–8.
[43] Abélès makes this point in relation to France, *Quiet Days in Burgundy*, p. 268.
[44] Ibid., pp. 81, 174.
[45] Ibid., p. 268.
[46] In May 2014 Andy Slaughter even wrote to the Prime Minister complaining that he visited

from different denominations spoke about the importance of community and the MP concluded the speeches by saying that the green has a pub one end and a church at the other end, symbolic of life across Britain. Then we strolled across the green to a tent with a local company selling beer and cider to drink a toast to the Queen. Within one small fete we had civil society (a residents' association) organizing an event to mark the endurance of the Monarch (the Queen's Jubilee) with the army (cadets marching), the church (opening speeches) and Parliament (the MP concluding proceedings). Free enterprise lubricated conversation between all these elements by selling refreshments, with plenty of quips about who was buying the drinks. The MP said to me afterwards that he had forgotten to say the one thing that you are supposed to say on these occasions – thanks to the organizers. It was for the MP to thank because he was the VIP at the occasion, symbolizing the link between this community group meeting at the grass roots, Parliament and the Monarch reigning over the nation. MPs represent conflicting ideologies but they are also the glue that holds our governance together.

Like very nearly all MPs, with the exception of the handful who don't see constituents, in his 'surgery' Andy Slaughter provides a link between private and public worlds, the individual or family and the state. By listening to our trials when dealing with the housing department or Home Office, he is repre-senting our interests to the local council or central government in a way that creates a social relationship – a human bridge – over the chasm between faceless bureaucracy and us citizens. It means the inhuman face of the state becomes meaningful and even bearable. He, or his caseworker, even gives the state a name when he says: 'I will write a letter to Mr Williams at the Housing Department and see how your case is progressing.'

At the same time, other meetings reveal him as also symbolizing specific political roles that he has in common with some MPs but that set him apart from others at any one particular time. In our area of London he stands for opposition to both the national government and, until 2014, the local government. He used to be Council Leader when Labour controlled it and for some years his former colleagues on the council have been locked in a battle with the Conservatives over housing, land and development. More recently he initiated a campaign to keep A&E departments open in the local hospitals, accusing the local council of colluding with central government to close them down. Residents eventually took over this campaign but the MP got it going, lent it support and remains the figurehead. So he, along with others in the opposition parties, symbolizes opposition at the local and national levels in a highly marginal constituency. He played a part in helping Labour councillors to win a majority on the

---

Hammersmith without giving notice, despite the Speaker recently clarifying this protocol. He included a copy of this letter in an email sent to constituents on 21 May 2014 at 15:25.

Hammersmith and Fulham Council in 2014 for the first time in eight years. Other MPs signify their own even more specific politics. Caroline Lucas MP is doing more than just articulating environmental policies; as the only Green MP she is a symbol for the green movement in Parliament. Similarly, the nationalist MPs from Wales, Northern Ireland and Scotland may be considered of little importance in Parliament by other MPs but to nationalists in the electorate, their symbolic importance can't be overstated.

In some ways we want MPs to be like us. One of the candidates at the Eastleigh by-election responded to this clamour when he said during a hustings: 'If you want to speak to Westminster then I am your chance. I am you. I'm not a party person. This would be true democracy, I will speak for you. I am one of you.' Most of us are not particularly party political, and getting less so, but we see ourselves as belonging to a particular locality so, unsurprisingly, we want our MP to hail from our local area and we mind less about their individual attributes or their gender.[47] In early 2014 Conservative MPs Anne McIntosh and Tim Yeo were deselected by their local associations; journalists claimed that she fell out with party members and he did not give enough attention to his constituents.[48] There may have been other reasons, but local expectations of MPs are growing.[49]

One reason the selection of MPs can provoke such tensions is because the whole concept of what representation signifies is contested. In the summer of 2013 one of the architects of New Labour, Peter Mandelson (former Labour MP), worried that the unions would give mass backing to Old Labour candidates and lose Labour the 2015 General Election. The General Secretary of one of the unions involved, Unite, explained why they had encouraged people to join the party and vote for union-nominated candidates:

> Labour MPs look less and less like the people they seek to represent. The big strides made in securing more women Labour MPs have also, unfortunately, been paralleled by a decline in those from working-class backgrounds.[50]

---

[47] Philip Cowley, 'Why not ask the audience? Understanding the public's representational priorities', British Politics, vol. 8, 2013, pp. 138–63.

[48] http://www.dailymail.co.uk/news/article-2551013/Tim-Yeo-ousted-Conservative-MP-grassroots-revolt-second-Tory-backbencher-rejected-week.html and http://www.conservativehome.com/parliament/2014/01/anne-mcintosh-mp-deselected-by-thirsk-and-malton-conservatives.html [both accessed 1 September 2014].

[49] Conservative MPs have fallen out with local associations for other reasons. In 2013 some of the executive of Crispin Blunt's local association tried to deselect him, the final straw being his decision to come out as gay. But the attempt did not succeed, http://www.theguardian.com/politics/2013/nov/18/gay-tory-crispin-blunt-defeats-campaign-deselect [accessed 1 May 2014].

[50] Len McClusky, 'Peter Mandelson's selection argument is about politics not procedure', Guardian,

If MPs are not like 'us', we worry that they will not understand our concerns. Most MPs are alert to this. Gyles Brandreth (former MP) recounted that fellow Tory Ann Widdecombe marched him out of a first-class carriage to second class on a train, advising him sternly that MPs should not set themselves apart.[51] As Dunn puts it, the idea of democracy implies that 'in human political communities it ought to be ordinary people (the adult citizens) and not extra-ordinary people who rule'.[52] And yet, ironically, once citizens become MPs they can only survive by becoming extraordinary. So at the same time, we require our politicians to be different and set apart from us in at least two senses. We want politicians to be authentically themselves – less eager to please and bend towards us, saying whatever they think even if we don't agree. Both politicians and journalists speculate that MPs needed to relearn authenticity, become less like those smooth, media-training politicians who give a robotic, impersonal and flawless performance.

---

politicshomeuk (politicshomeuk)

03/10/2012 12:48

Lord Falconer: 'An absence of authenticity is dangerous in politics; Boris is strong because he's an authentic character.' #bbcdp

Politicshomeuk is a political news website

But secondly, and somewhat contradictorily, we need MPs to be different from us in the sense of specialist career politicians. The nature of the job is to wage a continual battle against the falling sands of time. A politician has to respond to endless requests from constituents, whips, interest groups, local supporters, as well as proactively find out what they think and need, without having enough time to do justice to any of these demands. According to one, 'It feels like Genghis Khan attaching four horses to your limbs and you are pulled in four directions'. The more inclusively you listen, the more directions you will be pulled in. The better you represent, the more you sink under the weight of many voices.

In practice, MPs do not literally listen to everything; they use various strategies for filtering out, analysing and privileging some voices. This week she

---

21 May 2013, http://www.guardian.co.uk/commentisfree/2013/may/21/peter-mandlesons-selection-argument-politics-procedure [accessed 7 July 2013].
[51] *Today* Programme, BBC Radio 4, 20 October 2012.
[52] John Dunn (ed.), *Democracy: The Unfinished Journey, 508 BC to AD 1993* (Oxford: Oxford University Press, 1992), p. v.

meets people in her surgery facing housing problems, so she rises to speak about that in a debate about the cuts. Next week she has booked a meeting with a pub landlord and might take up the need to introduce regulation to protect tied pubs from financial ruin. She will ignore 30 other invitations and possibilities. The important point about a constituency is that the interests of all people are unknowable and unguessable. The same is true, of course, when organizations such as unions or charities claim to represent a particular group. Save the Children can't literally represent the interests or promote the rights of *all* children. Their promises never live up to their rhetoric, but unlike politicians, charity workers are not to held to account with much rigour.

As Mike Saward eloquently explains, representation is not a one-way formal mechanism provided simply by an institution. It is process, a two-way relationship between representer and represented, within which the represented choose their politician in an election and the representers portray the represented in particular ways.[53] It is something performed within relationships that continually change. The claims made by the politicians – about themselves or the constituency – tend to be more compelling when they resonate with current cultural understandings. So while the conventional question is whether MPs are responsive to those they represent, as if their interests can be known, Saward's approach implies a different question: does the MP manage to silence or evoke the represented?

The French anthropologist Bruno Latour also challenges us to think about politics as one of the ways that we create society, so when people refer to a crisis of representation in democratic politics, they are undervaluing and perhaps taking for granted a process that is easy to misunderstand. When political utterances are portrayed as false, fickle and corrupt, we judge the conditions of one way of talking in relation to those of another. After all, 'political discourse appears to be untruthful only in contrast with other forms of truth'.[54] For example, if you are conducting a scientific experiment about what subjects said in relation to a given question, truth depends on faithfully recording and reproducing what they said. If you are doing politics, the representative can't faithfully produce the people's views; she has no option but to betray them in order to convert multiple views into one. There is no alternative. So to pretend that political talk can be guided by reason, evidence, straight talk and the literal representation of multitude of interests is dark and dangerous. Latour ends with this warning:

> By replacing distorted representation by faithful representation, impossible obedience by pedagogy, composition of new groups by rectilinear transfer

---

[53] Mike Saward, 'The Representative Claim', *Contemporary Political Theory*, vol. 5, 2007, pp. 297–318.
[54] Bruno Latour, 'What if we talked politics a little', *Contemporary Political Theory*, vol. 2, 2003, p. 147.

of 'relations of domination', we may well finish off politics for good or, in any case, cool it down to the point of it dying of numbness, without even noticing, like a careless pedestrian lost in a blizzard.[55]

Representation of other people is not usefully seen as a mechanical articulation of the interests of a group but as a changeable relationship between a constituency and the person symbolically creating it, within which claims are made, contested, thrown out and remade. Could MPs engage in fuller dialogue and debate with different groups within the constituency and within Parliament? Could Parliament contain greater diversity to improve its credibility? Of course, to both. Possibly we should be debating more fully what it means for representation, and democracy more widely, if the likely increase in women MPs means MPs will spend more time doing surgery work in the future. But if we see representation as utterly broken, it is possible we have misunderstood what democratic politics is about.

---

[55] Latour, 'What if we talked politics a little', p. 162.

4

Rulers and Whips

MPs preside over and scrutinize government. The assumption is that government will get its legislation through by whipping, but not before the opposition in both Houses have asked them to think again. The whips are losing power, backbenchers are gaining clout through influential committees, government consultations are more common and petitions are on the increase. So is government subject to greater scrutiny or still too dominant due to the tyranny of the whip? The Coalition of two parties in government intensifies the temptation to rebel with consequences that look disastrous but also please all within Parliament.

****

Powers of government have passed from the Sovereign, nearly. The British Monarch has only few prerogative powers: the prorogation of Parliament and the appointment of the Prime Minster are the most regularly used. But she could even declare war. Our Monarch uses her powers on the advice of the PM, so doesn't really use them, as long as the democratic process works. If it doesn't – for example, if no party achieves a majority at the General Election and we have a 'hung Parliament' – then what the Monarch can or can't do is a matter of debate. Politicians go to great lengths to avoid embarrassing the Queen and the monarchy and government have worked on an 'extremely fluid base of instantly invented precedents'.[1] And conventions in the House prevent the Monarch's name being brought into debate. She avoids expressing her opinions, although occasionally rumours circulate about what she may think or have said about politics. Claims that she was against Scottish Independence were reported by journalists just before a Referendum on leaving the Union in 2014, but her spokespeople were careful to say that she had expressed no opinion.

Our elected rulers emerge as they win seats in the House of Commons at a General Election; the party with the largest number of winning MPs forms a

---

[1] Peter Ziegler, as quoted by Peter Hennessy, *The Hidden Wiring: Unearthing the British Constitution* (London: Phoenix, 1996), p. 50.

government. If the MPs in government have an overall majority, then they know they can pass the laws that allow them to raise taxes and regulate society. But the government gets its business only when the Members of the government party (or parties) vote as instructed. What is seen as the dominance of the executive in Parliament – as expressed by their control of the business agenda, time during sessions and whipping their flocks – is voluntarily sustained by government backbenchers. Although they usually support their leaders, backbenchers have rebelled against their party's instructions more frequently in recent years and the two-party system is weakening, while various forms of media get more powerful. So not only is the dominance of the executive relative to opponents in a slight decline, there is little that the government can do about it.

With our first-past-the-post (FPTP) electoral system, coalitions are supposed to be rare. Those supporting the two large parties like FPTP because it is designed to produce a clear winner – either Labour or Conservative in recent decades – and a strong government. Those in smaller parties prefer proportional representation systems, which tend to give them more seats and sometimes influence. Contrary to these tendencies 2010 had a hung Parliament, the first since 1974. The election gave Conservatives 307 seats and Labour 258, so it was the third largest party – the Liberal Democrats with 57 seats – who decided who would rule. Their influence is less surprising when you look at the share of the vote (Con 36 per cent, Lab 29 per cent and LD 23 per cent) but this clout was bitterly resented by the two main parties, who saw themselves as the natural and reliable rulers. Not only did LD join the Conservatives in government but also they negotiated an agreement that formed the basis for many of the policies and laws developed during their term.[2]

It is the Prime Minister, the leader of the largest party, who appoints the Ministers in the House of Commons and the House of Lords. The most senior Ministers sit in the Cabinet, the collective decision-making body chaired by the Prime Minister, while more junior ones support these Secretaries of State. In the UK political system, unlike the US Congress, Ministers sit in Parliament and report directly to it. Their reports to Parliament take the form of statements and replies to questions, responding to debates, appearing before Select Committees and explaining the content of legislation in the Chamber and in Public Bill and Delegated Legislation Committees. The most famous question time puts the PM on the spot for 30 minutes every Wednesday, while other Ministers rotate to take their place at the despatch box to deal with this ferocious form of scrutiny on other days. Treasury questions always get considerable attention as the Chancellor is such a heavyweight, those topics that concern

---

[2]HM Government, *The Coalition: Our programme for government: Freedom, Fairness, Responsibility*, 2010, http://www.instituteforgovernment.org.uk/sites/default/files/publications/The%20Challenge%20of%20Being%20a%20Minister.pdf [accessed 2 October 2013].

constituents attract a fair amount (transport, health, education), while questions about the House administration or constitutional reform tend to have a small cult following. After statements their counterparts in the main Opposition party (or parties before the Coalition) then reply, following which backbenchers can ask questions.

These are just a few of many ritualized form of interactions that take place in Parliament. The diversity in form, style and substance is dizzying. Just to give a flavour of how the stages in the theatre of Parliament set different tones: the main debating Chamber is the place for gargantuan tribal clashes on the 'floor of the House', the Westminster Hall Chamber contains a large horseshoe for more measured, non-votable debates, and the committee rooms in the Palace of Westminster or neighbouring Portcullis House hold in-depth and often collaborative meetings of Select Committees, general committees or parliamentary groups. The order and timing of all these rituals are highly struc-tured and regulated – the stages of bills are scrutinized in a set order and at conventional intervals – but there is also some room for manoeuvre about what happens when. The government controls the order and timing in the House of Commons, although the Standing Orders stipulate that time must be allocated to opposition business, backbench business and private members bills, and the Speaker has the power of granting urgent questions. Whether or not they horse-trade time with other parties depends on the size of their majority. The key performances and conversations that are due to take place in these theatres are announced by the Leader of the House each week on Thursday morning and listed on the internet and on the 'order paper'. This Thursday business statement, as it is called, is an opportunity for MPs to challenge the government's priorities in their use of time but also to raise the profile of any issue close to the heart of an MP, and most likely her constituents, and then copy the transcript on to their website.

When the parties distribute information about what debates are coming up, they let their Members know when their presence is required. The whips also form the usual channels who are responsible for arranging the business of the House in consultation with the Leader of the House. The key figure behind agenda setting is the Private Secretary to the Chief Whip, who some say is the second or third most powerful person in Parliament after the PM. However, the well-worn and simple view of power in the British political system is that government, and within it the whips and business managers, have too much of it and the backbenchers (and ultimately citizens) too little. Like most things in the House of Commons, everyday reality is rather different from the abstract generalities made by remote pundits. The power hierarchies are more complex, and look quite different above and below the surface and from different people's viewpoints. This changeability will be revealed in this chapter on Ministers and whips as well as the subsequent one on scrutiny by different groups.

Ministers

A Minister holds public office in government; they serve the public, as the Latin origin implies, and rule us at the same time. Each Secretary of State, the most senior Ministers of the Crown, heads a government department and attends the Cabinet. After the Prime Minister (PM) and the Deputy Prime Minister, the most senior Ministers all have nicknames: Secretary of State for Foreign and Commonwealth Affairs – the Foreign Secretary; the Chancellor of the Exchequer – the Chancellor; and the Principal Secretary of the Home Department – Home Secretary. Departments also have junior Ministers – Minsters of State and then one rung down, Parliamentary Under Secretaries of State.

The Queen meets the PM once a week and has a group of advisers who make up the Privy Council. Privy Counsellors (PC) are mostly MPs and Lords with a sprinkling of bishops and judges and you know when an MP is a PC because they are addressed as the *Right* Honourable Member. You take an oath requiring that you keep secret anything told on Privy Council terms, but in practice this rarely happens; when members of the Council meet, their orders are put in the public domain.[3] If it weren't for the involvement of Ministers, and the presence of the Queen at court in Windsor Castle, the business of the Privy Council would appear rather humdrum. So the formal power of the Privy Council is immense in theory if they choose to use it, but the everyday practice limits it to a small role relative to an average government department.

How do Ministers get their positions? First you have to get into Parliament. Some only fight to get into the House of Commons as a route to government, so they told me, although rather few will admit to that publicly. Conversely, others did not particularly intend to aim for government but once in the highly competitive arena of Westminster, caught the feverish longing to have clout and change things. Rather few are completely uninterested or realize rather quickly that they are unlikely to be offered a 'job'. Former MP Tony Wright pointed out to me that when MPs say they want a 'job', they mean in government; being a backbench MP is not seen as a proper job by many MPs. Ambitious politicians are a larger proportion of MPs than they would have been in the past; as many MPs put it, the Tory stalwarts from the shires continuing in a family tradition and the union officials seeking a second career as Labour backbencher are few and far between these days. However, in the last few years Select Committee Chairs take their role seriously and receive a small salary. These roles are increasingly being seen as an alternative to government positions.

Many of those who aspire to government jobs seek experience as special advisers (SpAds) to Ministers partly to gain knowledge of Whitehall and

---

[3]http://privycouncil.independent.gov.uk/privy-council/orders/ [accessed 12 September 2013].

endorsements from senior figures. All three party leaders during the 2010–15 Parliament were once SpAds: Cameron to the then Chancellor Norman Lamont; Clegg to Leon Brittan in Europe; and Miliband to PM Gordon Brown. It is a good training, because you work closely with your Minister and senior civil servants on policy, but also communications. In many cases civil servants find it useful to have SpAds in the department who know the Minister well, understand the politics of policy and have a link to the party. In a small number of cases SpAds cause havoc. Damian McBride, a Special Adviser to the Labour government, not only fed stories to the press to undermine some of Gordon Brown's rivals, but also planned to publish stories about Tories that turned out to be completely untrue. SpAds at the Department for Education are rumoured to have smeared opponents, allegedly partly through a Twitter account called @toryeducation and one of them, Dominic Cummings, admits to attacking Nick Clegg MP both before and after he was working for Gove, even though they were in the government coalition together.[4]

As an MP you usually have to wait some years before you acquire a departmental brief. Or at least you used to. Both Edward Heath and Margaret Thatcher were MPs for 20 years before being PM, Tony Blair was 14 years, David Cameron only nine, Ed Miliband was in the Cabinet within two years and Rachel Reeves was made a Shadow Minister only six months after entering Parliament. You may catch the attention of the Chief Whip, or be pushed forward by a senior patron, or belong to a chronically under-represented group and get in early. But if in the government party, even then you often have to do a stint as a Parliamentary Private Secretary (PPS) or whip. I will come back to whips later in this chapter, but a PPS is the link between a particular Minister and Parliament: a bag-carrier, intelligence agent and advocate. When your Minister speaks in the Chamber you sit behind them and pass notes to or from the civil servants sitting in the officials' box. Even in committees officials can't advise Ministers directly during the session and if they require information, they have to pass notes via their PPS who sits directly behind them. If the PPS is dozy, or – even worse – absent, then the Minister's command of the situation can easily unravel. The PPS writes down the constituencies of the MPs present so that when the Minister speaks they get the terms of address correct. You spy for your Minister to find out what backbenchers think about them and their policies and you promote his/her interests by plugging both their achievements and causes across the party. In the case of Conservatives or LD, the Coalition

---

[4]Damian McBride, *Power Trip: A Decade of Policy, Plots and Spin* (London: Biteback Publishing, 2013) and http://dominic.wordpress.com [accessed 30 May 2014]. As further evidence of the links between the Twitter account and DoE SpAds, after Gove gave evidence to the Education Select Committee, claiming that complaints about his SpAds were politically motivated, @toryeducation tellingly tweeted 'win'.

means there is a remote but unlikely possibility that the PPS might liaise with backbenchers in the Coalition partner party. Mainly you stick to your own. The whips use you as reserves, getting you to make speeches in all the Chambers and committees and ask questions that put the leadership in a good light. You might prepare notes with civil servants in advance of a session in the Chamber to make it as surprise-free as possible. Some go to Ministerial team meetings in the department. Some find it exciting, relishing the experience of being almost on the inside or at least on the way up. But one described it as the worst job in Parliament. You are on the payroll, which means you are expected to vote and speak for the government, but with no pay. The theory is that it helps you get into government, but you do not have the freedom to campaign for your own interests, sound independent or threaten rebellion unless given promotion.

A backbencher will not get a position unless either they are perceived to be loyal to the party leader or they have a significant following of their own. It can be safer for a PM to put an MP with a large number of supporters into Cabinet, and therefore force them to support the government, than have them complaining and fomenting trouble on the backbenches. It would have been dangerous for PM Tony Blair (1997–2007) to sack Chancellor Gordon Brown because of the damage he and the Brownites could have caused him and his government. Not only that, he had to allow his own but also Brown's supporters to have government positions to sustain the loyalty of his Chancellor. In a similar vein, in 2010 an LD MP wanted a position in government but was not offered one because LD Cabinet positions went to those who had been in the Commons for a long time and had built up a following: Clegg, Alexander, Laws, Cable, Huhne and Moore. Conservative positions mostly went to David Cameron's allies (such as Osborne and Gove) and heavyweights with a supporter base (Clarke and May). Rivals will speculate about the injustice of promotion and demotion: 'He got the job because he went to the same school' or 'She only got the job because she slept with a whip'. Others point out that the PM with a small majority has a relatively small pool to choose from when you discount the unreliable and incompetent. Although the number of women in government posts tends to be roughly in proportion to their total number (less than one quarter of MPs), many MPs and observers claim – sometimes with resentment – that they have been given preference in recent years to correct their under-representation.

If you are in opposition, then the rules for promotion have been different for the two main parties but also continually change. Labour MPs used to vote to put their favourites into the Shadow Cabinet until 2011 when Ed Miliband persuaded the party to abolish elections. He wanted to stop Members campaigning against each other. The people who voted for Ed Miliband in his leadership contest tended to be the MPs offered a place on the Opposition frontbench, with a few exceptions.[5] However, both Ed Balls and his wife Yvette Cooper voted for Balls and the leader gave them key roles. Such significant players, with aspirations to work in government at the highest levels no doubt, would be dangerous and divisive to leave fuming on the backbenches. After all, they were in the top three the year before when Labour MPs voted on who should have positions in the Shadow Cabinet.[6]

When PM Gordon Brown put his old foe Peter Mandelson into his Cabinet, it was supposed (or at least spun) to symbolize the creation of unity within the party – to outsiders but to his own party as well. It was surely also because he was a Minister of unusual ability, according to several civil servants and observers. Caution is needed before accusing leaders of promoting only those who support them in a cynical bid to consolidate their power – said of both Ed Miliband and David Cameron – as it may be that they agree with them and mutually respect each other, even if they don't like each other. Most politicians have an extraordinary ability to forgive past hostilities – although some are stubborn exceptions – in a way that is more like families than work organizations.

Closeness to the party leader is always good for your prospects as long as she or he stays there. If you are not close, the leader may find ways to undermine you. The leader chooses who to put in her or his Cabinet, while there is more scope for others to influence the choice of junior Ministers. The Chief Whip identifies those to be placed on the lower rungs with the assistance of their whips acting as talent scouts. They look out for MPs in their flock who are loyal to the leadership, vote with the party and speak well. Whether or not this qualifies them to be good leaders, managers and administrators in departments is another question, and is not normally known until they are tried and tested, but MPs are continually having to prove one set of skills (e.g. electioneering to get into Parliament) in order to then apply another (e.g. holding government to account as backbenchers). MPs win office for political reasons rather than due to their executive experience.[7]

How do MPs experience Ministerial office? The endless disagreements over policy, and competition for both parliamentary time and the backing of the PM and the more powerful Ministers to get things through Cabinet, consumes huge amounts of time for Ministers and especially PMs. Doing deals and leaking to the

---

[5]See here for a list of the Labour Shadow Cabinet: http://www.labour.org.uk/shadow-cabinet and here for how Labour MPs voted in the leadership campaign: http://www2.labour.org.uk/leadership-mps-and-meps [accessed 9 February 2015].

[6]http://www.newstatesman.com/blogs/the-staggers/2010/10/john-healey-balls-votes-cooper [accessed 25 September 2013].

[7]K. Theakston, as cited by Peter Riddell, Zoe Gruhn and Liz Carolan, *The Challenge of Being a Minister*, the Institute for Government, http://www.instituteforgovernment.org.uk/sites/default/files/publications/The%20Challenge%20of%20Being%20a%20Minister.pdf 2011, p. 19, [accessed 2 October 2013].

media are well-established traditional tactics. When Barbara Castle MP wanted to get trade union reform through in a hurry in 1969 and met resistance within the Cabinet, either she or the PM Harold Wilson told the press that it had been approved.[8] After angry exchanges between Barbara Castle MP and Richard Crossman MP during the Industrial Committee, with the latter defending the rights of trade unions, a critical Cabinet meeting had to decide which to back. With the PM's support already in the bag, the vote would swing towards Castle if the Chancellor, Roy Jenkins MP gave his support. He explained later that he agreed with Crossman, but had made a deal with Wilson to support Castle on the condition that his own legislation went through. So she won ten to six. Crossman suspected that the PM just wanted to gain popularity with the public, who might like a curb to union power, in advance of an election.

The telling of such stories by politicians is itself political work. Crossman is telling his version of the Labour government from 1964 to 1970 in a bid to ensure that his world view prevails, preferably with his contribution to the country at the centre. In a parallel way Conservative former Minister Ian Gilmour's devastating critique of Thatcher's dogma, which from his viewpoint imposed sacrifice on the poor for the benefit of the rich, is a plea in part to his own party. He is championing the One Nation Tory idea of satisfying the 'aspirations of people in all walks or layers of life' against an ideology he saw as divisive and destructive.[9] Minsters even more than backbenchers wage more painful ideological battles *within* their party (or coalition) than with other political parties. Even the amusing diaries of Alan Clark and Chris Mullin expose bitter rivalries, with the former trying to persuade Conrad Black to lean on the *Telegraph* to withdraw support for Heseltine and the latter railing against the incompetence of other colleagues in government, leaving their stories, ideas and personalities stamped on our national memory and the image of some of their fellow party Members somewhat tarnished.[10]

When Thatcher died, her supporters were determined to reshape her legacy. They secured her a ceremonial funeral and bandied about a declaration that she was the greatest post-war Prime Minister, while Labour countered with Clement Attlee MP as number 1. As journalist Steve Richards puts it: 'Politics never stops, not for a moment. When a leader dies the debate about his or her legacy becomes much more about the present and the future than about the past.'[11] When Prime Ministers produce memoirs, they are trying to shape their legacy as statesmen and women and ensure their ideas triumph. The cover

[8]Antony Howard (ed.), *The Crossman Diaries* (Basildon: Magnum Books, 1979), pp. 559–68.
[9]Ian Gilmour, *Dancing with Dogma: Britain Under Thatcherism* (London: Simon and Schuster, 1992) pp. 337–41.
[10]Alan Clark, *Dairies: In Power 1983-1992* (London: Phoenix, 2003), p. 284, and Chris Mullin's three-part diaries published by Profile in 2010, 2011 and 2012.
[11]Steve Richards, 'The battle over Thatcher's legacy is a battle for the future', *Guardian*, 10

blurb on Blair's autobiography does so immodestly: 'Tony Blair is the politician who defines our times … Few British prime ministers have shaped the nation's course as profoundly …' Blair presents himself as a global leader but also rather above the nasty fray of politics, more moral and interested in religion than his rivals.[12] He aims to refute the claim by his critics that he betrayed Gordon Brown. Before becoming PM Blair persuaded Brown to give up his claim to be leader, against the Parliamentary Labour Party's preference, on the understanding that Blair would win the country's support and then hand over the crown. The delay was valid, in Tony's version of history, because Gordon was flawed and plotted against him. He describes his erstwhile friend and latter enemy as cautious, conventional, introspective, too political and having 'analytical intelligence, absolutely. Emotional intelligence, zero.' The rest of the book implicitly argues in favour of Tony's comparable brilliance. Over ten years he learned to move from courting popularity to 'doing what was right' and saw himself as leaving at the height of his powers.[13] Such lengthy rationalizations reveal more about how politicians justify their actions, rather than what goes on behind the scenes. Churchill put it pithily: 'For my part, I consider that it will be found much better by all Parties to leave the past to history, especially as I propose to write that history.'[14] At the same time Blair's narrative makes it plain that the impossible contemporary ideals of leadership – visionary planning, control, and mastery over events – get lost in the maelstrom of 24-hour media, public reaction and unpredictable events. Like many PMs, his arrogance was his undoing.

The tendency to diminish collective Cabinet responsibility by turning to others for advice and making 10 Downing Street an important source of policymaking goes back to Harold Wilson and his 'kitchen cabinet', according to the US historian George Bernstein.[15] Power shifted further away from Cabinet during Thatcher's and Blair's time, partly in response to the furious pace of 24-hour media. Recent PMs Blair, Brown and Cameron all rely heavily on their closest advisers and friends. When the PM sets a less collaborative tone, other Ministers tend to follow. Another former Cabinet Secretary, Lord Butler, points out that when decisions are taken without proper discussion in Cabinet three problems tend to arise. First the potential impact on other government departments and the people they serve tends to get overlooked. Secondly the Minister taking the decision fails to get enough advice from other senior politicians. Thirdly

April 2013, http://www.independent.co.uk/voices/comment/the-battle-over-thatchers-legacy-is-a-battle-for-the-future-8567289.html [accessed 9 October 2014].
[12] Blair, *The Journey*, p. 690.
[13] Ibid., pp. 58, 60, 68–9, 616, 659, 657.
[14] Winston Churchill MP, *HC Debates*, 23 January 1948, col. 557.
[15] George L. Bernstein, *The Myth of Decline: The Rise of Britain since 1945* (London: Pimlico, 2004).

the other Ministers are not bound by the decisions if they haven't taken part in them.[16] The decline of the Cabinet as a decision-making body is indicated by the shortening from two long meetings every week in the 1970s down to one brief discussion in the present. On the other hand, another Cabinet Secretary – Lord Turnbull – considers it surprising how much collective responsibility still remains in contrast to the USA, for example, and his successor, Lord O'Donnell, points out that Gordon Brown favoured a more collegiate approach, so much so that he passed a note at the first Cabinet meeting saying: 'if we go on like this, Prime Minister, we will be here until midnight.' The 2010–15 Coalition has revitalized Cabinet discussion, in the sense that it is where the two parties thrash out some of their differences, but maintained the limits to collective responsibility because big decisions are taken by only a few (Cameron, Clegg, Osborne and Alexander being the core) and due to the endless leaks about those decisions.

The job of PM has become hugely demanding compared to the days when Harold Macmillan claimed it was so easy he had plenty of time to read Trollope. The business of contemporary government is burdened with difficulties. The PM and Ministers are constrained by a wide range of groups and institutions all disagreeing about what is best for their department and, more broadly, for the country. Gerald Kaufman MP explored such pressures and constraints in his guide about *How to be a Minister*. He warns of two diseases to beware of: Ministerialitis, whereby the car and driver and attention of brainy civil servants can give you ideas of grandeur, and Departmentalitis, which induces you to ruthlessly promote the interests of your own department at the cost of others.[17] Instead of being seduced into such ego-enhancing states, he counsels new Ministers to give their attention to standing up to officials. At the same time, you have to seek their co-operation because, despite the perception on the left that Whitehall is conservative and on the right that it seeks consensus or avoids risk, the same civil servants will advance socialism and then demolish it as long as it is practical, if that is what their Ministers have been elected to do. So civil servants ensure continuity and stability and they are also the people who make things happen. They constrain and enable. When you go to a Cabinet meeting your officials and advisers will give you a briefing with a 'Line to Take'; Kaufman reports that on occasions when the subject was highly complex, Ministers gave up any pretence to a view themselves and simply read out their respective briefs.[18] Conversely a Tory Minister told me that despite the intelligence of civil servants, you have to rely on your own political antennae as they can ignore the political implications: they fail to consider whether an issue would be misunderstood or upset too many

---

[16] Interviewed by Lord Hennessy and Dr Anthony Seldon 2013, http://www.cabinetsecretaries. com [accessed 2 October 2013].
[17] Gerald Kaufman, *How to Be a Minister* (London: Faber and Faber, 1997), pp. 10–17.
[18] Ibid., pp. 35, 57.

people. If you do have your own view, and when you meet strong opposition to it either from colleagues or from within your department, then you resort to canvassing. In fact, MPs are *always* canvassing. The extent to which Ministers get their way (at least in the short term) depends in part on how good they are at canvassing support through persuasive communication and developing relationships.[19] Plus getting the backing of the PM can be dynamite but only if used sparingly – even the threat of action from No. 10 can galvanize people.

Showing appreciation to your supporters is important for any politician but especially for Ministers. Whether it is your government backbenchers, or party members outside, again and again Kaufman stresses the importance of maintaining good relationships with people on the same side. To avoid being remote he writes about sharing information, meeting people face-to-face and talking to them. After all, 'you cannot suddenly construct a close and trusting relationship during a crisis'; if you have established trust already, on the other hand, then you can pick up the phone when you need something and ask for it.[20] Even if you are not in a supplicant's position now, you might be in a while. If you run into trouble in Parliament, broad support in your party will save you. When Chief Whip Andrew Mitchell MP was accused of swearing and calling a policeman a pleb, his job was on the line. According to gossip around Westminster at the time, backbench Tories in the 1922 Committee were asked to support him, but too many kept quiet (see Chapter 5). It was said by many that he did not get along well enough with colleagues to be an effective Chief Whip. He had been International Development Secretary since 2010 so many new MPs did not know him. The indignation from colleagues was not loud or broadly based enough to save him. Whether this version was true or not, it confirms at least the perception that a strong platform of support within the Parliamentary party is important to a Chief Whip and perceptions have a habit of influencing people irrespective of the truth. MPs told me that working the tearoom to nurture your relationships with your colleagues, and maybe even converting your critics once in a blue moon, is useful to any Minister. Those who don't find the time to do this, or keep away because they don't relish Parliament's strange eating places, may be vulnerable when in trouble or as a reshuffle or election approaches. As a politician you incur debts, particularly so if you are Prime Minister, according to Lord Callaghan. You ask people to do things and once you are voted or pushed out you spend your time repaying them by being patron, giving lectures or lending your support.[21]

---

[19] In the everyday work of Ministers and civil servants depicted by the political scientist Rhodes the importance of gossip, rituals and networks shines through, all vital for ordering relationships through communication and interaction; see R. A. W. Rhodes, *The Everyday Life in British Government* (Oxford and New York: Oxford University Press, 2011).

[20] Kaufman, *How to Be a Minister*, pp. 113, 118.

[21] Although there was another former Prime Minister he could think of who simply said no or charged huge fees: interviewed by Emma Crewe, 20 January 1999.

Ministers become skilled at judging what is politically practical and acceptable – having a nose for how different groups will react – by getting to know the people around them. One former Cabinet Minister talked of 'not running a policy until you can find a civil servant who will work with you on it and you have to form the basis of a relationship. If you come up with an idea, you can't run it against the department – you have to persuade somebody.' Another former Minister told me how she used to establish trust and motivate people. Giving credit to others for their ideas is part of building good relationships with officials and others working for you; 'The price for taking the blame, and getting caught in the crossfire, is that you restore trust between Ministers and civil servants', she said.[22] If fronting a press conference, she would be sure to say when a senior official or one of her junior Ministers thought up a good scheme. When they get something wrong but acknowledge their mistake, then you should back them publicly. If you are autocratic and pick fights with civil servants, you can look strong as a politician but then you fail to motivate your staff, which weakens you in the long run, she counselled. The cost may be that you advance more slowly than colleagues who promote themselves more vigorously. Home Secretary Theresa May MP has publicly blamed her officials for mistakes, for example, but it does not seem to have done long-term damage to her reputation with most of the media and other politicians. When he was Secretary of State for Education Michael Gove apparently found his officials hostile to his proposed reforms; he replaced four out of five of the most senior ones before he was satisfied.[23] Morale within the education sector continues to decline, but he survived – due to his backing from the PM – until he had a row with the Home Secretary.[24]

The business of establishing relationships within departments is often disrupted. Ministers tend to be thrown into departments with no warning and then shuffled to another department just when they are getting to grips with the subject matter and making good relationships (27 months is the average).[25] In effect, the endless disruption to their relationships within and around the department caused by reshuffles makes it difficult to be effective. Sir George Young gives an example:

> The logistics of a Government reshuffle are complex. Although an outgoing Minister will have known for up to a day that he or she is heading for the departure lounge, secrecy is meant to be preserved and the Minister has to

[22] Interviewed by Emma Crewe, 20 November 2012.
[23] Charles Moore, 'David Cameron's lonely Ministers have been abandoned by Downing Street', *Telegraph*, 15 February 2013, http://www.telegraph.co.uk/news/politics/david-cameron/9873325/David-Camerons-lonely-ministers-have-been-abandoned-by-Downing-St.html# [accessed 2 October 2013].
[24] See results of a YouGov poll held with teachers, http://www.theguardian.com/politics/2013/jan/02/education-policies-hitting-teachers-morale [accessed 2 October 2013].
[25] Riddell et al., *The Challenge of Being a Minister*, pp. 10–12, 17, 20.

remain at his post until his successor arrives. The time of that arrival is not known in advance; nor indeed the identity of the new incumbent; but, once both are known, things move quickly. I had about 15 minutes to get some champagne out of the fridge, share it with my hardworking staff and make a short but sincere valedictory oration of appreciation for their support for the last two and a half years. I strode out of the office with my head held high; and then realised I had nowhere to go … I telephoned the Whip in charge of accommodation in order to solve the problem and get a proper office. There was no reply. He too had been reshuffled.[26]

Politics in government, like anywhere, is about making and losing friends but also foes. I talked to former Foreign Secretary Sir Malcolm Rifkind about surviving in a shark pond without behaving like a shark yourself. When I asked him how he handled others who behaved badly, he replied: 'I make a mental note never to be dependent on that person. If asked, I will warn others about the person as well.' There was a junior Minister who was obsessed with his own career progression. He said that later he was asked for advice about whether this more junior Minister in his department should be promoted. He felt he had to speak the truth as he saw it: 'He is charming and intelligent but he has a personality flaw so can't be entirely trusted.' That person did not progress.[27]

When in Parliament, Ministers' work is to face the public antagonism from their opponents in other parties and sometimes from critics on their own side. Your opponents in other parties are far more straightforward and can be useful. Former Home Secretary, Jack Straw MP pointed out that when his opposite number was ineffective, the Chancellor's response was that everything appeared fine and he wouldn't give his department more money. When Ann Widdecombe took over with her hyperactive approach, it not only put him on his mettle but also helped him get more money out of the Treasury.[28]

Matthew d'Ancona (MatthewdAncona)

11/12/2012 13:51

Parliamentary masterclass by @Maria_MillerMP in not rising to the bait and killing her opponents with cream #equalmarriage

Matthew d'Ancona is a journalist and former deputy editor of the *Sunday Telegraph*

---

[26] Sir George Young's website, http://www.sirgeorgeyoung.org.uk/articles/newsitem.cfm?newsid=4120 [accessed 2 October 2013].

[27] Interviewed by Emma Crewe, 4 September 2012.

[28] Jack Straw, Speaker's Lectures, Great Offices of State, http://news.bbc.co.uk/democracylive/hi/house_of_commons/newsid_9688000/9688423.stm [accessed 15 May 2014].

Despite this everyday reality of Ministers' attention being taken up by making and breaking relationships with those around them, they also aim, of course, to bring about change from within government. A Minister is measured by immediate outcomes rather than longer-term effective administration of the country. Politicians, the media and advocacy groups all demand change, reform and innovation by government. As an example, the Institute for Government lists examples of effective Ministers as those who have 'made a difference' – selling council houses or establishing academies – as if Ministers are project managers rather than managers of huge state institutions that provide everyday services.[29] So Ministers announce policy changes, new interventions and projects and proposed legislation. Former Ministers talk about taking their first bill through Parliament as an event of huge significance as if it symbolically represents their power, influence and prospects. So symbols of modernity are seen as more important than efficient administration to building a reputation as a Minister. The work undertaken by the government departments of which they are in charge are not necessarily easily measurable or turned into evidence of success. And yet ignoring the everyday administration in favour of huge reform programmes may have damaging consequences.

Eye-catching reform initiatives as well as loyalty to the boss will make promotion more likely for a Minister. Tim Loughton may have made the mistake of failing to disguise his irritation with his boss. He spent many years preparing as Shadow Children's Minister, consulting with a range of professionals working with children. Once he became Minister his diary was even more pressurized, frenetic and jammed with meetings, as his official diary secretary can confirm.[30] Rather unusually for a Minister, he was hugely popular with professionals working with children, probably as a result of this hectic schedule of discussions with teachers, social workers, NGOs and young people. But in the Autumn 2012 reshuffle he was sacked. His Twitter image changed abruptly from a sober grey-suited photo to a picture of him face-painted as a lion. The official line was that other MPs had to be given a chance and new blood was needed in government, but MPs, peers, journalists and professionals working with children gossiped that he was being sacked for the wrong reasons. He did not sit easily with former Secretary of State Michael Gove MP, because he was too close to the very teachers and interest groups that Gove distrusted. The groups did not always agree with Loughton's politics, but professionals appreciated his style of working because he put so much work into building relationships. In contrast, Gove's approach was to wage political war on the interest groups who got in the way of reform; if Loughton takes sides with those groups, and works more co-operatively with them, then he is not supporting his boss, so the gossip

---

[29] Riddell et al., *The Challenge of Being a Minister*, p. 10.
[30] http://www.timloughton.com/tims_track_record/aweekinthelife.htm [accessed 2 October 2013].

concluded. Whatever Gove's and Cameron's motives for sacking Loughton, such gossip feeds the idea that Ministerial success is linked more closely to your relationship with your boss, and those close to her or him, and the media than your abilities as a manager.

Whips and the usual channels

The usual channels consist of the party managers and their whips' offices. Their collective job is to keep the parliamentary show on the road. The key public figure in the usual channels is the Government Chief Whip (also known as the Patronage Secretary). All Chief Whips need three strengths to do well, according to a close observer: a good relationship with the PM; good knowledge of procedure; and a network of links across their own party.[31] The relationships within the usual channels not only change over time but with different Chief Whips. In the words of a former Chief Whip, speaking about the 1980s:

> The whole agenda of politics is managed, as far as possible, so that the debate may be free and fearless and purposeful. That's the Whips' role and that's the Leader of the House's role. And so you fix it all up ... the business of the House is settled by the Government Chief Whip with the Opposition Chief Whip secretly and privately before it ever goes to the Cabinet. They fix it up between them, what would be acceptable.[32]

In his view, a successful government CW delivers deals to his PM by making sure that his counterpart is influential with his/her own side. In discussion with the Opposition Chief Whip he might concede two more days on a debate if he will let some minor bills through with no discussion and neither of them let on within their own Cabinets that this is what they have agreed already. They present these as their aims to colleagues and when they then pretend to wrestle concessions from their opponent, they both appear to be tough and effective negotiators. If the Opposition CW came into his office saying his side was angry, this government CW would reply: 'Oh well, in which case we'd better have a row, hadn't we? When shall we have it? How are we going to start it? But most important of all is, how are we going to finish it?' This particular CW adored deals, whereas others are less inclined to fix the whole timetable, and even sometimes outcomes, co-operatively or don't need to because their administration has a huge majority. But the co-operative discussions across the parties' whips, including through intermediaries, is more extensive than the public

---

[31] Interviewed by Emma Crewe, 20 September 2012.
[32] Interviewed by Emma Crewe, 15 May 2000.

realizes. When I asked the former CW whether his way of working was too manipulative, he said that it allowed discussion about the issues rather than the modalities. The whips focus on process so that the rest can argue about policy, success and failure. To illustrate what happens without stage-management, he told this story:

> I can remember an occasion when one of the junior whips on the opposition side started a great row in the House over defence. He got everybody going … I called the Opposition Chief Whip over and I said, 'What's going on?' And he said, 'Well I don't really know. This chap started this thing.' I said, 'Well, he's a fool, isn't he? What's the point of him starting a row if I can't deliver anything for him at the end of it? All I can do is crush him. I can't deliver anything. I can't have these whips making a great scene in an uncontrolled fashion. If he wants to make a fuss and a row he needs to negotiate in advance with us what can come out of it.

It is tempting to see this as either the admirable passion of the Opposition and control freakery of the Chief Whip or the naivety and vanity of the junior whip and the co-operative pragmatism of the Chief Whip. One of the complexities of politics is that both could be true simultaneously.

When the current Shadow Leader of the House, Angela Eagle MP (Labour) gave evidence to a Commons Committee, she said that most of the time the usual channels work effectively:

Mr Chope: Surely if you had really wanted to put the pressure on that particular issue and ensure that that Lords amendment was debated, for the very good reasons that you put forward, you could have, through the usual channels put a lot more pressure on and achieved your objective, couldn't you?

Ms Eagle: Well, no. With all due respect, the usual channels work very well in my view a lot of the time, but sometimes if the Government does not wish to grant an Opposition time to debate a particular thing, it just makes a decision and says no and there is not an agreement on usual channels. There is just an instance where the Opposition is told what is going to be happening. Thankfully, that does not happen very often, but there are examples where I am sure Governments of all colours have done that.

Mr Chope: However, then you can engage in reprisals, can't you? If you are done over by the Government like that, then you can engage in guerrilla warfare, which no Government wants to countenance because they want the usual channels to work.

Ms Eagle: Christopher, you are a past master at guerrilla warfare and probably one of the House's experts. You are right, but in general mutually assured destruction is not the approach that the usual channels take.[33]

But once again, working effectively can, at the same time, mean not much space is left for passion, spontaneity and improvisation. The occasional ambush is useful for reminding government that the opposition could create havoc if it wished to. For example, if the opposition call an unexpected vote and the Members that assemble in the Chamber do not reach the quorum of 40, then business stops for the day. So just the threat of an ambush requires government to maintain a bloc of supporters during all sitting hours.

Let's look at it first from the viewpoint of the usual channels. They do deals and use parliamentary procedure to ensure that the will of the majority prevails and that tiny factions do not gain more power than they deserve in a democracy. At the centre of this process is a civil servant, Mr Roy Stone, with the title of Principal Private Secretary to the Chief Whip. An MP told me that on taking up the post of whip she was handed a sheet of paper with names, photos and explanation of responsibilities and against Mr Stone's name it simply stated: 'Usual Channels'. When I googled 'Roy Stone+Parliament' in October 2013 I found only four passing mentions, two in evidence to a Commons committee, one in a library note, and one in a footnote of a book I wrote on the House of Lords.[34] His ability to keep under the radar is quite remarkable. Mr Stone is only the fourth PPS to the CW that has ever been. The first was Sir Charles Harris. During his first day as a 16-year-old in the whips' office he heard Lloyd George discussing the conduct of the First World War. He became so indispensable that he was employed as PPS in 1919 and stayed for nearly 60 years in post. He was followed by Sir Freddie Warren (1958–78), Sir Murdo Maclean (1978–2000) and then finally Roy Stone. Richard Crossman said of the PPS that it is 'a little round ball-bearing which makes the huge joint work that links the Opposition to the Government Whips' Offices'.[35] MPs say that these people are unsackable, as they know all the secrets in Parliament.

Just as the Clerk runs Parliament behind the scenes, for the Speaker who sits front-stage as the ringmaster, the Chief Whip appears to manage business but really leaves much of the backstage work to his PPS. Mr Stone goes from

---

[33] Political and Constitutional Reform Committee, oral evidence, 16 May 2013, http://www.publications.parliament.uk/pa/cm201314/cmselect/cmpolcon/82/82.pdf [accessed 7 October 2013]. The witnesses to this enquiry provide plenty of rich material about the range of MPs' opinions on the power of the usual channels and the whips.
[34] Jennifer Walpole and Richard Kelly, *The Whip's Office* (House of Commons Library Standard Note, SN/PC/02829, 2008).
[35] As cited by J. C. Sainty, 'Sir Charles Harris and the Management of the Business of the House of Commons', *Parliamentary History*, vol. 21, 2002, p. 239.

one Chief Whip or party leader to another and he learns the pressures, desires and frustrations of each party. It is not just deeply undesirable politically for the parties to expose their problems to the wider public, but they can't do so to other parties. Revealing their vulnerabilities to their opponents would be political masochism. A party's leader and managers may object to a proposal, but if hugely popular with the public it may be easier to keep their objections private. The parties can't trust each group en bloc to be discreet. As a non-political civil servant, Roy Stone can discuss the temperature of each party on different issues and make recommendations, or even propose solutions to intractable differences, without revealing the secrets to others. This go-between role depends on one crucial element: trust in his discretion. A PPS to a CW will only last as long as he/she is perceived to be utterly discreet by both sides. Discretion is not just a matter of keeping secrets to yourself; it is about knowing what is a political secret or sensitive in the first place. His/her job is to warn the government of possible trouble without impeding the necessary scrutiny by the opposition. From Mr Stone's viewpoint, careful planning, consultation and scrutiny by all parties reduces the risk of trouble for the government. So his brokering of deals relies on discretion but not blanket secrecy, on trust and ambiguity but never dishonesty.

After the agenda is set, with or without deals, then the whips set about getting their troops to comply with the plan. Once a week Members of each party receive information about upcoming business and their party obligations in Parliament. A whip is not only a piece of paper but also a person, whose job is to nurture a good relationship between Members and their party, as well as a description of that relationship. So MPs take the party whip in an abstract sense, receive a weekly whip on paper, and are whipped by other party Members who are led by a Chief Whip. The more lines to the paper whip, the more you are expected to comply: one line is desirable, two is expected, three is seriously obligatory unless your health or life are in danger. The whips make it clear when your presence is required in the Chamber, sometimes to avoid a vote rather than win it, but also which way to vote. If you have a fantastic excuse for absence, then you ask your whip for a 'slip'. If you absolutely can't square the voting instruction with your conscience or your constituents' demands, then you have to let the whip know. They will try and talk you round or get some senior MP to do so, or you may get escalated up to the Minister if the vote is close and issue important. You got into Parliament on the back of your party, and you are reminded in all parties that it would be arrogant to forget that or think otherwise, so you owe loyalty. For the whips, defiance is the whimsical conceit of an over-inflated ego or a misplaced desire to put your local party above the national party/leadership. If you lazily vote against the whip while colleagues are biting the bullet and voting even when they or their constituents disagree, then you should at the least agonize and chew it all over with colleagues.

The world view according to whips and loyal party Members puts far greater stress on the importance of government 'getting its way' and, unsurprisingly, being loyal to your party. The whips mediate between backbenchers and front-benchers; they act as the glue that holds the political party together so that the frontbench can run government, or oppose, with controlled conflict and the minimum of fuss. Democracy depends on a government delivering on its promises and it can only do this if Parliament votes through its finance bills and laws. That is the abstract rhetoric of the whips. A former Labour MP voices the morality of whipping on a more pragmatic note: 'You have to appease the party even if you don't believe in their position. It would be sanctimonious to expect otherwise, you can't simply have politics decided on the whim of the individual. Parliament is a leveller, eminent people have to win reputations.'[36] Again and again I heard loyal party members talk about the arrogance and conceit of serial rebels. Those who support the party – which effectively means those who support the group who currently lead it – also want it to succeed for political reasons. They believe their party will save the economy, protect poor people, stop climate change, ensure independence for their part of Britain or whatever their galvanizing mission happens to be. Their party will keep out the other lot and prevent the harm that they would otherwise cause.

Or, if you worry that the executive dominates our political system too easily, then from that viewpoint whips are the scheming bullies who collude across the parties to prevent MPs from holding government to account. These contrasting views about the whips are continually aired both in private and public:

Mr Peter Bone (Wellingborough) (Con): Does the Deputy Leader of the House agree that a more important reform with regard to amendments would be to allow Members on both sides a free vote in Committee and to not subject them to whipping? Would that not produce better legislation?

Tom Brake: That is an interesting point. I suspect that allowing free votes on amendments in this place would lead to chaos.[37]

Peter Bone MP is a champion of the rights and duties of backbenchers to hold government to account, in part influenced by their constituents and in part by their own view of what is best for the country. That is rendered difficult by the ambitions of most MPs, who want a job in government rather than staying on the backbenches and have little interest in the workings of Parliament.[38] Bone even introduced a bill to abolish the whips and leave the management

[36] Interviewed by Emma Crewe, 10 November 1999.
[37] Peter Bone and Tom Brake, *HC Debates*, 12 September 2013, col. 1153.
[38] Interviewed by Emma Crewe, 26 March 2013.

of the timetable to civil servants. Votes are easily won by government due to a combination of the payroll vote and the obedience of ambitious MPs, the rules that allow government to control time in Parliament and the behind-the-scenes machinations of the whips, he explains. The 'payroll' vote consists of those with government jobs (limited by law to 95 in the Commons) and their PPSs (46 in November 2012), who have to follow the whip to stay in position but are not paid. The size of this payroll vote climbed from 42 to 129 during the last century and reached 140 in 2010.[39] Others add that Mr Bone is on the right of his party, often disagrees with his leadership and intensely dislikes the Coalition with the Liberal Democrats, so of course he would think that facilitating his government – or, even worse, a Labour government – would merely enable them to govern badly. Unsurprisingly other MPs, too, who follow Bone's criticism of a overweaning executive and favour reform of the rules, tend to be critical of their own party's policies as well as against those of the Opposition.

Various political developments have dramatically affected the context of whipping. As long ago as the 1960s, when UK government had far more clout than it does now, Ian Gilmour argued that the system provided stability and its failings were most in evidence when the executive failed to act. It is the evasiveness of the UK government, the fact that it fails to use its power, which can cause problems, he wrote.[40] Gilmour points to the secrets battles between government departments, the growth of private organizations and interest groups, so that the government is more like a merchant than a general, making bargains and negotiating deals rather than giving orders. He warned that if the Liberals were ever to revive, then promising them electoral reform in return for support would be dangerous. This is exactly what happened in 2010, except that Cameron only agreed to a referendum on a watered-down form of proportional representation, which the public voted against in any case.

Since the 1960s the political power of the executive has weakened and the power of the whips has declined. Why? There are many possibilities probably acting in conjunction. First, the decline in political parties; the main ones have suffered declining membership and funding, public cynicism towards their tribal battles, and questions about how they differentiate themselves ideologically. Those on the left of both Labour and Lib Dems and the right of Conservatives would argue that, since Mrs Thatcher, all their leaders have betrayed the ideological traditions of their gang. The Coalition has accentuated this tendency. Sarah Teather explained to a journalist that she was voting against the whip,

---

[39] Keith Parry and Oonagh Gay, *Parliamentary Private Secretaries* (House of Commons Library Standard Note, SN/PC/04942, 2012).
[40] Gilmour, *The Body Politic*, pp. 2–3, 6.

and even resigning, because the party had abandoned all its values under the pressure of public opinion and the compromises of coalition. She was even offended to be asked for loyalty, the journalist reported:

> Teather says she was dismayed to be told by her party to back the recent motion paving the way for in Syria because it was an issue of 'loyalty'. 'If it was a minor aspect of administrative policy then fine – talk to me about loyalty. But if they are wanting to launch military action on another country you can't tell me I need to give permission on the basis of loyalty ...', she says.[41]

Secondly, couple this with hugely more demanding constituents. Both constituents, and as important to the business of staying in a parliamentary seat, their local party, expect MPs to listen to them and not exclusively to their whips. They don't want an MP who is mere lobby fodder. If they ignore constituency demands to vote in particular ways too much, MPs worry that they may become unpopular or even become deselected. Whips no longer threaten to write to the local party and suggest they should deselect their MP; they would take no notice if they did. Thirdly, both these trends are intensified by both the mainstream media and the ceaseless evaluations on social media, that attack government and encourage backbenchers to be independent-minded. The greater exposure of government's failings and MPs' voting patterns – partly due to 24-hour media but also as a result of the Freedom of Information Act 2000 and websites that publicize how MPs vote – also put MPs under pressure to defy their party's whip. Fourthly, the decline in deference in British society more generally, and the allied shift from a hierarchical, macho-style culture in the whips' office, means that MPs are losing their fear of their whips. Fifthly, recent party leaders, and specifically Cameron, Brown, Blair and Clegg, are not seen by MPs as keen on Parliament as an institution. They spend little time on wooing Members to their cause in the tearooms or even being seen in Parliament at all, according to many MPs. Add to this the changes in hours; MPs spend fewer evenings in Parliament, because the sitting hours start and end earlier in the day. Arguably this reduces the time MPs spend bonding with each other as party members. These trends have each contributed to a steady increase in rebellion by MPs, and especially government backbenchers, since the 1940s. Whatever whips do, it can have counterproductive effects. When they send MPs off to their constituency to stop them plotting, this has the effect of MPs listening to their local parties and constituents more than to the whips.

---

[41] http://www.theguardian.com/politics/2013/sep/07/lib-dem-sarah-teather-step-down [accessed 30 May 2014].

Paul Waugh (paulwaugh)

21/05/2013 08:49

One big bit of luck for Cameron. Commons rises for another break (Whitsun) today: much harder to plot when in yr constituency

Paul Waugh is a journalist, was Deputy Political Editor of the *Evening Standard* until he became Editor of the politicshome news website

Phil Cowley's extremely thorough dissection of voting patterns reveals that defiance of the whip in the Commons has risen during every Parliament since 1945. The 2010–12 session was the most rebellious since 1945. The following session saw a slight dip, but that may have been more because the government withdrew unpopular legislation, such as the House of Lords reform bill, rather than greater obedience on the part of backbenchers.[42] The 2010–15 Parliament remains on course to be the latest most rebellious Parliament since 1945, just as the previous Parliament was, even if you take account of higher levels of obedience as the General Election approaches. Cowley's long study of rebels reveals at least two other significant aspects. First, in the 1997 Parliament Labour women were half as likely to rebel as men in the Parliamentary Labour Party and did so about half as often.[43] Confidence or arrogance play a part in rebellion and since women MP face greater obstacles within the world of politics, it is perhaps unsurprising if they hesitate to anger or show disloyalty to those controlling the party. Secondly, after you have rebelled once, you are far more likely to do so again. If you have overcome such hesitation, and realized that rebellion comes with certain advantages and friends, it becomes easier and easier as time goes on. Once established as serial rebels, Members have nothing else to lose.

The 2010–15 Parliament presented particular challenges to the whips. Fewer peerages can be promised as the House of Lords is overflowing. Changes brought about on the recommendation of the 2010 Wright reforms stole a few weapons away from the party leaders and whips. Whips no longer appoint the Chairs and Members of the Select Committees so they can't offer these to wavering MPs who could be tempted towards greater loyalty than otherwise. The creation of a Backbench Business Committee in 2010 has encouraged backbenchers on all sides to introduce cross-party debates. The idea that

---

[42] For information about 2012–13, http://www.conservativehome.com/platform/2013/05/philip-cowley-and-mark-stuart-for-1000am-tuesday.html [accessed 7 October 2013] and for other Parliaments and a longer view see their website on voting: www.revolts.co.uk.
[43] Phil Cowley and Sarah Childs, 'Too spineless to rebel? New Labour's women MPs', *British Journal of Political Science*, vol. 33, no. 3, 2003, pp. 345–65.

those in opposing parties might be referred to as 'Honourable Friends', and the process of discussing issues with those in other parties, undermines the whips' mission to paint other parties as the enemy. Finally, while the Coalition has probably made less difference to the job of the Labour whips, which is always easier when in opposition, it has greatly complicated the task for government whips. Whenever a measure is seen as Conservative, Liberal Democrat whips have to cajole their MPs into biting the bullet and keeping the government show on the road or persuading them why what appears to be conservative is actually liberal. When a government bill appears too liberal, Conservative whips have to do the reverse. Or, when the cause is too hopeless, and they face a rebellion, explain to their leaders why defeat was inevitable.

So whips are losing some of their weapons and gaining critics. Partly due to the growing number of more soothing women MPs, but also because the combination of deference and occasional violence that once characterized the whips' office is evaporating, whips have become less intimidating. The infamous story of a whip squeezing Jack Straw's balls until he promised to vote the right way would cause outrage today. In the late 1980s a Tory whip, David Lightbown MP, also called the Terminator by the tabloids, was spotted kicking a man at Members' entrance. When the victim asked why he did it, Mr Lightbown said: 'Because you are a Tory MP going in the wrong direction', to which the man replied: 'No, I'm a Monsignor from Westminster cathedral.' Whips were tough in the old days; even severely ill people were expected to attend, as Joe Ashton related about a vote in the 1970s:

> I remember the famous case of Leslie Spriggs, the then Member for St. Helens. We had a tied vote and he was brought to the House in an ambulance having suffered a severe heart attack. The two Whips went out to look in the ambulance and there was Leslie Spriggs laid there as though he was dead. I believe that John Stradling Thomas said to Joe Harper, 'How do we know that he is alive?' So he leaned forward, turned the knob on the heart machine, the green light went around, and he said, 'There, you've lost – it's 311.' That is an absolutely true story. It is the sort of nonsense that used to happen. No one believes it, but it is true.[44]

Whether or not it is true, such stories about the ruthlessness of past whips still circulate. They created an air of intimidation, but were actually used rarely and only by certain whips. But some MPs told me that if such tactics were ever used, they were only a measure of last resort and have their main effect as the threat of what once was and could be again.

---

[44] Joe Ashton MP, *HC Debates*, 4 June 1997, col. 507.

The threat of exposure was also a more useful weapon for whips in the past. To avoid bad press, MPs have to put on a façade to hide their financial difficulties, the strains on their marriage or struggles with alcohol, always protecting their reputation and that of the party. Some whips make it their business to find out how the stress is manifesting in particular MPs. The Conservatives put information about MPs in a black book, although according to Patrick McLoughlin MP, Chief Whip (2005–12), it is blue.[45] Another CW working some decades ago even went out of his way to try and solve such problems – finding some consultancy work for MPs in debt or perhaps a loan from a richer MP. He would keep an eye on debts, including accounts in the House of Commons restaurants, as a way of identifying possible trouble brewing. Then he might check that MP's expenses claims and if they looked fishy he would say: 'There's a bit of a blitz on mileage allowances, old chap. Just check you've got yours right. I mean, some damn fool's charged his wife's mileage in as well as his own', thereby averting disaster.[46] But since allowances have been handled by an external authority since 2010, and claims are published on the internet, whips no longer look at MPs' expenditure. To defy the whip still means relinquishing the protection of the party; the whips will be more likely to jump to your defence if you are loyal and co-operative. But since secrets about MPs' personal lives have become almost impossible to keep, and parties can no longer risk concealment in our more morally censorious age, the possibility of protection by the whips has greatly diminished in recent decades.

Whips are seen by many as bullies, marshalling their own side like the 'whippers-in' they were supposedly named after. In fox hunting, whips assist the huntsman, who is in charge of the hounds, by keeping the pack together and preventing dogs from straying off. But if whips in Parliament were ever an imitation of these fox-hunting whips, they are no longer. They are now even less authoritarian than sheepdogs because when one of the group repeatedly wanders off, whips have to accept it and report back to the Chief Whip that they have lost a vote. The good whips find out how their flock are likely to react to policies far in advance of votes and let they party managers know where dissent may emerge. Thus, the retention of the title 'whips' is part wishful thinking; they are more like intelligence-gathering sheepdogs herding cats.

Jeremy Corbyn MP, frequent rebel, talked about how the approach to whipping has changed, even in the last 15 years. While Hilary Armstrong (former Labour MP) was Chief Whip the regime was stricter. He tells a story that she once called him into her office and threw a book on the table in front of him:

---

[45] Interview by Paul Goodman, 26 October 2010, http://conservativehome.blogs.com/thetorydiary/2010/10/by-paul-goodman-during-the-summer-there-was-a-kerfuffle-about-the-work-of-the-whips-office-and-i-wrote-a-defence-of-whips.html [accessed 1 June 2013 but since mysteriously removed].
[46] Interviewed by Emma Crewe, 15 May 2000.

Chief Whip	
(angrily):	'Do you know what that is?'
Jeremy:	'No, what is it?'
Chief Whip:	'It is our manifesto. And what are you doing to help get it into law?'
Jeremy:	'If we were getting our manifesto into law then why are we privatizing everything? That is not in the manifesto. You are not my employer.'
Chief Whip:	'You are incapable of loyalty.'

Towards the end of the last Labour administration a phone call between then whip Sadiq Khan and Jeremy Corbyn tended to go something like this:

Whip:	'Hello there Jeremy, just wanted to check how you are planning to vote on Tuesday.'
Jeremy:	'I'm going to vote against.'
Whip:	'OK.'
Jeremy:	'I mean against the government.'
Whip:	'Yes, I know.'
Jeremy:	'Sadiq, at this point you are supposed to persuade me to support the party.'
Whip:	'I can't be bothered. Would you consider abstaining?'
Jeremy:	'No, sorry I can't do that.'
Whip:	'OK.'

Aggressive indignation no longer prevails. These days whips might occasionally shout or even more infrequently get accused of doing a little mild shoving. A Conservative whip contrasted the tactics of former military whips who used to get MPs by the scruff of the neck and push them against the wall. Now they look ahead and try to anticipate trouble beforehand. When they see they might have a problem, then the Chief Whip will decide whether to do an 'operation' – meaning ringing around everyone, especially those who might present trouble. It is highly methodical, one whip added: 'We need the numbers – it is a numbers game. If they might abstain that is only half as bad as a vote against.' One of the major concerns for all parties is to avoid political humiliation; they would rather not have a vote at all if they anticipate a rebellion.

Rewards are scarcely in their gift any more. They no longer choose Select Committee Chairs or members, and although they place people on the Public Bill Committees this is often tedious work that is not seen as a reward by many. Verbal threats and promises still have their place; there is always the unsaid possibility that whips may refuse MPs a slip – that is, permission to be absent for something important like a football game or their children's event at school – or they might arrange meetings at less convenient times or even cancel them, if you show little team spirit. Their approach is based on the mostly unspoken contract between whips and their 'flocks' that obedient backbenchers will be cared for in a general sense – given slips, trips abroad and promotion if they vote with the party. Loyal Members are more likely to get good offices within the parliamentary estate, party funding at the next election or, far more unusually, government assistance or backing for projects in their constituency. Long-term loyalty may reward an MP with a peerage or at least a knighthood. Conversely, disloyal backbenchers may get less support when the press attack, may be briefed against, and may be denied slips, promotion, treats, trips or funding. Promotion is always a more urgent issue if the party can offer government positions rather than places on the shadow frontbench. However, even this doesn't work with some MPs. One new MP related a conversation with a whip:

Whip: 'We have been watching your career with interest. You show great promise. But it will be difficult if you don't do x or y.'
MP: 'Do you realize how dysfunctional that is?'

This MP was put in the 'awkward box' early on. When the MP asked for a document from the party HQ, advisers sent through a summary with 'lines to take'. On asking for the full document, the adviser claimed the person who had it was away from their desk. However, further down the email thread someone higher up wrote: 'Don't send the full document. Not on message.'

For serial rebels the whip sits lightly on their shoulders. Kate Hoey MP (Labour) explained to me that party loyalty is not necessarily about complying with the wishes of the party leadership as communicated by the whips.[47] Being loyal to the party entails weighing up the views of leaders, local party association, party members, local councillors in your party, as well as considering other constituents and your own personal views. She has voted against her party on numerous occasions: the first time was difficult, but it gets easier. When she voted against her party as a junior Shadow Minister and against the Maastricht Treaty in 1992 John Smith called her at home:

'Kate? John Smith here.'
'Hello John, I am just watching the football.'
'I would like you to resign.'
'If you would like me to resign then why don't you sack me?'
'OK, you're sacked.'

---

[47] Interviewed by Emma Crewe, 16 May 2012.

She lost her job but made it more likely that her local party would reselect her. She has always informed her whip when she planned to rebel and so once Labour were in government she became Minister of Sport under a different leader in any case. She continues to rebel and has fewer qualms about defying the whip if the issue was not in their manifesto. Like many rebels, she has a hinterland – a life beyond politics, as Denis and Edna Healey called it – and socializes with plenty of people outside Parliament, which may make it harder for the party to discipline her. After all, obedience to the whip is more about a sense of belonging to the party and its leadership rather than a calculation of self-interest.

As the power of the whips recedes, they continually innovate with different tactics. Labour MPs related how during the Blair administration the whips struggled to keep their backbenchers occupied during the long hours in Westminster waiting for votes. Many government backbenchers drank heavily, especially those far from home, and the sitting hours encouraged it. So, since they had a huge majority they tried a rota, giving a section of their MPs time off in their constituencies. However, encouraging MPs to get too close to the local party means that loyalty to the leadership (and, therefore, to the whip) can diminish, so they stopped this. I asked another whip, a Conservative this time, what she does when people don't vote with the party.

'Talk to them, find out why.'
'A bit like canvassing?'
'Yes. You go to the tearooms but you can't *just* do that because some of them don't go there. So you get on the phone.'

She added that about half of MPs are self-important and so think they are above party and have no problem voting against it. You may not be able to reduce that proportion but you have to find out why. Others find defiance more of a struggle so the whips offer sympathy and coaxing. Former MP Paul Goodman's analogy is of the life of MPs as comrades in arms as 'a Parliamentary Party's in some ways a regiment. MPs are members of it together, fight battles, get scars, are wounded. A few take to the bottle. Others crack up. Such work creates a rough, often mute, understated sympathy.' In that case, the whips are the Sergeants.[48] Whips in all parties describe a large part of their function as equivalent to pastoral care or a human resources department for MPs, as well as conveying commands.

When Paul Tyler (now a peer) was an MP and Chief Whip of the Liberal Democrats in the House of Commons he persuaded the party to agree to a

---

[48] Ibid., Goodman, Interview on 26 October 2010 [accessed 1 June 2013].

new addendum to their Standing Orders. The gist was that if MPs couldn't support the party's line, they: (a) have an obligation to discuss with the lead spokesperson (to make sure that it is not a simple misunderstanding); (b) should explain why, how and what to the whips; and (c) if a three-line whip, consider abstaining.[49] Once you know a backbencher is threatening to vote the wrong way, and if you understand why, then you can offer a meeting with the Minister; on critical votes, such as the Iraq War, possibly even the PM. But even if such meetings fail, at least the whip-spies can predict with accuracy the way the votes are likely to go, then the leaders/whips can take account of this when deciding whether to call divisions and what kinds of concessions to ask for when negotiating with other parties.

In addition to the black arts of whipping and soothing HR, whips are intelligence agents. As a former Chief Whip operating in the 1980s puts it:

> Successful whipping is about anticipating the problems and heading them off or finding ways round them, or converting them, talking to people. It is only when you've made a mess of it and you've got it wrong that you might have to bully somebody to go and vote. The whole business is about collecting this information.[50]

At around the same time a Deputy Chief Whip held a list of the institutions where the MPs in his party could be found at all times. While the bullying has dwindled, the intelligence-gathering has become the core of whipping. Every MP I spoke to confirmed that the courtesy of informing your whip about your intention to vote was almost universally followed. The crude assumption of some outside Westminster may be that MPs have the whip withdrawn if they vote against the party. The reality is that the greatest sin is failing to keep them informed. In the Autumn of 2012 Nadine Dorries had the whip withdrawn (which effectively temporarily banishes you from the party) not for rebelling – which she often does – or for appearing in a TV programme (as reported by the BBC), but because she failed to get agreement for her absence from the whips.

So whips can be bullies when working with their own flocks, but are more often like HR managers these days. The configuration is quite different when working against their opponents. All pastoral HR is dropped, of course, and the instructions and spying are all geared to a continual process of bullying the other parties. A constant responsibility of the whips' office is to make sure that both frontbenchers and backbenchers are present in the debating Chambers, ready to speak, follow agreed messages and lines to take, heckle or vote, all at the right time. The extent to which whips get embroiled into organizing attacks

---

[49] Interviewed by Emma Crewe, 24 July 2012.
[50] Interviewed by Emma Crewe, 15 May 2000.

on the other side depends on the culture of their office, which in turn is linked to their boss, the Chief Whip. Towards the end of the 2000s one male whip used to hold up a photo of a Tory MP at the beginning of each week saying: 'This is the wounded wildebeest of the week.'

With the huge demands of constituencies and Select Committees, making sure that your backbenchers are there to support the party has become more difficult. The tradition of regular pairing – whereby MPs from opposing parties could be let off attendance on a two-line whip and thereby cancel each other out – has not been used so systematically since 1996. During the 1990s it exasperated the newer MPs who did not have a pair, and especially if they were in marginal seats so wanted to be in their constituencies, as well as the Liberal Democrats. But it has been resumed in an ad hoc way by whips' arrangement. The accommodation whips make decisions about MPs' offices while the pairing whip gives permission for MPs to be absent. Rotas are organized, for both whips and backbenchers, and messages are sent daily. In the two largest parties, whips are assigned to particular bills. Where once whips had to rely on letters and catching people in the tearoom, technological change has allowed whips to use pagers, smartphones and now ipads to communicate with their Members.

Another male Labour whip claims that whipping has completely changed in their party thanks to Rosie Winterton MP (Opposition Chief Whip). Winterton was elected unopposed by the party in 2010 and since then the operation of the whips has been more co-operative in all directions. Sir George Young has also brought a gentler style to the government's whips' office. A whip told me that from the moment he chaired his first meeting in the whips' office he restored an amiability and team spirit between Conservatives and LDs that was lost during Andrew Mitchell's brief reign. However, whatever the gentle management and persuasive skills of the government whips, controlling increasingly rebellious MPs – and government backbenchers always have more cause to rebel than opposition ones – in coalition is a challenging task. The government's defeat on House of Lords reform will illustrate the difficulties.

A rebellion

The difficulties of whipping during a coalition were on full display during the Lords reform rebellion in 2012. The proposals for introducing a mostly elected House of Lords appear modern, democratic and rational; most Lib Dems, some Labour and a few Conservative MPs supported them. The House of Lords Bill (2012–13) proposed a House that would eventually have 360 elected Members (based on the electoral districts used in European elections), 90 appointed Members, and 12 Bishops and an unspecified number of ministerial Members, all serving 15-year terms. The link between the peerage and places in the House of Lords would be broken and the hereditary peers would no longer have the right to sit as peers. However, neither the majority of peers nor a sizeable proportion of MPs in the two main parties liked the proposals, for two main reasons. First, if you strengthen the perceived legitimacy of the upper House, it might exercise its powers more vigorously. Secondly, if you have some kind of proportional representation in the House of Lords then the LD will gain places at the cost of the two main parties and the Crossbenchers. This proposal was presented as a government proposal but was really seen by most as a Liberal Democrat initiative.

Unsurprisingly the proposed reform alarmed existing peers. Following the 1999 reform, which evicted most of the hereditary peers, the House of Lords had 572 life peers, 26 Bishops and 92 hereditary peers and a total of 690 peers sitting in Parliament.[51] By 2012 the size of the House had reached 775 with a huge proportion visiting regularly. While nearly all peers see the need for some sort of change, not many favoured the reform introduced in the House of Lords Bill. Bearing in mind that all three parties had reform in their manifestoes in 2010, peers prepared for resistance long before the reform was introduced. They knew that it is difficult for peers alone to stop reform to their House – it might look like turkeys campaigning to abolish Christmas and the Parliament Act could always be used to force it through – so it was MPs who were needed to stop it in its tracks.

The House of Lords and House of Commons are variously entangled. Constitutionally the House of Lords is primarily a revising Chamber, with secondary roles played by junior Ministers and committees, and politically it is where some of the deals between parties are made and put into effect. It is also where MPs can be deposited if no longer needed, or supporters can be rewarded, so it serves other political purposes too. Socially quite a number of MPs (especially Conservatives) are connected to peers by marriage, birth or friendship. Peers knew that to defeat the reform they needed both Conservative and Labour backbench MPs to support them. All Lib Dems were likely to support it – after all, the Bill was proposed by their leader – and the Conservative payroll vote would have to back it because it was in the Coalition Agreement. Meanwhile significant numbers of both Conservative and Labour MPs favour an elected House. So a multi-pronged strategy was required to attack this measure. The Joint Committee on the Draft House of Lords Bill, a mix of MPs and peers, reported in April 2012 with only 13 out of 22 in support of the new House having any electoral mandate.[52] By this time parliamentarians were telling

---

[51] This does not include those on leave of absence or disqualified. Feargal McGuiness, *House of Lords Statistics* (House of Commons Library Standard Note SN/SG/3900, 2012).
[52] http://www.publications.parliament.uk/pa/jt201012/jtselect/jtdraftref/284/284i.pdf p. 150, [accessed 11 November 2013].

me that the reforms, like so many before, did not have a chance. Twelve of the committee members produced an alternative report. Since minority reports are not allowed, according to Erskine May, they released it on the internet. They held a news conference and blogged about problems with primacy and PR.[53]

The resistance to Lords reform attracted some impressive organizers: new MPs Jesse Norman, Nadim Zahawi and Penny Mordaunt, as well as longer-established MPs and peers with an interest in the constitution, some of whom had sat on the Joint Committee scrutinizing the proposals. They called themselves the Sensibles. As the Bill approached the Commons, MPs began lobbying – the 2010 intake talking to other new MPs, old hands talking to MPs from earlier intakes. Once they had Malcolm Rifkind's support, spirits were buoyed; if he did not like the proposals, it hardly felt disloyal to consider voting against the Tory whips. In the early stages nothing was written down, emailed or texted – they just got people on side through informal conversations, gossip in the corridors and the tearoom. One of the organizers had once been a whip so arranged to divide potential supporters into flocks of between ten and 12 and encouraged them to talk to others too. For three evenings before the vote they met informally, always arranging meetings at the last meeting, and in between they canvassed other Conservative MPs. Jesse Norman published an eloquent letter in the *Guardian* on 1 July 2012 warning: 'This bill will pile a constitutional crisis on top of an economic crisis.' Privately critics did more than criticize it as a piece of flawed legislation; they attacked the fact that it was led by Lib Dems and backed by a Coalition that was bitterly resented (especially by Tories on the right).

The pressure from the whips in the other direction was intense. The Conservatives did not particularly want House of Lords reform, according to both backbenchers and outside observers, but they were worried about losing the pending boundary changes. These changes had emerged out of the work of the Boundary Commission and all parties had agreed to the Act that gave them instructions to review where the boundaries of constituencies should fall, making adjustments in response to changes in population to make them more equal in size.[54] YouGov's Anthony Wells calculated on the basis of 2010 results that the boundary changes (which also reduced the number of MPs by 50) would have meant a loss of seats for each party as follows: Conservatives 4, LD 6 and Labour 36 (others 4).[55] So Conservatives were a lot keener on them than the other two parties. This became critical. Not only did the Conservative

---

[53] As examples, http://www.huffingtonpost.co.uk/2012/04/23/eleanor-laing-lords-reform-nick-clegg-tories-are-stupid_n_1445145.html?ref=uk; http://nortonview.wordpress.com/2012/05/01/debating-the-lords/; http://www.conservativehome.com/platform/2012/04/oliver-heald-mp-a-reformed-house-of-lords-should-be-indirectly-elected.html [all accessed 9 October 2014].
[54] Parliamentary Voting and Constituencies Act 2011.
[55] YouGov, *Boundaries update*, 24 October 2012, http://ukpollingreport.co.uk/blog/archives/category/boundary-review [accessed 8 November 2013].

rebels let Labour know informally that if they joined them in defeating the programme motion of the House of Lords Bill then boundaries changes might be abandoned by the Liberal Democrats, but a former LD adviser confirmed this to the newspapers. On 6 July 2012 former Strategy Director, Richard Reeves told the press that if Tories voted against Lords reform then the Lib Dems would retaliate.[56] Thus he created an incentive for Labour to vote against reform.

Despite this threat to boundary changes, the Sensibles persisted. They persuaded 70 MPs to sign a letter warning colleagues about the flaws in the Bill, which was published in the media – broadcasting their message to all.[57] They took to Twitter. Jesse Norman tweeted: 'any MP who says: "House of Lords reform is like a dose of the clap" deserves a follow.'[58] On the evening of 8 July Jake Berry MP (Conservative), who favoured reform, warned: 'Dark forces are massing at the gates, to defend the HOL from lordsreform. The establishment knows how to fight.'[59] On the day that MPs were due to debate Lords reform, Jesse Norman tweeted: 'Fact 1: Blair gvmt defeated 4 times in Commons, 460 times in Lords. Does anyone really think a party-list elected Lords wd do better?'[60]

When DPM Nick Clegg MP opened the second reading debate on House of Lords reform, a mix of laughing and aggressive heckling by Conservative MPs began almost immediately. Interventions were thick and fast, with Jesse Norman drumming home the point he made in his tweet. The Speaker complained about the 'permanent cacophony', which then became even more ribald when Pete Wishart MP (SNP) asked whether senior LDs would refuse to join an unelected House if reform were to fail. When Nick Clegg quoted Winston Churchill in support of his reform, his grandson Sir Nicholas Soames MP stood up – to absolute quiet – and asked him to stop. Labour MPs intervened to say it did not go far enough or that the Lords should be abolished altogether. Their spokesman, Sadiq Khan MP mentioned that the DPM's lofty and hectoring piety made it difficult. Most devastatingly, Sir Malcolm Rifkind MP encouraged the rebels by saying:

> The Bill is a puny measure ... if Christopher Columbus had been a Liberal Democrat, he probably would have been content with discovering the

---

[56] Andrew Grice, 'Exclusive: Reform Lords – or it will cost you 20 MPs, David Cameron told', *Independent*, 6 July 2012, http://www.independent.co.uk/news/uk/politics/exclusive-reform-lords--or-it-will-cost-you-20-mps-david-cameron-told-7917993.html [accessed 13 November 2013].

[57] http://order-order.com/2012/07/09/exclusive-that-letter-signed-by-mps-opposing-lords-reform-signatories/ and http://www.dailymail.co.uk/news/article-2170499/Nick-Clegg-House-Lords-flawed-undemocratic-institution.html [accessed 14 November 2013].

[58] Jesse Norman, tweet, 06/07/2012 17:56.

[59] Jake Berry, tweet, 08/07/2012 19:59.

[60] Jesse Norman, tweet, 09/07/12 08:03.

mid-Atlantic … I have not voted against my party on a three-line Whip for a very long time. I last did so in the 1970s. I do not know what effect it will have this time on my future ministerial career. All I can say is that the last time I did it, in the 1970s, two years later Margaret Thatcher appointed me to her Government. So my right hon. and hon. Friends should be of good heart and vote as they believe, and that means voting against the Bill and against the programme motion.[61]

The following day the debate was due to continue. I observed the Speaker's conference – a daily meeting he has with his deputy speakers and the top three Clerks to consider how to handle the business of the day – and they discussed the programme motion that loomed. If the vote was tied, the Speaker had to cast his vote. It was agreed that the Speaker cast his vote in accordance with precedence to allow for further discussion. But it did not come to that. Jesse Norman sent this email during the day:

Dear friends,

We have the chance at 10pm tonight to help the PM by voting against this Bill. One single decisive action now will kill this Bill outright. It will be a vital blow for the authority and strength of the back benches. Then we will have the recess, and a chance to reset the compass and allow our government to govern this country again.

   Please join me, and dozens of your colleagues, by voting AGAINST this Bill tonight.

All best,

Jesse[62]

The government realized that the rebels wouldn't be able to stop the Bill proceeding to the next stage, because Labour would support it, or at least need to look as if they were in favour of an elected House of Lords. But the rebels could defeat the programme motion – a measure that defined how many days would be given to debate this Bill, ensuring that it couldn't be talked out by MPs filibustering – to kill the Bill. Not only did the Labour Party refuse to support the motion on the grounds that this constitutional bill needed greater scrutiny but they wouldn't say how many days they wanted, so the government couldn't

[61] Malcolm Rifkind MP, *HC Debates*, 9 July 2012, cols 52–3.
[62] Nick Robinson, 'Lords reform: now it's handbags', 11 July 2012, http://www.bbc.co.uk/news/uk-politics-18793452 [accessed 12 November 2013].

adjust the motion. Labour MPs who favoured reform were told by their whips to vote against the programme motion. When one Labour MP protested to his whip that he supported reform he was told: 'You are the only one, do you want to be the one that lets boundary changes through?', only to find out later that there were quite a few in that position. Given the choice between constitutional reform and saving 36 Labour seats, the vast majority planned to vote to preserve their colleagues and give their party a better chance of winning in 2015. They knew that they could still vote for Second Reading, which would allow the Bill to progress, and tell their constituents that they had supported reform. Caroline Lucas MP proposed an amendment, which increased the number of days in the programme motion, which the House accepted on paper, but it was not selected. The programme motion was not moved because the government knew they would lose. Before the vote on Second Reading the Conservative whips had suspected there were 70 rebels in their party. But they were seriously taken aback by the vote, which revealed that their own rebellion had grown to over 90, with only 80 in the party voting yes. Two rebels were Parliamentary Private Secretaries in the government, so they resigned. But the Second Reading of the Bill was passed, with the support of Labour, which meant it could proceed in a technical sense.

As I left the gallery with some peers, we bumped into a LD MP coming out of the whips' office who said: 'Get your P45s ready chaps.' But this followed a short interchange I had with one of the anti-reform peers as we were walking down the stairs:

Emma:	'What happens now?'
Peer (beaming):	'It's over.'
Emma:	'But they did not defeat it.'
Peer:	'No, but that was only Second Reading. They didn't get the programme motion so there is no timetable and it can be talked out. And they will get even more voting against Third Reading.'

Since Conservatives had told me that David Cameron wasn't particularly excited by this piece of reform, I was puzzled by reports that later that evening the PM raised his voice to Jesse Norman, telling him he was not honourable. Whips even asked him to leave the Palace on the night of the vote. But it may not have been Lords reform, or even boundary changes, that fuelled his irritation. He did not like Mr Norman encouraging MPs to 'help the PM', as if Cameron was intentionally and deceitfully betraying the Liberal Democrats. The PM needed to hold the Coalition together to remain in power and it was his relationship with the LD he was worried about, rather than this particular bill. He told the backbench Conservative 1922 Committee that they had to save Lords reform to avoid losing the extra MPs that boundary changes should bring.[63] When he suggested that they should remember that Labour, not the LDs, were the enemy, Sir Peter Tapsell (Father of the House) pointed out that Labour were opponents and not the enemy. It may have reminded those in the room of the cliché that MPs are quick to point to when talking about parliamentary politics – that your opponents are across the House while your enemies are all around you.

Although you might think the LD would have been furious that their measure was sabotaged by backbenchers within their Coalition partner, their feelings were mixed. It allowed them to vote in the Lords to end boundary changes – saying that it was part of the package of constitutional reform – thereby avoiding an automatic loss of seats in the 2015 election. Privately some LD peers didn't like the Bill; some wanted a fully elected Chamber, for example. But above all, it kept the Coalition together, which is vital for the Lib Dems. They want to prove they are a party of government, and not just opposition, and that coalitions can be effective; they want to secure their position as one of the parties running the country in the future.

So to what extent was this all choreographed? Sources close to the action told me it was anticipated, if not stage-managed – all except the venom and scale of the rebellion. The Conservative leadership knew they had to support Lords reform to keep the Coalition going. Since 2010 LD had been supporting a raft of Conservative measures, to the fury of some of their activists, and their biggest impact on government was stopping or watering down measures in private. They lost the referendum on the introduction of PR in our electoral system in 2011. So they badly needed a success or the appearance of success – or at least to look as if they were striving hard for success. It seems highly likely that senior LD MPs who worked on this bill, the Deputy Prime Minister above all, believed in it and wanted it to pass. Whether they really thought it had a good chance is another matter. How hard did the Tory leadership really try to make it happen? One MP told a *Telegraph* journalist:

> … it was 'remarkable' and 'extremely odd' that the Government whips' office had not yet started the traditional ring-round ahead of the key vote. One whip, after being told by an MP of his plans to vote against, replied, 'Thank you'.[64]

---

[63] http://www.conservativehome.com/thetorydiary/2012/07/tories-must-deliver-tiny-elected-element-to-lords-or-lose-boundary-changes-cameron-tells-1922-meetin.html [accessed 14 November 2013].
[64] Christopher Hope, 'David Cameron faces biggest ever rebellion by Tory MPs over Lords reform', *Telegraph*, 6 July 2012, http://www.telegraph.co.uk/news/politics/9382313/David-Cameron-faces-biggest-ever-rebellion-by-Tory-MPs-over-Lords-reform.html [accessed 14 November 2013].

But either the MP, or this journalist, may have political reasons for highlighting Tory reluctance. This article was written a few days before the critical vote, so may have been encouraging MPs to rebel. Conversely, another article about how the LD shocked the Conservatives by supporting a Labour amendment that would kill boundary reform, thereby putting the Coalition in terrible jeopardy, made good journalism but doesn't seem wholly convincing.[65] The Coalition survived after all.

Few Labour MPs would shrink from Lords reform, but not many liked this particular bill and all greatly appreciated the sabotage of boundary changes. So the course of the House of Lords Bill suited practically everyone, at least in some important ways, even if reformers were disappointed that reform had failed. Even Jesse Norman came out well. To his critics he says that no harm was done: 'Fact remains that, Lords Bill or no, LibDems wd have killed boundary reforms.'[66] He went on to publish a book about Burke and how representation by MPs involves judgement and not slavish obedience to constituents or to the whip. He was chosen as Backbencher of the Year by the House Magazine in 2012 and asked to join the Conservative Policy Board in 2013 (but sacked when he voted against the government on Syria). Perhaps on this one occasion MPs bucked Peter Hennessy's wise warning about Lords reform when he described it as the Bermuda triangle of British politics from which no politician emerges unscathed.[67]

Power and constraints in government

Blunders in government are inevitable and academics and journalists serve an important purpose in pointing them out. King and Crewe chart some of the most absurd mistakes committed by governments in recent decades, adding their view of some recent ones by the 2010 Coalition government, such as the West Coast Main Line franchise having to be done twice, limits on immigration costing universities and businesses, and the incompetence of private company contractors.[68] Some blunders are more of the public relations kind, like taxes proposed for hot pasties and caravan tax in the 2012 budget, which was so unpopular it left the Treasury looking foolish.

King and Crewe theorize about why these come about. Some blunders are

---

[65] http://blogs.telegraph.co.uk/news/benedictbrogan/100187967/cleggs-tit-for-tat-retaliation-could-bring-about-the-coalitions-end/ [14 November 2013].
[66] Jesse Norman, tweet, 04/10/2013 02:42.
[67] http://www.theguardian.com/politics/2012/apr/23/lords-reform-committee-divided-reports [accessed 14 November 2013].
[68] Anthony King and Ivor Crewe, The Blunders of Our Governments (London: OneWorld, 2013), pp. 399–415.

common to all governments. Ministers do badly because they have Messiah complexes, move around departments too often, compete against each other and are in a hurry to be able to shout about positive results. There is often a time lag between a government blunder and people finding out about it and Ministers lack incentives for thinking far enough ahead.[69] Too many government politicians and civil servants are ignorant about the lives of those they rule over and oblivious to their own flawed assumptions: 'The man in Whitehall not only did not know best: he did not know that he did not know that which he badly needed to know.'[70] Tax credits were designed on the misplaced assumption that most people have a computer. A policymaker at the Department of Social Security said of the equally catastrophic Child Support Agency that they had no idea so many people had complicated family structures, with large numbers of women having children by several men.

One of the antidotes to such a chronic disconnect between people's real lives and the way policymakers imagine them is wide consultation and piloting ideas. This might have helped government avert many disasters but also raises an ethical point about democracy. Consultation by government has become a matter of course for most policies and laws, but its depth and timeliness is sometimes lacking – as we will see in the next chapter, even when government is at its best – and one group is consistently marginalized from political debate. The UK government regularly violates the United Nations on the Convention of the Child by failing to consult children about decisions that affect their lives, a theme I return to in Chapter 6.

As society become more complex, fragmented and fast-moving, successful management of policy, services and the economy through government departments becomes more challenging. From the viewpoint of those who are in the hot seat – one of the MPs with a Ministerial position – blunders come about partly because they have far less control over events and other people than they expected. Power tends to be disappointing, as Asquith revealed when he said: 'Power, power? You may think you are going to get it but you never do'.[71] In some ways they wield tremendous power – after all, Ministers are responsible for huge plans, budgets and large numbers of civil servants and through their access to the media they can decide which issues come to the attention of citizens. But in other ways and contexts they are severely restricted. Even Prime Ministers are endlessly constrained by the conflicting demands and agendas. Satisfying diverse interests within and outside the UK means government involves compromise at every turn. Within Parliament, Ministers who make

---

[69] Ibid., pp. 348–53.
[70] Ibid., p. 244.
[71] Peter Hennessy, *The Prime Minister: The Office and its Holders Since 1945* (New York: Palgrave, 2000), p. 271.

mistakes, or face disasters over which they had no control, will only be defended if they have the support of the PM and usually a sizeable number of backbenchers within their party.

To measure success, as it is often done, against plans in our increasingly complex and unpredictable world becomes more and more absurd, as Griffin points out.[72] It feeds the phenomenon, found across both public and private organizations, that we attribute idealized cult values to leadership but then turn on our leaders and denigrate and blame them when they fail in our eyes. The state is not only reified in everyday discourse but often assumed to be either evil or our saviour. Paul Ricoeur points out that it can be both. Societies need to organize themselves politically into states to reach their potential in stable ways, but paradoxically that inevitably leads to domination by rulers and possibly to violence or evil. In his essay on the 'political paradox', Ricoeur wrote:

> The problem of the control of the state consists in this: to devise institutional techniques especially designed to render possible the exercise of power and render its abuse impossible. The notion of 'control' derives directly from the central paradox of man's political existence; it is the practical resolution to this paradox. To be sure, it is, of course, necessary that the state should be but that it not be too much. It must direct, organise, and make decisions so that the political animal himself might be; but it must not lead to the tyrant.[73]

David Runciman reminds us that democracy shouldn't be taken at face value or judged by how it is portrayed on the news and at elections.[74] You have to take a longer view. When economic times are good, it is possible that democracy does quite well, but therein lies a problem; politicians get complacent and out of touch, which then causes crises. Democracy muddles through crises less well but they are necessary to shake politicians out of complacency, so they are good for democratic ways of doing politics. Politicians may ignore the lessons that crises could teach them, but at least the energy that is intrinsic to democratic engagement – as Tocqueville wrote about so long ago – is stirred by disaster. When the Scots voted in a referendum in 2014 about whether Scotland should be independent, those campaigning in favour of keeping the UK together panicked as they seemed to be losing ground in the polls. The Scots voted to stay with the UK, despite the perceived neglect and misunderstanding by Westminster, and although the divisions created by the referendum were bitter, the turnout of nearly 85 per cent of the electorate revived democracy. So an

---

[72] Doug Griffin, *The Emergence of Leadership: Linking Self-organisation and Ethics* (London: Routledge, 2002) pp. 200, 218.
[73] Paul Ricoeur, *History and Truth* (Evanston: Northwestern University Press, 1965), p. 262.
[74] David Runciman, *The Confidence Trap* (Princeton: Princeton University Press, 2013).

ironic aspect of the political paradox is that if democracy were too successful in its administration of the country, then it would start to fail as a political mode. Some failure, and exposure of it, is inevitable and healthy, as Chair of the Liaison Committee, Sir Alan Beith puts it:

> All Parliaments will always incur a great deal of public unpopularity, public dislike and public cynicism ... only when law and order is collapsing and democracy is denied do people start to see the merits of a Parliament ... looking for a good opinion poll rating for Parliament is not really how we should view this issue.[75]

It is a paradox worth understanding, because then we can focus on criticism of our political leaders for poor judgement, arrogance and aloofness rather than morally censure them for being politicians. That is why it is so important that the processes of scrutiny, exposure and criticism within Parliament from the opposition and even their own side, as well as from within the media and civil society, restrict Ministers' exercise of power, as I explain in the next two chapters. This is not only relevant to the scrutiny of plans, law and administration. It is also a vital challenge to government's more fundamental power to dictate the terms and content of debate inside and outside Parliament. The space for citizens' ideas and demands to bubble up into local and national discourse is an important aspect of democracy that has been expanding but remains limited and dominated by the usual suspects. In the meantime, the way backbenchers (and peers) hold government embraces complexity, unpredictability and the paradoxes of democratic politics in ways that deserve more recognition.

[75]Page 38, http://www.publications.parliament.uk/pa/cm201314/cmselect/cmpolcon/82/82.pdf [accessed 5 May 2014].

5
Scrutiny and Making Trouble

Scrutiny by MPs is a key role for the opposition and backbenchers. The dizzying range of scrutiny rituals attended by MPs is given some continuity by riffs and rhythms. Some are antagonistic between political parties but many are cross-party, and increasingly so, with the result that the dominance of the executive is kept in check. Media attention is moving away from scrutiny and into aggressive politicking through collusion and mimicry.

****

In the eyes of a Whip, 'scrutiny' means 'making trouble'.

Andrew Tyrie[1]

As a check against absolute power, and in a bid to prevent governments committing blunders, various processes and people scrutinize, evaluate and oppose. As Winston Churchill famously said about the House of Commons Chamber: 'This little room is the shrine of the world's liberties.' The opposition parties within Parliament sit to the left of the Speaker (if looking from his viewpoint) while the government sits to the right, and oppose except when the country unites against a foreign aggressor. The right-hand side is customarily the position for people of higher status in British culture. Parliament scrutinizes three main areas of government business: policy, administration and lawmaking. The opposition and backbenchers across the House scrutinize proposals and bills, as well as administration by government departments, and raise the profile of issues neglected by the executive, as individual MPs, as members of Select Committees or Public Bill Committees, in small groups taking issues to the Backbench Business Committee, as All-Party Parliamentary Groups and via the media. The House of Lords is tasked mainly with asking the government to think again, especially when it makes laws, although it can initiate government

---

[1] Andrew Tyrie MP, *HC Debates*, 22 February 2010, col. 100.

business in bills when uncontroversial. (The various rituals and rules of scrutiny are comprehensively explained in Rogers and Walters's *How Parliament Works*, so I will not duplicate.[2])

King and Crewe are typical of politics scholars in describing such opposition and scrutiny as weak: 'there is at the heart of the British system a deficit of deliberation.'[3] The opposition that checks government is not so much within Parliament as outside; the anticipated reaction of the voters, as influenced by the media, makes governments cautious and populist, they claim. However, I argue in this chapter that Parliament has increased its power to embarrass government, partly due to Select Committees, and despite the increasing clout of backbenchers their work remains scarcely visible to the public. I will analyse what goes on in this world of scrutiny and in the next chapter see how it works as one particular bill travels through Parliament.

The riffs, rhythms and rituals of scrutiny

The three main modes of scrutiny and debate in the House of Commons take place in the main debating Chamber and in a smaller Chamber off Westminster Hall: the committees (Select and Public Bill); and the advocacy meetings (APPGs, small meetings between MPs and others). The lowest levels of scrutiny are achieved by Early Day Motions – or parliamentary graffiti, as some call them – when MPs sign written motions but which are not debated, and Written Private Questions asking the government for information. The rules, conventions and cast for each of these processes are completely different. From the viewpoint of the MPs, adapting to these various sites requires knowledge of the endlessly complex procedural rules and different styles of performance for multiple audiences and demands. The sketchwriter Norman Shrapnel wrote about politics as theatre in the 1970s; Parliament 'acts out the national conflicts like a form of expressionist theatre. So what we have is a famous but ever-struggling national repertory company, busy dramatizing an era, improvising its way through a mistily discernible plot.'[4] Many MPs remarked on the need to adapt their mode of performance. Sir Malcolm Rifkind advises MPs to sound confident and adjust their style to the context. If you dry up in the Chamber, then stop and turn it into a dramatic pause. He continued:

> If you are speaking on the TV it is not good speaking as if you were performing to the nation, with a dramatic declamatory style, you need to talk

---

[2]Robert Rogers and Rhodri Walters, *How Parliament Works* (London: Routledge, 2006), p. 9.
[3]Ibid., p. 386.
[4]Norman Shrapnel, *The Performers: Politics as Theatre* (London: Constable, 1978).

as if you were speaking to one person in their sitting room. You need to be conversational. When Winston Churchill spoke in his dramatic declamatory style he was a figure of fun until 1939. His style was appropriate for war time.[5]

There are three processes that provide some continuity for MPs between and across all this chaotic diversity and dynamism. The first are the riffs that MPs develop to make sense of ideology and communicate as policies and arguments, each improvised for different audiences. The second are rhythms that organize the work of MPs by creating repetition in time and space but allow for adaptation and variation at the same time.[6] The third are the rituals – as examples, debates in the Chamber, interviews in TV studios and speeches in party conferences – that punctuate the daily routine with riffs and rhythms of particular political, social and cultural significance.

So what are these riffs, rhythms and rituals? Like jazz musicians, MPs create riffs, as Chris Bryant MP (Labour) put it to me, perhaps seven or eight at any one time. For example, at one point he had to become an expert on pensions and so he developed a 90-second linguistic riff, which could be extended to several different lengths. It is OK if people hear the same points in different contexts, but 'if you have a reputation for using formulas, then you are going nowhere',[7] he adds. Riffs can be useful for any occasion but your style and tempo need to change completely in the different sites because different relationships are being formed or maintained. So a good MP has riffs but has to appear as if she doesn't, as if being spontaneous, otherwise she is acting impersonally. You have to be able to respond to an intervention in a highly personalized way to be considered a good performer. You need to have an awareness of specificity – the audience, the mood and the relationship – and to express a coherence of your self, and your ideology, which glosses over the fact that all human beings have ups and downs and changes of heart and circumstances.[8] Both political parties and Select Committees have to do this too, which means that individuals have to interlace their own riffs with those of their colleagues. Often they have to feign a consensus view over time by establishing riffs in the face of diverging opinions and changing membership.

Riffs are not only created by individual MPs, their factions, political parties, Select Committees and both government and opposition; they can also develop across political divides. The popular view of MPs as locked in antagonistic and polarized battle underestimates how much there is a shared discourse between

[5]Interviewed by Emma Crewe, 4 September 2012.
[6]Tim Edensor, 'Introduction', in T. Edensor (ed.), *Geographies of Rhythm* (Farnham: Ashgate, 2010) pp. 1–20.
[7]Interviewed by Emma Crewe, 25 January 2012.
[8]Erving Goffman, 'Social Life as Drama', in Charles Lemert and Ann Branaman (eds), *The Goffman Reader* (Oxford: Blackwell, 1997), p. 101.

all parliamentarians that they tend to take for granted. Most obviously, *all* MPs speak publicly about the need for change when trying to win support from the public. Modernization is a taken-for-granted riff for all members. Although traditionally Conservative philosophy tends towards the protection of national institutions, since Thatcher's reforming zeal they have championed change almost as much as Labour. In contrast, with austerity and cuts in funding for state institutions such as the NHS and the BBC, the Labour Party is arguing for protecting those national institutions that constitute the welfare state. In one sense Labour may be becoming more conservative, while many (perhaps even most) Conservatives are even more impatient for sweeping reform of the EU, of immigration policy and of the way that the state provides services than they explain publicly. So the parties are moving in different directions, in part in opposition to each other, but the shared riff is that none praise British traditions or spurn modernity as they once did: modernity has become a taken-for-granted dominant riff for all politicians. When MPs were discussing the management of the Commons itself and recruiting the next Clerk, every MP rationalized their proposal by claiming it was more modern than the last.[9]

While riffs give shape to the speech-interactions between politicians – that is, the content of their social performance – their bodies have to navigate time (parliamentary calendar and seasons) and space (a vast estate in Westminster and the streets of their constituencies) by following routines and timetables or refusing to do so. These rhythms create continuity and disruption in the work of MPs and their importance is revealed by the status of diary secretaries. Although some do it themselves, most MPs have a member of staff who arranges when, where and with whom they meet, and patterns emerge when you look at MPs' diaries. Groups of MPs share rhythms in common. Most rhythms are planned in advance, such as attending a Select Committee; some are impulsive, like sitting regularly with your mates in the tearoom; and others are idiosyncratic to specific MPs, whether planned or not. One MP may visit a particular business in their constituency annually while another always goes to Business Questions on a Thursday. Like riffs, these rhythms allow room for adaptation or can be disrupted[10] and transformed, but in the everyday work of MPs they provide some continuity. While riffs create the content, rhythms provide the form, which makes it possible for MPs to navigate their sociopolitical world. Together these allow MPs to develop and maintain key social relationships and have some continuous sense of self in relation to the world around them.

Finally, the more events are politically, socially and culturally significant, the more they are ritualized. This usually means they will be charged with symbolic

---

[9]*HC Debates*, 10 September 2014.
[10]Shirin Rai, 'Disruptive democracy: analysing legislative protest', *Democratization*, vol. 20, 2013, pp. 385–91.

meaning, regulated by rules, and reproduce or challenge a sociopolitical hierarchy (as I have argued in a book about the House of Lords[11]). While an unimportant APPG may be run informally, with few rigid rules and minimal sense of hierarchy, an important political event – Prime Minister's Questions (PMQs), a Select Committee enquiry meeting or a party political conference – is replete with strict rules, symbols of power or rebellion, and status hierarchy.

Let's see how this works in the most dramatic ritual of parliamentary scrutiny, PMQs. Oral questions are posed by MPs to the Ministers in a department or, on Wednesday, to the Prime Minister. The main party leaders prepare beforehand with their allies and advisers, developing linguistic riffs with the aim of humiliating the other side and its leaders. Opposition MPs devise questions to humiliate and expose flaws, while government backbenchers are encouraged to pose questions that allow the Minister to champion successes. The Prime Minister does not know what questions will be thrown at him from the other side, whereas his/her own MPs will usually send copies to his/her advisers, although the list showing the questioners will give the civil servants some clues about what will be asked even by opponents. Still the PM is briefed on all the major issues facing government. Even if it achieves nothing else, PMQs makes sure that the PM is up to speed on the key issues of the week. When PM Tony Blair changed the timing of PMQs to once a week, the number of minutes of scrutiny stayed the same but the briefings on key matters were cut in half. The opposition identify government's vulnerable spots and craft verbal attacks; in this context words become deeds and riffs become weapons. The rhythm of PMQs is identical – every Wednesday for 30 minutes with carefully regulated questioning and answers given by the PM, usually leaning against the despatch box, which aim to humiliate the other side.

Despite the promises of incoming PMs to tone down the aggression, PMQs remains famous for gladiatorial verbal combat, always witnessed by packed benches of MPs. When the leaders do tone it down, the hacks describe them as dull and ineffectual.[12] It is a ritual, rather than just a routine, because it is charged with cultural, social and political significance, the best-attended political event by MPs and most observed by outsiders. It is seen as a way of taking the temperature of the fortunes of government versus opposition, the parties and the leaders all at the same time. Along with elections and party conferences, which tend to be infrequent, it is the key regular public occasion for evoking party unity – inspiring social *communitas* within parties through antagonism to others. PMQs is the most concentrated and theatrical ritual within which government leaders defend themselves, and publicize their occasional triumphs, and opposition accuse them

---

[11] Crewe, *Lords of Parliament*.
[12] Hansard Society, *Tuned In or Turned off? Public Attitudes to Prime Minister's Questions* (London: Hansard Society, 2014) pp. 49–50.

of arrogance and incompetence. Underneath all that, various hierarchies are on display. Frontbenchers surround their leader while the banks of backbenchers behind boost (or occasionally undermine) their superiors in the party, egged on by the whips. It is this ritual above all others that has been criticized for its macho, aggressive style; women MPs, in particular, describe it as infantile and excluding. But not only women. The Speaker argues: 'I do think there's an inverse link between decibels and decorum; screaming is not scrutiny', and asked the three party leaders to meet to discuss how to improve it. This has been partly inspired by Hansard Society research indicating the public are not at all impressed by the point-scoring noisy ill-mannered bluster; in the words of one member of the public, it is 'farce drama to see who can outdo the other'.[13] Some people even wondered whether the whole event was scripted. The challenge will be to discourage aggression without losing the political punch and significance. But for the parties, another problem is that the event stirs up strong emotions and party loyalty among some MPs; losing that in a climate of increasing rebellions could be dangerous for the whips. But it might force them to find even subtler ways of winning the support of their MPs, for example by taking account of their views even more often.

At the other extreme, we have a scrutiny ritual with no drama and scarcely any audience: Public Bill Committees. I was warned by all MPs, journalists and parliamentary officials that Public Bill Committees were the most dismal parliamentary occasion. Once principles underlying a bill have been aired in a 'second reading' debate in the Chamber, the bill is then sent to a committee for more detailed scrutiny. However, the government always has a majority and the committee members are chosen by party whips. They tend to choose backbenchers whose views align with those of the government. When one MP asked to be on a particular Public Bill Committee the whips said: 'only if you don't rock the boat. We can give you amendments to put.' The MP declined. The result is that loyal government backbenchers do their best to block any opposition amendments. Your presence is required, especially if on the government side, to prevent any ambushes by the opposition – such as unexpected calls for a vote – and you are asked not to speak unless making brief remarks of support. This doesn't always stop government backbenchers intervening, especially if they know about the subject or have been lobbied by constituents. The opposition backbenchers are encouraged to object, speak and amend but to leave it mainly to the frontbenchers so that they can focus on their agreed key concerns. The result can be ponderous, repetitive and predictable. Government committee members sign Christmas cards, answer constituents' emails or write speeches; some MPs feel that there is little point in them engaging much with the discussion, which tends to be mostly an interchange between the opposition proposing amendments and

---

[13] Ibid., p. 6.

the Minister then rejecting them. This was the picture of Public Bill Committees that MPs had painted for me.

In September 2012 I dragged myself along to a Public Bill Committee meeting expecting to fall asleep. The wooden seats in the otherwise sumptuous Committee Room in the Palace of Westminster were far too uncomfortable for dozing, but I became captivated in any case by a love-in between the Coalition Government and the Official Opposition (Labour) over the problem of the theft of metal monuments. Richard Ottaway MP (Conservative) had introduced a bill to regulate scrap metal dealers. Conservatives don't usually like regulation, but everyone agreed that something had to be done because all constituencies were affected. The meeting was so co-operative that David Winnick MP (Labour) voted with the government and Graham Allen MP (Labour) even sat with the Coalition MPs, saying it was a cross-party issue. The only person who struck a rather negative note about the Bill was Simon Hughes, who spoke up for scrap metal dealers in his constituency.[14] David Hanson, speaking for the Opposition, asked whether they would accept an amendment after 20 years of having them refused. When he was a Minister, he admitted, he only accepted them in the sense of reintroducing them as government amendments to improve the drafting or make it looks as if it was their idea. To his amazement the Minister accepted it. The Chair was so taken aback he couldn't quite remember what procedure followed next.[15] But this committee meeting was unusual because the Bill had strong cross-party support. Even when opposition amendments are not accepted, the spokesperson may well still take Public Bill Committees seriously as an opportunity to prove themselves and enhance their reputation.

The Select Committees that scrutinize the government departments are informally ranked by MPs in terms of status from the most senior, the Treasury Committee, down to Welsh Affairs. The ranking is linked to the size of department, the amount of money they spend, but also how much press attention they get. But the ranking is changeable; some MPs want to be on the Welsh Committee more than any other. The Select Committees range from providing melodrama to deliberative investigation. A politically significant event is the termly questioning of the Prime Minister by the Liaison Committee, a committee made up of the chairs of all other committees. Public perception of this form of questioning is complimentary – they saw it as informative, honest and authentic, when asked by the Hansard Society.[16] One pointed out that the

---

[14] Although Simon Hughes' local party association received donations from scrap metal dealers in his constituency that he failed to register, he was cleared of breaching the rules of lobbying for reward and consideration by the Parliamentary Commissioner for Standards, http://www. publications.parliament.uk/pa/cm201314/cmselect/cmstnprv/805/80504.htm [accessed 17 September 2014].

[15] *HC Debates*, PBC (Bill 009), 11 September 2012.

[16] Hansard Society, *Tuned In or Turned Off?*, p. 36.

PM can't hide and wriggle out of the questions. Sir Alan Beith MP, Chair of the Liaison and Justice Select Committees, has the ability to question with forensic ferocity if it is the Prime Minister accounting for his record and gentle patience when it is a social worker talking about child abuse. Not all committee chairs and members adjust their style with such observant deftness, but it is increasingly the case that Select Committees are adapting to their multiple roles and audiences. Some witnesses complain that when MPs arrive late for the meeting they sometimes ask a question that has already been asked, which rather ruins the air of efficient interrogators. But mostly witnesses are impressed and giving written and oral evidence is taken seriously by both visitors and MPs.

The most reliably uncompromising committee is the dry-sounding Public Accounts Committee chaired by Margaret Hodge MP (Labour). This committee is tasked with interrogating government about how it uses public money and since it has the support of the National Audit Office, the inquiries are well-informed and catch media attention. When questioning a Minister or senior civil servant, the committee has the appearance of a court. They 'take evidence' from 'witnesses' through a form of inquisition, with MPs taking it in turns to put questions. After the NAO publishes reports it produces a briefing for the committee by highlighting key sections. Although it suggests questions that the MP committee members might ask, a task usually carried out by Clerks and advisors on their own in other committees, MPs often devise their own questions either in advance or on the spot, even more than they do on other committees. If MPs sound a little like barristers in court, they lose this appearance when witnesses are evasive; committee members can be irritable, even aggressive, if they don't get answers. When a senior solicitor at HM Revenue and Customs refused to reply to a question about a tax deal done with a global company on grounds of legal privilege, Margaret Hodge told him Erskine May (the bible of parliamentary procedure) trumps legal privilege. When he said he was accountable to his Minister, she retorted that he was ultimately accountable to Parliament so should answer the questions. She became so exasperated that she and her colleagues bullied him into swearing on oath to tell the truth. Hodge and colleagues were breaking the wonderfully named Osmotherly Rules,[17] which stipulate that Ministers but not civil servants are directly accountable to Parliament (unless they are Accounting Officers), but there was little the witness could do about it. When reprimanded by a colleague the next day, the Chair Margaret Hodge looked abashed but said they received fantastic media coverage, so I was told by a third party.

The Public Administration Committee is chaired by a Conservative, Bernard Jenkin MP, and has been almost as critical of government, or more specifically

---

[17] These rules were christened by then *Times* journalist Peter Hennessy in 1980. He named them after Edward Osmotherly, the civil servant who issued them, but they were written by Sandy Russell.

the way the civil service is run, and also gets entangled in the question about whether civil servants can be forced to answer questions. Neither Hodge nor Jenkin shrink from hammering government and although she is Labour and he is no particular fan of the current leadership of his party, so supporters of the government claim they have their own agenda, both have attracted plenty of positive media attention to Parliament's scrutiny role. But, as one shrewd parliamentary observer points out, the saying 'you catch more flies with honey that you do with vinegar' may apply to the scrutiny of government, so some of their aggression may incline government to ignore them.

These Select Committees are not the only ones flexing their muscles. The Culture, Media and Sport Committee got huge audiences when it interviewed the Murdochs, who only appeared reluctantly and allegedly gave incomplete answers, raising questions about what should be done if people tell less than the whole truth. Other committees may be quieter but are growing in influence, especially within their fields. A former Prison Inspector told me that he considered attendance at the Justice Select Committee a vital part of his job and his direct accountability to Parliament was what gave him clout. A very senior Judge told me that he was always impressed when giving evidence to that committee, partly because the MPs were well informed about the issues and in touch with the problems facing their constituents. Committees appear as if they operate rather like a court in their most common mode, establishing facts through the interrogation of witnesses, but they are also innovating in the way they find out about perspectives, problems and solutions. They run sessions around the country, commission research and occasionally even take evidence from young people in more informal ways.

Oral questions, written questions and Select Committee sessions all rely on questions mediated by Clerks. Parliamentary Clerks are unique to legislatures. If MPs and peers are the Rajputs or rulers of the parliamentary social order, then in one guise Clerks are the Brahmans whose knowledge of the sacred texts of procedure means that they guide like priests or teachers. But there are significant differences between Commons and Lords Clerks. While the Lords police their procedural rules collectively, the Commons Speaker and Deputy Speakers do so in the Commons. This means that Commons Clerks tend to be in greater demand, giving advice more frequently in response to questions and especially to the Speaker. At the same time they are more cautious in their responses; they are serving elected parliamentarians and never lose sight of MPs' democratic mandate. To serve Parliament, MPs always make the final decisions. In the Lords, in contrast, some Clerks respond to the limits to peers' governing power by more proactively giving advice when answering a question posed by a peer.

Clerks still wear eighteenth-century court attire when sitting at the Table in the debating Chamber, giving them the air of lawyers. An extension of the operation of the Table can be found beyond the corridor behind the Speaker's Chair, a tiny office with two Clerks and one assistant who get MPs' oral and written questions into good shape. A narrow-sighted MP will assume that these Clerks block any feisty questions by stripping out any radical language because they are conservative, tradition-bound pedants. A broad-minded MP will realize that these Clerks are determined to hone every question into a weapon of scrutiny, getting a government into a place where it might become more difficult to evade the question.

Foolish MPs fail to see that Clerks have extraordinary powers of observation and political savvy. They don't see this because Clerks disguise both. They ration their advice, so as not to appear presumptuous, and present it as party politically neutral. But they are only too aware of the political sensitivities and subtleties of different strategies. If an MP presents a fuzzy or tendentious question, then a Clerk will correct it. If an MP goes and asks 'how can I ask this question in the most awkward way for government', the Clerk will obligingly advise. Above all, Clerks are discreet. So often they can't explain why they are advising the way they are – it would reveal what they know about other players and parties – and consequently MPs tend to underestimate Clerks' knowledge to their own detriment.

The journey that a question takes once submitted by an MP is exhaustive. First of all, when questions arrive at the Table Office the Clerks check they are 'admissible'. If not – it is offensive or does not concern government – then the MP is sent a blue card so that she or he can edit it. There are always more oral questions drafted than can be put. In the long 2010–12 session there were over 100,000. So they are then sent to the Upper Table office for the Shuffle. They put the MP's name and question number into the computer and once all the questions for a particular day are in there, they set it to randomly select a manageable amount. Then they retrieve the hard copies and return them to the Clerks. The editing Clerk marks those that are already perfect with an e. Those with imperfections, she corrects. Her edits make the language consistent, avoiding capitals where possible, for example, and removing redundant words. Argumentative questions are out of order. A Clerk changed a question about people being silenced to 'not discouraging whistle-blowers from coming forward' and a 'delay' to 'time taken'. MPs can't ask about discussions between civil servants. They correct imprecision. One changed a question about 'when government will legislate' to 'when Parliament will legislate' because only the latter can pass laws. And finally, they avoid vagueness. One question had 'action' changed to 'steps', another was more specific about the effect of an action rather than a general question about impact, and several had more specific timescales introduced to avoid the Minister giving a vague answer. One had its timescale shortened as too long a time period becomes unreasonable in terms of the cost of compiling the answer. The most common edit was designed to minimize the Minister's room for evasion. Then the re-edited question is sent back to the MP. Ninety per cent of the time they are happy, but some then get into discussion with a Clerk about the final draft.

Once agreed, the full list of questions is forensically investigated for flaws at a Haroosh, a meeting of Clerks to check the questions one last time and then approve them. I asked the Clerk, Sir Robert Rogers where the word came from and he told me it was coined in the 1960s by fellow Clerk and former army officer Frank Allen, who claimed it was an Arabic word for palaver. According to one web forum it is an old colonial word meaning 'a general process of bureau-cratic disturbance, confusion, fear, suspicion and agitation ... initiated by the nabob at the apex of the administrative pyramid in reaction to the incompetence or political incorrectness of an underling or underlings'.[18] The Haroosh I watched was relaxed and laced with arcane knowledge and jokes about the pedantry of Clerks, whether or not the nabob – Paul Evans, the Table Clerk in this instance – was present. But still the word captures something of the urgency of the Table Office getting it right.

While the Clerks correct MPs' written words in preparation for the ritual of questions, their speech is regulated by other MPs. In each significant ritualized debate, an elected Chair always presides. Within the main debating Chamber it is the elected Speaker or Deputy, within a Select Committee it is a Chair also elected by the whole House, and for APPGs an MP is elected by the members of that group. The Speaker, the highest authority in Parliament, and his Deputy Speakers ensure that backbenchers have their say in debate or questions. When canvassing to be one of the Deputy Speakers in 2013 Eleanor Laing MP said: 'I would like to be part of the Speaker's team, not just to keep order in the Chamber but to stand up for the rights of the backbenchers ... against overbearing governments.'[19] The Speaker mediates the political rituals of scrutiny in the main debating Chamber with the assistance of the parliamentary Clerks, who sit at the Table.

John Bercow MP, who was elected as Speaker in 2009, has championed backbenchers and the scrutiny of government more than most.[20] He allows 'urgent questions' far more than any other Speaker in recent times, putting into practice the advice of the then Clerk of Legislation (later the Clerk 2011–14) Sir Robert Rogers.[21] This has probably led to Ministers making statements more often, partly to avoid responding to an urgent question where they are in responsive rather than proactive mode. He has encouraged Ministers to make announcements in

---

[18] https://listserv.ucsb.edu/lsv-cgi-bin/wa?A2=ind0404&L=nabokv-l&F=&S=&P=13367 [accessed 17 February 2014].
[19] *The Daily Politics* programme, http://www.bbc.co.uk/news/uk-politics-24520070 [14 November 2013].
[20] Interviews held in December 2011 and January 2012.
[21] www.parliament.uk/briefing-papers/SN05110.pdf, June 2009 [accessed 28 May 2014].

the House before they do so to the media or on Twitter. Observers of Parliament confirm these changes, but so do some numbers. Between 2004 and 2008, a range of two and eleven 'urgent questions' were allowed by the then Speaker annually; in 2011 40 urgent questions were asked. Between taking office in 2009 and December 2013 Speaker Bercow granted 154. He encourages a fast pace as MPs move through questions, giving as many backbenchers as possible a chance to put Ministers on the spot. Some Conservatives perceive his approach as biased against his own party, and specifically against David Cameron, given an impetus, they claim, by his Labour-supporting wife. He can be rude, vain and pompous, many MPs told me. At the same time few would dispute that he has contributed to a revival of the Chamber and made it more respectable to support the role of backbenchers.

Changing the rules: Backbenchers flex their muscles

The Commons Speaker has talked about how the House of Commons has experienced a Doctor Who-like regeneration since 2010 for three reasons.[22] First, the Coalition has challenged both Westminster and Whitehall to devise new norms and opened up space for backbench ingenuity. Secondly, the large intake of new Members arriving in 2010 into the two main parties were not only more diverse than ever before, but determined to bring about change. Finally, changes in the rules of the game have transformed the way it is played, including the Speaker's revival of the Chamber – with far more urgent questions and snappier interventions at question times – and reforms that have cleaned up expenses and empowered backbenchers. In 2009 Parliament threw out the old expenses system and created a new body to regulate MPs' pay and allowances – the Independent Parliamentary Standards Authority. They also introduced reforms to the way Parliament works to create a good news story about parliamentary business. This came about because in 2009 Tony Wright (then a Labour backbench MP) wrote to PM Gordon Brown with some suggestions. Nine days later, on 10 June, Professor Wright was sitting in the Chamber and Jack Straw came up to him and asked: 'Did you know that the PM is about to announce the establishment of a committee on reform and you will be Chair?' He didn't. The Wright Committee, as it came to be known, worked at tremendous speed with the skilful guidance of the then Clerk of Committees, David Natzler.

The Wright Committee members were champions of the backbenchers at a moment when a new Speaker was clearly taking their side as well. Most of the

---

[22] http://www.hansardsociety.org.uk/wp-content/uploads/2013/11/Designing-a-Parliament-for-the-21st-Century-Hansard-Society.pdf [accessed 4 December 2013].

members were approaching retirement – they had nothing to lose by opposing the whips and the interests of government. They came up with a series of proposals to challenge the dominance of the executive, even if only mildly. Mindful that whips favoured loyal party members on committees, and even removed two troublesome Committee Chairs in 2001 – Gwyneth Dunwoody MP and Donald Anderson MP – only for them to have been reinstated by backbenchers, the Wright Committee recommended that the whole House should elect Chairs to committees. They knew that some MPs would worry that MPs might vote mischievously to elect unpopular people in other parties. They braced themselves for a campaign.

The other main proposal was for a Backbench Business Committee to plan the use of backbench time and a House Business Committee, with backbenchers represented on it, to agree government time. The idea of a Backbench Business Committee came from Australia via the Committee's Specialist Adviser, Meg Russell (a University College London researcher).[23] The Committee also encouraged action on the stalled process of introducing an e-petitions system. They had not forgotten how such reforms had been sabotaged in the past by whips, who saw them as anti-democratic, weakening party accountability and giving too much clout to whimsical backbenchers. So some Members sought support from party leaders as they went along and prepared themselves for a struggle.

Gordon Brown welcomed *some* of the proposals. When first put to the House, the motions were stopped in their tracks by Hilary Armstrong (once a Labour Chief Whip but at that point a backbench MP). The Wright Committee managed to bring about a second debate before the General Election but the frontbenchers conspired to try and water down some of the changes.[24] Backstage canvassing ensued in the tearoom. Not only did backbenchers defeat them on an amendment to halve the number of days to be put into the hands of the Backbench Business Committee (BBBC) but they passed all the recommendations of the Wright Committee. The next set of hurdles would ensure the proposals were put into practice. The elections to committees had already been secured. After a long delay by the Brown Government, Standing Orders for establishing a BBBC were ready to be passed, but when they came to be debated the then Leader of the House, Harriet Harman MP said there was not enough time. She did not want to sacrifice government bills by wasting time on this motion, which had swelled because Members had put amendments down. If they would withdraw them, it could be carried, she promised. But one of the anti-reformers was a former Chief Whip, who had left the building and was

---

[23] Meg Russell, '"Never allow a crisis to go to waste": The Wright Committee reforms to strengthen the House of Commons', *Parliamentary Affairs*, vol. 64, no. 4, 2011.
[24] Ibid.

unobtainable, to the irritation, if not fury, of the reformers. It was clear that the frontbenchers colluded with pro-whip backbenchers to defeat reform without appearing too obstructive. So Parliament dissolved with no Backbench Business Committee.

The General Election of 2010 ushered in 227 new MPs; more than a third of the House were new and intent on healing Parliament and politics after the expenses scandal. Former members of the Wright Committee, including Graham Allen, kept working away behind the scenes to make it happen. A group of NGOs working on governance – including the Hansard Society, Democratic Audit and UCL's Constitution Unit – had written in March that year to all MPs arguing for change.[25] The new Coalition had promised to implement the Wright proposals and some of the anti-reformers left the House at the election. New ones were desperately trying to get to grips with the onslaught of being MPs and the Leader of the House, Sir George Young was a reformer and even sat briefly on the Wright Committee (before being promoted). So, the proposal for a new BBBC committee was passed without a vote.

The first Chair elected to the Backbench Business Committee was Natascha Engel MP (Labour). She had sat on the Wright Committee and wrote a minority report expressing disagreement; she had been worried that the BBBC might take power away from accountable party leaders and hand it to an unaccountable backbench elite. She put down an amendment to make sure the BBBC had its sessions in public but was defeated. So she stood as Chair to ensure this transparency by creating it herself. How did she do this? Mainly by talking to her own Committee members, MPs in the tearooms, whips and the Leader of the House. With the guidance of a Clerk, Andrew Kennon, Natascha designed the Committee from scratch, persuading the whips to go along with the innovations when they expressed doubts. For example, they wanted Chairs of Select Committees to announce their reports in backbench time but whips wondered whether it would work. 'What happens if there is a vote?' the whips worried. 'Why should there be one?' Andrew asked. They agreed to try it.

Once set up, the Committee took control of non-government time in the Chamber and in Westminster Hall. They allocated the time with a newly designed ritual. Every Tuesday cross-party groups of backbenchers queue to put proposals to the committee by making a pitch in public. It is a bit like *Dragon's Den* without the intimidation. Their criteria for giving time are:

1 Topicality.

2 Importance of the subject.

3 Breadth of interest: how many other Members supported the proposal and

[25]http://wrightreforms.files.wordpress.com/2010/05/support-wright-reforms-letter-2-march-2010.pdf [accessed 4 December 2013].

were they likely to take part in debate? Was there cross-party interest in this debate?

4 Was there support from Select Committees, campaign groups, constituents and others?

5 Was the subject unlikely to secure debate by other means (for example, by a debate in government or opposition time)?[26]

If they do not have cross-party support, the Committee politely suggests they acquire some and reapply. Once the pitches are made, the committee sit in private to discuss the applications. Those that match all the criteria are given green (debate as soon as possible) or amber (has merit but is not as urgent), while those outside their remit are given red (so no debate). A debate about trade union funding to the Labour Party was turned down because it had no Labour support. Another to drop the Health Bill was refused because it did not have Conservative support at a time when it was being debated in the Chamber in any case.

The debates always have both cross-party support and opposition, so express at least two sides to an argument but in new configurations. MPs and journalists agree that some of the backbench debates have been among the best of this Parliament. They voted to recommend an investigation into the Hillsborough disaster, the banning of wild animals in circuses and better regulation to protect pubs. I sat in the public (formerly 'Strangers') gallery to listen to the debate on pubs. There are 54,000 in the UK but 25 are closing each week, in many cases because pubs that are tied to breweries do not get a good enough deal to survive. In every constituency in the country, pubs are a vital social hub. So MPs from across the House passed a motion to ask the government to introduce regulation that protects pubs more effectively. Publicans in the gallery all looked decidedly relieved that backbenchers were championing their cause. Such debates have even inspired public interest. Typical viewing figures for BBC Parliament are 120,000 but backbench debates have attracted far more; 330,000 for Hillsborough and as many as 480,000 for the debate about an EU referendum.[27] Some are impressed by the way MPs use debates to force the government to pay attention to issues it wants to duck.[28] In

---

[26] Parliamentary website http://www.parliament.uk/business/committees/committees-a-z/commons-select/backbench-business-committee/suggesting-debates/ [accessed 9 December 2013].

[27] David Foster, 'Going "where angels fear to tread": how effective was the Backbench Business Committee in the 2010–2012 parliamentary session?', *Parliamentary Affairs*, published online 9 June 2013, [accessed 4 December 2013], p. 7.

[28] The only critic appears to be Quentin Letts, who has it in for Natascha Engel for sounding too sympathetic, e.g. http://www.dailymail.co.uk/debate/article-1350512/Natascha-Engel-Backbencher-work-pet-grievance-counsellor.html#ixzz33HmFttvY

Sir George Young's words, backbenchers have gone where angels fear to tread, choosing topics that the government would prefer to avoid.[29]

The committee has been canny in parrying the government's attempts to downplay their role. They encourage backbenchers to choose their words carefully – not to be either anodyne or aggressive – and to embarrass the government with motions that they can't easily vote against. Thus, they successfully forced the government to award funding to the BBC World Service because it would be too embarrassing not to. They made sure that backbenchers had votable motions so that their debates could not be marginalized. The frontbenchers whipped against them in the early days but following several defeats, they then tried to ignore them. Most of the debates gradually become motions encouraging the government to take note rather than motions for decisions that might be voted on. The Committee decided that the mover would open debate and a Minister would reply at the end. However, government put up whips to speak, saying it gave them the chance to practise speaking from the frontbench. The BBBC insisted that it was disrespectful to Parliament for Ministers to decline to speak, so the government gave in.

Even so, government has constrained the BBBC in several ways. They rarely give more than one week's firm notice about backbench time (the same as it is for government time), making it difficult for the committee to plan in advance.[30] They have given them a potentially contradictory role in finding time for MPs to debate public petitions that attract more than 100,000 signatures. So, on the one hand backbenchers are involved in representative democracy, holding government to account, but on the other hand they are responding to participatory democracy in the form of citizens' petitions. Further confusion is caused by the petitions sitting on the government website, as if the onus is on them to respond, but being dealt with by this parliamentary backbench committee. The BBBC tries to square this circle by inviting backbenchers to champion the e-petitions.

In March 2012, when MPs were due to re-elect Members to the BBBC, the Conservative whips jumped on the opportunity to evict Members who seemed too eager to embarrass their own government. They did this by a last-minute manoeuvre to change the rules so that the party, not the whole House, voted for Members to sit on the BBBC. I met several Conservatives on the left of the party who were only too happy to get rid of right-wingers like Conservative MPs Peter Bone, Philip Davies and Philip Hollobone. One was less certain:

[accessed 30 May 2014], but the bitter-sounding nature of his criticisms towards women politicians generally makes it hard to take him seriously.
[29] As cited in ibid., Foster, 'Going "where angels fear to tread", p. 9.
[30] Ibid., p. 13.

Con MP: 'The whips are saying that it means they can choose our best people while the backbenchers say it is a stitch-up by the whips. Which is it? What do you think?'

Emma: 'Is it possible that both are true from their respective viewpoints?'

Labour MP Chris Bryant described the contradictory status of Bone, Davies and Hollobone: 'On most issues, I would consider these three as the axis of Eurosceptic, lefty-bashing, "political-correctness-gawn-mad" evil – but, in relation to the business of the House, I have to admit they are saints.'[31] The Conservatives replaced them with three new Members. Whether or not these more loyal replacements have tamed the BBBC is a matter of heated debate.

Wrestling with Crocodiles: MPs and the media

In 50 years the political media has become unrecognizable. In the 1960s, Prime Minister Harold Macmillan and his colleague Selwyn Lloyd walked off a plane after an overseas trip. A BBC journalist greeted them with: 'Prime Minister, have you got anything to say to the BBC?' Macmillan replied: 'No, I don't think so. Selwyn, have you got anything to say to the BBC?' 'No, I don't think so', Lloyd replied.[32] For the PM to have nothing to say to the BBC today would be unthinkable, political suicide. Although some say Bernard Ingham was the first Prime Minister's press secretary and spin doctor, Margaret Thatcher, whom he served, was the last PM who did not obsess about media reaction, according to former Cabinet Secretary Robin Butler.[33] She listened to the *Today* programme while having her hair done but did not pay too much attention and used to say she planned to lead, not follow. If you give people what they want, they want something different five minutes later, she said. Tony Blair's press secretary, Alastair Campbell, took spinning to a new dimension. He told the Leveson Inquiry that they did not lie, but in managing thousands of stories every day, he acknowledged that they made mistakes.[34] Combine that with the IT revolution which brought with it 24-hour news and social media, and you have a complete

---

[31] Matthew Barrett, 'The Government's attempt to fix the Backbench Business Committee would take back power for the executive', 12 March 2012, http://www.conservativehome.com/platform/2012/03/the-governments-attempt-to-fix-the-backbench-business-committee-would-take-back-power-for-the-execut.html [accessed 9 December 2012].

[32] As told by Sir Malcolm Rifkind, interviewed by Emma Crewe, 4 September 2012.

[33] Interviewed by Anthony Seldon, http://www.cabinetsecretaries.com [accessed 15 May 2014].

[34] Leveson Inquiry, 14 May 2012, http://webarchive.nationalarchives.gov.uk/20140122145147/http://www.levesoninquiry.org.uk/hearing/2012-05-14pm/ [accessed 15 May 2014].

transformation of the relationship between MPs and various forms of mediated communication.

A sting was introduced into this relationship by the expenses scandal; it eviscerated the reputation of MPs when it was already flagging. Thirty per cent of people in a survey were dissatisfied with MPs in 2001, but after the expenses scandal it was 71 per cent.[35] Following a leak of millions of pieces of information, the MPs' expenses scandal in 2009 began with an heroic exposé by the *Telegraph* newspaper of a few rogue criminals who falsified their expenses claims and some who broke the rules inadvertently. Journalists in the *Telegraph*, and subsequently other newspapers, also pointed to some rather ridiculous rules about expenditure, which grew up historically to compensate for MPs' relatively low salaries. The result was a culture of generosity with expenses, both claiming and approving with the encouragement of the whips in all parties. With the daily revelations Parliament sank further and further into panic and despair. Particular stories became charged with potent moral fury. Douglas Hogg MP claimed expenses for having his moat cleaned, his piano tuned and stable lights fixed at his country home. Others were accused of flipping the definition of their main home to gain expenses. Jacqui Smith's husband claimed for two porn films. Anthony Steen MP did not help his situation by suggesting that the outcry was based on jealousy of his large house. The stories were staggered so that scandal was dragged out for as long as possible. MPs became so terrified that they feared answering their mobiles in case it was the *Telegraph*. In contrast to the instances of clear wrongdoing, some hardworking and honest MPs were vilified for going along with rules that the journalists decided were too generous. An MP told me that vile reports about her husband's infidelity were less upsetting than unjust accusations about financial dishonesty; they go to the core of one's reputation, she added. One MP felt that it was partly David Taylor's unfair treatment in the press that led to his fatal heart attack.

The Archbishop of Canterbury poured reason on troubled waters. He wrote that MPs who claimed that all was well because rules were not being broken were clearly morally wrong, but care should be taken. The daily humiliation of MPs could permanently damage our confidence in democracy.[36] Four MPs were eventually imprisoned for false accounting and one found guilty but not fit to plead. So politicians were – and were clearly seen as – subject to law as much as anyone else. Furthermore, a new Independent Parliamentary Standards Authority took responsibility for pay and allowances. But still the media obsession with expenses continues. IPSA, and some MPs themselves, publish all MPs' claims on the internet, which provide ammunition for the local press to

[35] House of Commons, *Rebuilding the House, House of Commons Reform Committee*, First Report of Session 2008–9, 12 November 2009, HC 1117, p. 7.
[36] http://news.bbc.co.uk/1/hi/uk/8064828.stm [accessed 4 December 2013].

write scurrilous reports about MPs' claims. Making fun of MPs spending money on toilet paper or on sugar to sweeten their constituents continues in a formulaic fashion. To give an example of the kind of media coverage given to expenses, the claims of MPs in one county were studied by a group of journalists and published in a local newspaper in September 2012. They complained that there were increases between 2010–11 and 2011–12 despite the fact that 2010 would have been a shorter year because they were only elected in May and took some time to (re)establish their offices. They picked out specific expenses from the information about each MP, implying that some wrong had been committed, including the following: two computers (£1,900), stationery (£638.92), newspapers (£23.30), sugar (61p), recycling bags (£2.40), a bus fare (£1.60), advertising an MP's surgery to constituents (£1,710), desk and office chair (£330.95), a Dictaphone (£52.99), cork boards (£17.46) and food and drink for an intern (£3.85). It is completely unclear why these amounts have been singled out or why they might be worrying or even surprising to constituents. They appear to be linked to the accusation of increases, as if higher expenditure is linked to unnecessary items. But wouldn't most offices have these or similar items? The whole article gives the impression that MPs are continually extravagant with taxpayers' money whereas in reality they subsidize constituency costs, knowing that all claims are made public. They mostly pay for anything that is likely to be picked on out of their own pocket, such as occasional taxis or toilet paper. Such reports resonate with a well-worn stereotype of MPs as corrupt, greedy and venal, but if they earn money it is not through allowances – it is by having a second job outside Parliament. So journalists persist in a form of auditing of MPs that once served a purpose, but is long past its usefulness. Taking a closer look at the additional sources of income of some MPs would be more revealing but would require more serious and costly investigation. Expenses now provide cheap weapons for attack.

Alongside media attacks can be found co-operation and collusion. Jack Straw, former Cabinet Minister, pointed out to the Leveson Inquiry that politicians always want to get close to the press because the media is the prism through which the public sees them. When in opposition MPs get close to certain journalists and cook up stories to attack the government, but it all changes once you get into government. You rely more heavily on special advisers to brief journalists privately, but you no longer find the media as co-operative once a Minister or even a government backbencher. They have a habit of changing their tune and launching attacks if it makes better copy. One government PPS told me she thought she was having an off-the-record conversation with a journalist and she mentioned that some constituents had been complaining about a government policy so she wrote on their behalf to a Minister. Although she expressly asked him not to use this, he took no notice. He twisted what was a private letter expressing the views of some constituents into a challenge she was making about her own government's policy. He either misunderstood, or chose to ignore, the nature of constituency advice and advocacy work.

Michael Fabricant (Mike_Fabricant)

16/02/2013 08:54

Daily Mirror hits real lows this Saturday. Only one thing worse than being an MP, being a 'journalist' on some redtops.

Michael Fabricant has been a Conservative MP since 1992

Whether distortion, selective editing, or occasionally simply making up stories, as some journalists admit,[37] politicians are at the mercy of an aggressive media in the UK. The motives for this aggression are mixed. They might be responding to the pressure to sell newspapers, get website hits and attract viewers; after all, playing into negative images of politicians gets more attention. They may be jumping on catchy phrases or amusing and embarrassing events. When a Tory politician complained about swivel-eyed loons among Conservative activists at a dinner party, the so-called 'row' trended on Twitter and we did not hear the end of it for days.

Matthew Parris (MatthewParris3)

18/05/2013 10:19

'Swivel-eyed loons'? A minority but we've all met them, they elbow meeker activists aside, & it's a huge problem. Can't we say so at dinner?

Matthew Parris was a Conservative MP (1979–86) and is a journalist writing for *The Times* and the *Spectator*

But the purposes of media rows can be political, in part if not entirely. Rebekah Brooks, editor of the *Sun*, called John Reid when he was thinking about running in the leadership contest and suggested he should think again. He didn't and they ran an eight-week campaign to trash him, saying he had no brain.[38] It is

---

[37] http://www.theguardian.com/media/2012/may/12/news-of-the-world-made-up-stories http://www.pressgazette.co.uk/node/47974 [accessed 11 February 2014].
[38] George Pascoe-Watson, 'John Reid's brain is missing', *Sun*, 7 September 2007, http://www.thesun.co.uk/sol/homepage/news/29723/John-Reids-brain-is-missing.html [accessed 11 February 2014].

difficult to imagine this was a coincidence. The ConservativeHome website has a tab called 'Left Watch', with regular articles bashing Labour and the Lib Dems. The process of twisting reality to show your opponent in a particularly bad light often involves taking their statements out of context and inventing a spin to aggravate a bad impression. Guido Fawkes has a similar approach to those he censures; he stated baldly that John O'Farrell's motivation for standing at Eastleigh was to have a massive ego trip.[39] In contrast O'Farrell's article made it plain he was doing it for love of politics, Labour and the possibility of change, and it was a massive ego trip along the way.

The media play a ferocious role as king and queen makers, often with the assistance of the aspirant MP's political allies or opponents. In 2012 the government leaked their budget in a bid to promote it to the press, but Labour's attacks on Chancellor George Osborne MP, especially by John Mann asking when he last ate a pasty at Gregg's during a Treasury Select Committee meeting, caught the attention of the media. John Thurso's more thoughtful questions about the budget received no coverage and Osborne was hammered by the media for being out of touch with ordinary people when introducing tax on pasties and caravans. It gets even more biting when family members are targeted, as Tony Blair's son was for drunkenness and his wife for having weird friends.

Politicians expect their opponents in other parties to use journalists to attack their ideas and even deem it legitimate. But when their own colleagues do battle with them by spin or leaking, the betrayal is harder to recover from. According to Alistair Darling MP it leaves a mark you can't erase.[40] Anonymous briefings from colleagues, or increasingly their special advisers, are difficult to rebut. Apparently former SpAd Damian McBride was annoyed by Labour MP Ivan Lewis having ideas about tax policy. When Lewis refused to be bullied, Damian planted a story in the *News of the World* about how he pestered a young civil servant. When Conservative MPs mused to a journalist about whether Home Secretary Theresa May might make a good party leader, the attack on Cameron was veiled but effective.[41] Whether negative or positive, or a mixture of the two, the journalism that makes and breaks politicians is not scrutiny – it is MPs and journalists colluding to do politics, making friends and breaking foes, to gain support for their own ideas and leadership.

'Plebgate' was the clearest example of politics by and through the media: journalists, the police and probably politicians may have colluded to bring down

---

[39] http://order-order.com/2013/03/04/quote-of-the-day-605/ for Guido Fawkes' version; and see http://www.theguardian.com/commentisfree/2013/mar/04/eastleigh-reasons-cheerful-general-election for John O'Farrell's article [accessed 30 May 2014].
[40] http://www.guardian.co.uk/politics/2011/sep/04/alistair-darling-memoirs-gordon-brown [accessed 11 February 2014].
[41] http://www.telegraph.co.uk/news/politics/conservative/9373105/Mrs-May-might-why-Tories-are-tipping-Theresa-May-for-the-very-top.html [accessed 11 February 2014].

a Minister. In September 2012 the newly created Chief Whip, Andrew Mitchell was trying to leave Downing Street with his bicycle and asked a policeman to open the main gate. The officer told him to use the pedestrian gate. Mr Mitchell says he muttered: 'I thought you guys were supposed to fucking help us', while the policeman logged that he called him a pleb and threatened that there would be consequences.[42] Gossip circulated shortly afterwards that someone in the Labour Party tipped off the Police Federation that Andrew Mitchell MP was not that popular so they might be able to oust the new Chief Whip. The Police Federation may have relished the opportunity for revenge at a government that was cutting police pay at the time. The police officer's version was leaked to the *Sun* and another policeman pretended to be a witness, sending in a false email to corroborate the story.[43] The media kept the spotlight on the incident for weeks.

Reports about reactions within Mitchell's party were contradictory. Labour MPs were claiming that at the Conservatives' 1922 Committee (the weekly backbench meeting of MPs) a senior MP said: 'Come on, chaps, we need to rally and support the Chief Whip', and the committee remained quieter than was necessary to save him. One journalist reported a leak that half the meeting supported him, others reported it was the majority, and another wrote that at least four backbenchers called for his resignation.[44] Backbenchers and some whips were worried that Mitchell, whose school nickname was Thrasher, would restore the old style of whipping favoured by former military men. His deputy, John Randall MP believed he should go, according to the BBC,[45] and some other Conservative MPs even said so publicly. The precise truth is not the point here – backbenchers were giving different versions to journalists – but it was clear that Mitchell had a mixed reputation. Five weeks after the incident, when it was clear that the various forces ranged against him were not going to back down, he resigned. In December 2012 a Channel 4 *Despatches* investigation reported that the police had fabricated evidence, with the collusion of various journalists, but by that time it was too late for Mitchell to reclaim his Cabinet post. Two years later a judge ruled that he did say pleb or something similar. Whatever he said, Andrew Mitchell's story is not one of scrutiny by the media to hold government to account, but collusion between journalists and his political opponents hell-bent on his scalp.

---

[42] Andrew Mitchell's resignation letter quotes himself saying this; see http://www.independent. co.uk/news/uk/politics/government-chief-whip-andrew-mitchells-resignation-letter-in-full-8218906.html [accessed 11 February 2014].

[43] Keith Wallis was prosecuted, found guilty and imprisoned for one year in January 2014.

[44] See Paul Goodman, 'Mitchell: This evening's 22 meeting "was divided 50:50"', 17 October 2012, http://www.conservativehome.com/parliament/2012/10/mitchell-this-evenings-22-meeting-was-divided-5050.html and http://www.theguardian.com/commentisfree/2012/oct/21/andrew-rawnsley-tories-made-andrew-mitchell-go [accessed 11 February 2014].

[45] http://www.bbc.co.uk/news/uk-politics-19922026 [accessed 11 February 2014].

---

politicshomeuk (politicshomeuk)

23/10/2012 10:32

David Mellor adds: 'There's a bloodlust out there ... Wounded creatures are there, and teeth are being sharpened in anticipation of a kill.'

Politicshomeuk is a political news website

The media politicking against politicians can take an especially personal form when directed at women. Lobby journalists, who are also over-represented by men, are drawn to develop close working relationships with male MPs. They tend to refer to the male MPs as the cerebral, clever and promising ones, while women are subject to personal jibes and patronizing assessments. One well-known journalist complains that a particular woman MP is a bore, but 'for any busy mum to hold down a top political job is surely a remarkable thing'.[46] On another woman, he writes: 'Though aged 60 (and counting), she teeters up to the Despatch Box in high heels, grinning girlishly at the Opposition benches before hesitantly lisping a few opening apologies for losing her place or some such calamity ... She invariably pulls at the bottom of her skimpy designer top, the better to accentuate her slinky torso.'[47] Thus, female attributes are insinuated into the criticism. When the journalist slams into male liberals, on the other hand, their maleness is not relevant. Nick Clegg is slippery, in his view, and gets compared to a flighty woman.[48] In other contexts, women MPs are rubbished when their different experience of life is glossed over. The *Sun* compiled a list of the top 10 laziest MPs on a superficial measurement of voting, including one when she'd been on maternity leave.[49] Another was described as 'frumpy' by a tabloid, adding that it wasn't surprising her husband left her, with an old photo from years earlier showing her eight months pregnant. These are just a few examples of an overwhelmingly clear pattern.

Sexism is not the preserve of male hacks. Some women journalists, too, appear to want to demonstrate their toughness by rubbishing women MPs.

---

[46] http://www.dailymail.co.uk/debate/article-2334069/A-Culture-Secretary-promoted-way-talents-Worse-shes-bore-QUENTIN-LETTS-asks--What-point-Maria-Miller.html#ixzz2tHaUbKUA [accessed 14 February 2014].

[47] http://www.dailymail.co.uk/debate/article-2125837/Ms-Featherstone-lightweight-party-dub-Lynne-Featherbrain.html [accessed 15 February 2014].

[48] http://www.dailymail.co.uk/news/article-2322716/How-Clegg-held-Britain-ransom-Nick-Cleggs-cynical-double-dealing-stabbing-Coalition-colleagues-By-QUENTIN-LETTS.html [accessed 16 February 2014].

[49] http://www.independent.co.uk/news/uk/politics/sun-apologises-after-branding-pregnant-mp-lucy-powell-lazy-9006002.html [accessed 14 February 2014].

Melissa Kite of the *Guardian* despairs at the number of women leaving Parliament and calls on them to toughen up: 'The problem is not that male politicians can be childish and offensive, but that today's female politicians don't seem to know how to handle them.'[50] She misunderstands why women are giving up. It is not male politicians that are always the problem – many are allies and male politicians have a hard time dealing with each other too, according to women MPs – it is relentless negative reports by the media and the devastating disruption to family life that are bigger factors in driving women MPs out. But to say so attracts further media attacks.

The media report frequently on women MPs' appearance but male MPs' political achievements or abilities. When members of the Treasury Select Committee were rated by *Guardian* journalists (one man, one woman) for their performance at their inquiry into Barclay's fixing of rates, the men were given between 4/10 and 8/10,while two women were given 4/10 on the grounds that they were insufficiently chastening.[51] However, one of them – former banker Andrea Leadsom MP (Conservative) – was focused, persistent and critical of the whole culture of the bank, and hit harder than some other members of the committee who scored higher. If men are attacked, it tends to be their behaviour that comes under scrutiny: their drinking, affairs or greed, all playing into a stereotype of dissolute male politicians. If they avoid alcohol, extramarital sex or claiming for toilet paper, then they have a chance of keeping their heads below the radar.[52] While journalists notice rakish male behaviour, it is women's perceived weakness of character or bad dress sense they usually criticize. Whether female or male, hacks can be strangely obsessed with women's appearance. If women MPs are plain or badly dressed then they are assumed to be bitter; if they are beautiful they must be dim; and if well-dressed then frivolous. When Stella Creasy MP criticized the depiction of topless women on page 3 in the *Sun*, the Editor, Tony Dunn retaliated by highlighting her bright blue PVC skirt.[53] One newspaper stooped as low as hunting for photos of an MP who posed topless as a teenager to make some money.[54] Do we really only want MPs who have been planning to enter politics in their teens and so avoid all embarrassing encounters, she warns?

---

[50] http://www.theguardian.com/commentisfree/2013/nov/28/women-mps-battleaxes-not-shrinking-violets [accessed 11 February 2014].
[51] L. Elliott and J. Treanor, 'MPs assessed. Chummy to chastening: how the committee measured up', *Guardian*, 5 July 2012, pp. 4–5.
[52] This was not true for former MP Lord McAlpine, however, who was mistakenly implicated in a sex abuse scandal in 2012 when the BBC claimed a senior Tory was a paedophile.
[53] http://www.itv.com/news/2013-12-11/mp-hits-back-after-sun-hack-criticises-her-choice-of-skirt/ [accessed 14 February 2014].
[54] http://www.gloria-de-piero.co.uk [accessed 31 October 2013].

---

stellacreasy (stellacreasy)

<u>23/12/2012 12:56</u>

MT @acortez1984: @stellacreasy If I say III vote 4 U because U have great tits, will U tell me you dont want my vote? Pls stop tweeting me.

Dr Stella Creasy has been a social psychologist, political lobbyist and a Labour MP since 2010

The denigration of women MPs by journalists is tame compared to the misogyny directed at them on social media. The comments in cyberspace, where anonymity is easy, can be threatening and violent. In January 2014 John Nimmo was jailed for abusing Stella Creasy MP on Twitter. Toby Young objected to her encouraging Twitter to ban tweeters who threaten rape or death, but his credibility was rather undermined by a reminder that one of his tweets asked: 'Serious cleavage behind Ed Miliband's head. Anyone know who it belongs to?'[55] When another tweeter called Creasy 'a dumb, blonde bitch', her plucky reply was: 'That's dumb Dr blonde bitch to you actually.'[56] Louise Mensch (Conservative MP until 2012) collected some examples of vile tweets: 'Louise Mensch is attractive but makes me want to hit her with a hammer in the face ...' and 'Louise Mensch is a dumb politi-whore'. A man emailed her a death threat saying she had to choose between her children unless she stopped using Twitter.[57] This is nothing new. Women MPs have always received threatening messages, whether via post or Twitter, as have black and Asian MPs and peers.[58] It is only the public nature and scale of abuse that has increased because privacy has shrunk and all communication with MPs has multiplied. It is not just women who receive the bile; all public figures do. Jamie Reed's top ten tips for the Twitter haters has at number five: 'emotional displacement: Twitter isn't the best place to exorcize the disappointments of your life'. So while some trolls are misogynists, not all Twitter abuse has that character, just as some of the negative journalism is sexist but some of the journalists' hostility has other sorts of fuel.

Journalists used to listen to politicians' indiscretions in restaurants over lunch and pass them on to other hacks in the bar. But meetings are hardly necessary

---

[55] http://politicalscrapbook.net/wp-content/uploads/2012/03/toby-young-cleavage-tweet.jpg [accessed 15 February 2014].

[56] She has a PhD in social psychology, http://www.independent.co.uk/news/people/profiles/stella-creasy--the-labour-mp-who-has-taken-on-the-internet-trolls-and-payday-lenders-8754945.html [accessed 17 February 2014].

[57] http://www.bbc.co.uk/news/uk-england-gloucestershire-18391970 [accessed 7 July 2012].

[58] Commonwealth Parliamentary Association seminar, House of Commons, 24 October 2012; Crewe, *Lords of Parliament*, pp. 126–8.

any more as gossip circulates in hours on blogs and in minutes over Twitter. The news machine has accelerated to such an extent that the gap between public and private scarcely exists and much of it is no longer mediated by hacks. When Tories were told to stop leaking news about the 1922 Committee live from the meeting, they leaked the letter:

Dear colleagues,

Earlier this year you elected me to serve on the Executive of the 1922 Committee. One of the reasons I decided to stand was my frustration, shared by a large number of colleagues, about the frequent leaks from 1922 Committee meetings.

These leaks, once unheard of, have now appeared to become the norm. However, I have been prompted to send this email after last night's meeting which was addressed by the Prime Minister. Details of this meeting weren't just leaked. It is clear that somebody was live leaking a minute by minute account of proceedings as they happened to journalists who then posted on Twitter whilst the meeting was still taking place.

Only Conservative MPs are allowed to attend 1922 Committee meetings. This means that one of our own is betraying the entire parliamentary party just to ingratiate him/herself with certain journalists.

These leaks must stop.

The 1922 Committee exists to provide a forum where backbench MPs can, in confidence, be frank with Ministers and vice versa. It has long been the cornerstone of a successful and united parliamentary party.

These leaks are not just undermining the 1922 Committee. They threaten to make it completely redundant.

How many backbenchers now feel unable to ask certain questions to Ministers as they know their name will appear on ConservativeHome within the hour? How many Ministers feel they need to be guarded in what they tell us because of these leaks?

In the long run, this can only have a negative impact on the party.

I urge whoever is behind these leaks to consider the consequences of their actions and stop.

Kind regards,

Graham Evans MP[59]

---

[59] http://www.huffingtonpost.co.uk/2012/07/12/tory-mps-told-to-stop-lea_n_1667229.html [accessed 15 February 2014].

'Certain journalists' means Tim Montgomerie. Tory MPs were keen to impress him because he was Editor of the hugely influential website ConservativeHome. com, read by the whole party including the Cabinet and many others interested in politics. The other much-visited right-inclined website that receives information from MPs is Guido Fawkes. This site is a more scurrilous version specializing in attacks, especially on left-inclined MPs, and has been described as Iain Dale on Ketamine. Tories also court Iain Dale, who writes a funny blog, hosts a radio show and publishes political books, but he is less interested in going in for the kill. Labour MPs read the Labour List but opposition MPs don't usually have as many secrets to leak, so it doesn't have the same punch. So in addition to courting the BBC political journalists – Nick Robinson and James Landale, the *Today* presenters or *Newsnight* journalists – the other channels and the press hacks, the bloggers and tweeters have to be kept sweet or at least entertained. They can be used to transmit messages that politicians don't want to be seen sending out – disloyal jibes at rivals in your party, for example.

Tim Montgomerie (TimMontgomerie)

22/10/2012 21:56

Further to last Tweet I think Tories in trouble for structural reasons but Fleet St's coverage of political trivia is now at epidemic levels

Tim Montgomerie is a Conservative blogger, founder of ConservativeHome and columnist at *The Times*

MPs are beginning to do their own media work through Twitter, with some of the big names acquiring a sizeable following. In October 2014 David Cameron had 816,000, Ed Miliband 348,000, Nick Clegg 191,000, and even some backbenchers get attention: Stella Creasy has 50,000, Zac Goldsmith 37,000 and Julian Huppert 15,000. With some of these sending out up to 50,000 tweets, most since the 2010 election, it is clear that, for some, Twitter has become a substantial part of their job. Although Creasy has attracted particularly nasty abuse, she had 1,000 newspaper articles written about her during a six-month period in 2013.[60] Twitter has become compulsory for any ambitious MP.

There is a less visible form of scrutiny by journalists who manage to be critical, but rely on analyses of complex political processes or causes of failure, rather than attacks on individuals. Robert Peston's *Who Runs Britain?* is an example of informed, hard-hitting scrutiny by a journalist with a profound knowledge of

---

[60] http://www.independent.co.uk/news/people/profiles/stella-creasy--the-labour-mp-who-has-taken-on-the-internet-trolls-and-payday-lenders-8754945.html [accessed 17 February 2014].

finance. He explains his own political predispositions, making it easier to understand where his views are coming from, and forensically takes apart the politics of finance. For example, when exploring the collapse of British occupational pensions he offers his perspective on what went wrong. Government departments relied on over-optimistic statistics, politicians from Lawson to Brown raided pensions, and cultural change in Britain resulted in companies showing less interest in the welfare of their staff.[61] The decline of paternalism and rise of individualism has benefitted the super-rich and their growing influence on politicians is a threat to our democracy. Such journalism is well-researched and worthy of debate. But it is easier to ignore such criticism, as fewer readers come across this than they do the lurid stories in the more popular newspapers or blogs. It is a reminder that effective democracy requires a free press, which has the right to protect its sources – a point that is easily forgotten when reading scurrilous carping.

The politics of scrutiny

Nick Robinson finds it difficult to get politicians to talk about substance – they are too impatient to rubbish each other. Everyone in Westminster obsesses about spin, sleaze and splits and he can't get the politicians to talk about substance.[62] When storms flooded and bashed the UK in early 2014, Ed Miliband blamed the government, Secretary of State Eric Pickles MP blamed the Environment Agency, Lord Smith (Chair of the EA) blamed the Treasury and those affected blamed anyone in authority. Not only do journalists join in with the finger-pointing, it is as if they mimic the politicians by taking sides and elevating the reputation of their own side by bringing down the villains in the other gang. Politicians are bound to do this; it is inherent to the way British representative democratic politics works. There is fierce competition between them, which has the benefit of galvanizing action. But when journalists mimic this antagonism then they lose their effectiveness as scrutinizers and critics.

    While the media drift further into a mix of political antagonism and collusion and away from detached scrutiny, politicians on the backbenches are moving in the opposite direction. In this chapter I have argued that the 2010 changes have increased the role and influence of Select Committees. In the last I suggested that the power of the whips has diminished. At the same time scrutiny by backbenchers is gaining momentum. This does not mean that the capacity

---

[61] Robert Peston, *Who Runs Britain?* (London: Hodder and Stoughton, 2008), pp. 3–4, 217–55, 347.
[62] http://www.theguardian.com/commentisfree/2012/oct/19/why-public-dont-trust-politicians [accessed 17 February 2014].

for parliamentary scrutiny will stand still. The power of the opposition waxes and wanes. The 2010–15 Coalition has meant that the Official Opposition has been made up of only one party rather than two, so has been seen as weaker, according to MPs on all sides. MPs' more specific rating of the effectiveness of the Labour Party in opposition depends in part on their assessment of Ed Miliband and those he has promoted.

Lisa Nandy (lisanandy)

20/03/2013 22:11

@SabrinaBranwood hi Sabrina, we basically keep an eye on the DfE, challenge them to do better for children and support them when they do.

Lisa Nandy has worked for voluntary organizations as a researcher and policy advisor and has been a Labour MP since 2010

But irrespective of the Official Opposition, Select Committees have grown in their role as scrutineers and get increasing coverage in the media for holding government and even companies to account. Some committees will probably continue to widen their circle of influence by seeking contributions from less visible groups via new technologies and by going to them around the country, by employing more staff and expanding their communications and media capacity.[63] Unfortunately other committees may be tempted by the media to continue to move further and further towards a more confrontational inquisitorial mode when questioning, perhaps influenced by two particularly significant wider modern trends. One concerns accountability. As the journalist Simon Jenkins observes:

> We now have a new form of accountability, to an 'inquiriat', a cackle of inquisitors and lawyers jumping to the bidding of public opinion, flapping round every executive's head and piling accusation on every error. This can only lead to ever more defensive behaviour in every sphere of public life. It is the paranoia of the modern state. Every document is 'open', every conversation 'on the record' and your friend today is tomorrow the witness against you.[64]

---

[63] The Liaison Committee reviewed various proposals for strengthening the effectiveness of committees. My evidence: http://data.parliament.uk/writtenevidence/WrittenEvidence.svc/EvidenceHtml/3815 [accessed 1 May 2014].
[64] http://www.theguardian.com/commentisfree/2012/oct/23/jimmy-savile-witch-hunt-paranoia?cat=commentisfree&type=article [accessed 30 May 2014].

The other relates to the way committees gather knowledge. Like all public bodies, Select Committees are under pressure to be guided by evidence. But the fashionable idea of 'evidence-based policy' can give an impression that research easily produces incontrovertible facts that can be turned into solutions. Many contemporary philosophers and social scientists argue that different groups of people in society produce truth, and therefore what they see as 'evidence', in different ways. Debating evidence is a vitally important part of political process. So rather than assuming Select Committees should be 'evidence-based', surely they should do scrutiny by investigating and debating different bodies of knowledge and contested claims and then making a judgment? Some of the time politicians are keenly aware of this – especially when doing politics by debating in the Chamber – but at other times they are seduced into thinking they can rise above this contestation and produce one impartial truth.

The French anthropologist Bruno Latour compares how lawyers and scientists produce knowledge (or what they both call 'evidence' when asserting its truth). Lawyers use documents and speech to establish what is true and false in a specific context even though the subject is not visible. The crime has already taken place.[65] Scientists are concerned with establishing universal truths by observing or deducing events or processes that do not depend on specific context and may be in the past, present or future. In law, form rather than content, in the shape of the *presentation* of evidence, is crucial to establishing truth in a particular case. In science, theories about the *content* of reality are what matter, whereas the way you present facts has no bearing on their validity. Thus objectivity is achieved in starkly different ways by these two professional groups. Politicians are influenced by both. When questioning witnesses who give 'evidence' in Select Committees, they sound like lawyers; when arguing for a policy position in debates, they can sound like scientists. Some MPs are influenced by other systems of truth, such as religion, where different assumptions again preside over knowledge creation. It is not the presentation or content of observable reality that matters for believers, but their transcendence. When people, including politicians, claim: 'But the evidence tells us x', the next questions are: 'Who says so?', 'How did they develop that understanding?', 'What assumptions underlie the interpretation within that understanding?' Unless you are believer in Absolute Truth – possibly a Christian, Muslim, positivist scientist or animist – in which case the knowledge produced by your own group is enough.

How do the different groups of scrutineers – the opposition, committees and the media – produce knowledge? Received wisdom implies that the Official Opposition has no other option in our democratic system but to gloss over the

---

complexity of evidence and present clear and stark choices for the public. Such choices are vital for our democracy to work, as Chantal Mouffe argues in *The Democratic Paradox*. Similarly, in the wrestling that goes on between journalists and politicians through spin doctors, both sides get fixated about truth or falsity – which has the appearance of urgent moral drama – but often lose sight of more important ethical questions of good or poor judgement, competence and efficient or inefficient administration. In contrast, backbenchers have the option, especially in Select Committees, to investigate evidence and demand further debate, but this gets less attention in the media. The result is the appearance of weak scrutiny. The most visible journalists mimic the tribal antagonism of politicians and even collude with one side to attack another. But the public do not see or hear as much about the journalism that forensically dissects the impact of government from a well-informed viewpoint, such as Robert Peston on finance as mentioned above. They don't see how the opposition (and of course government with its huge resources) builds up its knowledge of policy, services and the economy over years of canvassing, meetings, research and argument. This knowledge, and its alliances and contacts with outsiders, becomes critical to its role in opposing government and holding Ministers to account, in ways that often go unseen by the public. I will describe this in detail in the next chapter, taking a close look at the scrutiny of one clause in one bill that travelled through Parliament over almost two years.

6

In the Shadow of the Law

A narrative about what happened to one clause as it passed through both Houses of Parliament and was transformed from an idea into law. The clause directly addresses the welfare of children whose parents separate and go to court, but it is those who don't go to court – and will be in its shadow – who will be more numerous and potentially influenced in unknown ways. Under the text and formal process of lawmaking we find a range of complex relationships and conversations.

****

Every government Minister feels that presiding over the introduction of a huge law helps them accrue status, certainly in the present and possibly in the future. It leaves a permanent mark on the statute book. You can have a more tangible sense of changing British society (or some of the nations within it) for the better by laying down some new rules, even if it was civil service lawyers who drafted much of the bill.

Exceptionally a Private Member's Bill might get through, but it is extremely rare. A ballot decides who gets the chance to introduce a bill. If that fails you can queue through the night, sleeping in the corridor outside the Public Bill Office, to get a slot. When a new MP went along to queue at 11.30 at night she found three male MPs already settling down in their sleeping bags. In chivalrous fashion they reserved the fourth place for her if she returned at 6.30 a.m., which she did. Then your bill is discussed on a Friday, but you will find teams of backbenchers primed to talk out your brilliant idea, so that when 'the moment of interruption' comes – that is, time runs out – it is lost. If you got past that hurdle, the main parties would introduce huge numbers of amendments and kill it when it returned to the House. You can't get a Private Member's Bill through without government support, or at least indifference, although some important social reforms have been successfully introduced in this way, such as the abolition of the death penalty and legalization of abortions in the 1960s.

Standing Order 14 states that 'Save as provided in this order, government business shall have precedence at every sitting', and then offers the exceptions that allow some time for backbenchers and the opposition. It means that not only the vast majority of the results of votes but also the control of time, and therefore the agenda, is in the hands of the government. From the viewpoint of those in government, or in opposition but looking forward to another stint, this is democratic. It means that government will get its business and pass the laws that allow it to meet its manifesto commitments. From the perspective of the scrutinizers, Standing Order 14 is the tool and symbol of executive dominance. A similar split in attitude can be found in relation to programme motions. These were introduced in 1998 to agree how much time would be given to a particular bill. Again views polarize over these motions. Government and opposition leaders find them a convenient way to prevent maverick and rebellious MPs from wasting Parliament's time with tedious discussion and, in their eyes, relatively unimportant matters. In contrast, those who perceive government blunders and inadequate scrutiny of bills tend to be irked by programme motions that tip the balance of power towards government. They demand more time to discuss the legislation they see as dangerous or flawed.

Most agree that more careful scrutiny by Parliament would generally be a good thing, even if they disagree about how it should be achieved. Most academics, journalists and even MPs are scathing about the weakness of the House of Commons in scrutinizing legislation. King and Crewe portray Parliament as hopeless and our governance as generally lacking deliberation.[1] The Hansard Society concludes that scrutiny by Parliament has been recently enhanced but that government produces such a tidal waves of bills, in former Foreign Secretary Robin Cook's phrase, that MPs don't have the chance to improve it adequately.[2] The situation painted sounds so dire that it raises the question, is effective scrutiny ever possible? To answer this, I followed one clause of one bill to see what happened to it as it went through Parliament. While not typical – this bill inspired less partisan battles than most – this story shows what Parliament is capable of. It also illustrates the complexity of consultation, evidence and judgement involved in only one short section of one law.

'Section 11: Welfare of the Child: Parental Involvement'

The Children and Families Act 2014 is a huge piece of legislation covering family justice – cases when local authorities get involved (public law) and private cases where the court decides what should happen to children if parents separate

[1] Anthony King and Ivor Crewe, *The Blunders of our Governments* (London: OneWorld, 2013), pp. 399–415.
[2] Ruth Fox and Matt Korris, *Making Better Laws, Reform of the Legislative Process from Policy to Act* (London: Hansard Society, 2010)

(private law) – as well as special educational needs, the Office of the Children's Commissioner and parental rights at work. I was interested in a clause about parenting. It began its life with the heading 'Shared Parenting' and a provision requiring the courts to presume that children of separated parents would benefit by having both parents involved in their life, unless the contrary is shown. (Once a clause goes into law it is called a 'section'.)

Where did it come from? First, the transformation of family life in the last 50 years in the UK has seen greater involvement of fathers in parenting. In the 1950s middle-class British idealized families had men going out to work and women staying home to look after the children. By the end of the century both parents were expected to work, and usually had to for financial reasons, although many mothers often worked part-time and tended to retain the role as main carers. This change is reflected in children's arrangements on divorce or separation, which affects up to 350,000 children in the UK every year. Most parents agree between themselves where their children should live as well as how and when they see each parent. About 40,000 applications are made to the courts annually to settle a dispute over contact. It was once assumed that mothers would be the main parent, but the language changed to reflect cultural shifts, so that whichever parent had been the main carer was likely to provide the child/children's main home (the resident parent) while the other one (the non-resident parent) had the children to stay for shorter periods. An assumption that children benefitted from having one main home prevailed in the courts. Sometimes this is the only practical solution, as Baroness Butler-Sloss pointed out to me,[3] particularly if parents do not live close to each other. Children tended to live with their mothers (according to a report for the Ministry of Justice[4]) because they had been the main carer pre-separation, and saw their fathers typically every other weekend and one night a week. However, parents who once saw less of their children pre-separation often wish to spend more time with them once the family splits into two. Conversely, the parents who view themselves as the main carers are inclined to see more clearly (or sometimes invent) the potential for harm that the other parent may pose to their children. Throw acrimony, distrust and welfare concerns into this mix with the result that it has been estimated that 30 per cent of children have no contact with their non-resident parent.[5] The fierce contestation of the statistics on contact and court orders confirm the controversial nature of this issue.

What does the research say about children's well-being on separation? They are better off if parental conflict is low, they have a good relationship with at least one parent, their main parent is not suffering from mental health problems

---

[3]Interviewed by Emma Crewe, 22 October 2012.
[4]Joan Hunt and Alison Macleod, *Outcomes of Applications to Court for Contact Orders After Parental Separation or Divorce,* Minister of Justice, 2008, p. 1.
[5]Ibid., p.2.

and their family is financially secure.[6] Persistent conflict between parents, especially when children feel caught in the middle, is the main problem children face when families break down. Children also report that they are often not told what is happening or consulted about decisions, but it is good relationships between and with their parents that really matter most to them. They want to be involved with both parents if they get along with them, but not if they have a poor relationship with them or the parents with each other.[7] So from children's viewpoint, improving relationships and parenting, mental health programmes and financial assistance would alleviate some of the problems associated with family breakdown. But such work is difficult and expensive. The government is well aware of the issues, and tried to convey many of them on a website for separating parents,[8] so the hope of some politicians was in part to hand back the problem to families and reduce the responsibilities of the state. But in any case, it is adults, not children, who are making a bigger noise. MPs heard from mothers worried about domestic violence and met large numbers of fathers visiting their surgeries with horror stories about how they had been shut off from their children and required to pay unaffordable child maintenance by the Child Support Agency (since replaced by the Child Maintenance Group).

Fathers' rights have been given publicity, but also been damaged in the eyes of nearly all policymakers, by the campaigning antics of Fathers4Justice. They are known for dressing up as Batman and climbing buildings, disrupting traffic, throwing condoms filled with purple-dyed flour at Tony Blair (then PM) and, most recently, defacing a painting of the Queen. They also attack their opponents and even those who support fathers' rights and shared parenting and encourage people to post accusations about ex-partners, solicitors and social workers on a website. At an APPG meeting in the summer of 2012 one peer described them as the biggest impediment to fathers' rights because they are so destructive.[9] F4J may have attracted attention, but their theatrical tactics probably set their cause back until far more reasonable organizations came along, such as Families Need Fathers and the linked FNF Both Parents Matter Cymru. Their more child-focused approach, and even-handedness by supporting both men and women who have been denied access, won over support. The reputations of these organizations are important because, as we will see in this chapter, people are swayed not only by the logic of an issue, but by how they feel about the people advocating for it. At the same time, personal experience also played

---

[6]Ann Mooney, Chris Oliver and Marjorie Smith, *The Impact of Family Breakdown on Children's Well-Being, Evidence Review*, Research Report DCSF – RR113, Institute of Education, 2009, pp. 10–13.
[7]Ibid, p. 16.
[8]https://www.sortingoutseparation.org.uk/en/hub.aspx [accessed 9 October 2014]
[9]APPG on Children, 10 June 2012.

Table 6.1 The history of section 11: A timeline from 2011 to 2014

Sir David Norgrove (Chair) and the Family Justice Review panel publish their report on their review of family justice	November 2011
Government consultation on co-operative parenting	June to September 2012
Draft family justice clauses published without section 11	September 2012
Tim Loughton, Minister of Children and Families, replaced by Edward Timpson	September 2012
Justice Select Committee undertakes pre-legislative scrutiny of the family justice part of the Bill	September to December 2012
Draft clause on parental involvement published	November 2012
Coalition of anti-shared parenting NGOs meet for the first time	November 2012
Various APPGs hold meetings and undertake informal inquiries into the issues, including the APPG on Child Protection and the APPG on Children	July 2012 onwards
The Bill is published by the government	5 February 2013
First and Second Reading in the Commons	February 2013
Public Bill Committee considers the Bill in over 19 sitting days	March and April 2013
Report Stage and Third Reading of the Bill	June 2013
First and Second Reading in the Lords	June and July 2013
Lords considers the Bill in Grand Committee in 12 sitting days	October and November 2013
Report stage in the Lords takes 5 sitting days	December 2013 and January 2014
Third Reading in the Lords	February 2014
Ping-pong: House of Commons, final consideration of the House of Lords amendments including to clause 11	February 2014
Bill given Royal Assent, so becomes an Act	13 March 2014
Family justice provisions become effective	22 April 2014
Section 11 goes into law	22 October 2014

a part for some politicians. Some MPs were scarred by lack of contact with their own parents or children, or their close relatives had been.

As a result of these various threads of influence, the Coalition Agreement stated: 'We will encourage shared parenting from the earliest stages of pregnancy – including the promotion of a system of flexible parental leave', and their mid-term review reiterated these pledges.[10] It was apparently several middle-aged male Ministers who championed it – Iain Duncan Smith MP, Michael Gove MP and, at a more junior level, Tim Loughton MP – but it had considerable support in the Conservative Party more widely. Several MPs told me that David Cameron MP and Nick Clegg MP believed it sounded progressive. Others, including Ken Clarke MP, were more sceptical. The views within the Coalition, and even the Conservative Party, were varied and strongly held.

The government commissioned a review, chaired by Sir David Norgrove, which finally reported in November 2011. In the interim report they had proposed:

> No legislation should be introduced that creates or risks creating the perception that there is a parental right to substantially shared or equal time for both parents; and a statement should be inserted into legislation to reinforce the importance of the child continuing to have a meaningful relationship with both parents, alongside the need to protect the child from harm.[11]

They felt that legislation promoting shared parenting would dilute the principle underlying the Children Act 1989, that is that decisions should be based on the best interests of the child, and shift the emphasis from parental responsibility to parental rights. It is children's welfare that should be paramount, they emphasized, but a statement about seeing both parents could be positive. They subsequently took more evidence and decided to withdraw their second proposal, concluding in their final report that no statement at all should be made in law as it would probably be misinterpreted: 'It would be quite wrong and counter productive for children to make this area even more complicated and contested.'

The government consulted on shared parenting in any case. They received 214 responses on four options; more than half of them were in favour of introducing a clause about shared parenting but many of those were individuals promoting fathers' rights, whereas organizations representing children were against the idea of putting it into law. The government absorbed concerns about the risk of abuse in their final wording of the clause to strengthen the prevention

---

[10]http://www.gov.uk/government/uploads/system/uploads/attachment_data/file/229486/HMG_MidTermReview.pdf [accessed 15 January 2015].

[11]Family Justice Review, November 2011, https://www.gov.uk/government/uploads/system/uploads/attachment_data/file/217343/family-justice-review-final-report.pdf, pp. 137, 141 [accessed 18 February 2014].

of harm. The words were changed in the government preferred option from '... the court is to presume, unless the contrary is shown, that the welfare of the child concerned will be furthered by involvement in the child's upbringing of each parent of the child who can be involved in a way not adverse to the child's safety'[12] to 'does not put the child at risk of suffering harm', in the first draft of the clause, to recognize head-on the risk of domestic violence (see Table 6.2). Meantime two All-Party Parliamentary Groups – one on children and another on child protection – began a series of discussions with politicians, lawyers, social workers, managers of children's services, children's guardians, professional associations, academics and charities about the proposed Bill.[13] Decades of experience were articulated, weighed up and debated. Some presented the viewpoint of professionals or parents, but most centred on the welfare of children. The Children's Commissioner, Maggie Atkinson reported that children are crystal clear about what they want on separation – not to be used as weapons in battles between parents.

Table 6.2 First draft of the clause

1A Shared parenting

(1) Section 1 of the Children Act 1989 (welfare of the child) is amended as follows:

(2) After subsection (2) insert –

"(2A) A court, in the circumstances mentioned in subsection (4)(a) or (7), is as respects each parent within subsection (6)(a) to presume, unless the contrary is shown, that involvement of that parent in the life of the child concerned will further the child's welfare."

(3) After subsection (5) insert:

"(6) In subsection (2A) "parent" means parent of the child concerned; and, for the purposes of that subsection, a parent of the child concerned –

(a) is within this paragraph if that parent can be involved in the child's life in a way that does not put the child at risk of suffering harm; and

(b) is to be treated as being within paragraph (a) unless there is some evidence before the court in the particular proceedings to suggest that involvement of that parent in the child's life would put the child at risk of suffering harm whatever the form of the involvement.

The circumstances referred to are that the court is considering whether to make an order under section 4(1)(c) or (2A) or 4ZA(1)(c) or (5) (parental responsibility of parent other than mother)."

---

[12] http://media.education.gov.uk/assets/files/pdf/g/government%20response%20to%20 the%20shared%20parenting%20consultation.pdf [accessed 18 February 2014].

[13] For example, see the minutes of the APPG on Children held on 15 October 2012 with David Norgrove and Edward Timpson, http://www.ncb.org.uk/media/861509/121106_cf_bill_-_fam_ law_reforms_final.pdf [accessed 30 May 2014].

In early September 2012 an architect of the Bill, Children's Minister Tim Loughton MP, was replaced in a reshuffle by Edward Timpson MP. Loughton's attachment to shared parenting as a way of promoting fathers' equality as parents was ferocious. Timpson's view was more measured. As a family lawyer he had been unofficially advising on the development of Conservative Party policy on family justice since 2008 (when he entered Parliament in a by-election). His experience in the courts and through listening to various groups in his constituency and at Westminster told him that the status quo was not working quite well enough. He looked at it afresh when he became Minister – along with the rest of this monster Bill – and formed a more nuanced perspective on the subject. He wanted legislation to address the perception of bias in the courts, and thereby improve relationships between parents and children, but not to promote shared parenting as, although definitions vary, the phrase implies for many that children divide their time equally between separated parents. Some would argue for a broader meaning including shared responsibility and involvement, which might entail different allocations of time. It was already becoming clear that the concept was slippery; the interests of mothers, fathers and children were tangled but sometimes in conflict, and emotions were already running high.

Draft clauses for inclusion in the Bill were sent to four Select Committees for pre-legislative scrutiny: Justice and Education in the Commons, Adoption in the Lords and the Joint Committee on Human Rights. The shared parenting clause went to Justice, which had already carried out an inquiry into family courts but from a slightly different perspective and recommended that no legislative statement should be added to the Children Act 1989 to promote shared parenting, taking the same line as the final version of the Norgrove report.[14] Select Committees are composed of MPs from all parties, coming from completely different political directions, but like political parties they are inclined to link impact with consistency. They have a tendency to assume that producing contradictory recommendations might eat away at their credibility. The starting point of those Members involved in the earlier inquiry was a cautious attitude towards stating a presumption about shared parenting in legislation. At the same time, they were looking afresh at a new variant of the principles, so they took evidence and re-examined the arguments.

Lisa Nandy (lisanandy)

13/09/2012 14:57

justice sel comm conducting pre-legislative scrutiny on family justice proposals, encourage anyone interested to submit

Lisa Nandy has worked for voluntary organizations as a researcher and policy advisor and has been a Labour MP since 2010

---

[14] House of Commons Justice Select Committee, *Operation of the Family Courts*, Sixth Report of Session 2010–12, HC 518-1, p. 25.

They invited the public to submit written evidence and received 67 replies. Then they chose key stakeholders to give oral evidence with a tight focus on the draft clauses in three sessions. At this stage Fathers4Justice, who had not submitted written evidence, demanded that the committee invite them to give oral evidence so that they could give their views not just on the issue of shared parenting but on other aspects of the family justice system outside the committee's pre-legislative scrutiny work. The committee did not invite them, offering them instead the opportunity to submit written evidence after the deadline, but they declined that offer, tweeting misleadingly that the committee had refused to allow them to give oral evidence.

The witnesses spoke both for and against shared parenting. Mr Justice Ryder, the judge in charge of modernizing the family justice system, was wary of a new presumption and pointed to the irony in the shared parenting clause. It is the most co-operative parents who are least likely to go to court but most likely to make shared parenting work. However, for some embittered parents who do go to court, a 50:50 split in the time children spend with their two parents may be the only way to take the heat out of the conflict (even if an equal split in time was not the government's intention). Families Need Fathers liked the direction of travel and anticipated that even if decisions in the courts remained unchanged, parents in the shadow of the law would be influenced by the clause. Others too looked into the future, using their imagination to guess what responses the clause might elicit filtered through their experience, hopes and views. When the government Ministers Edward Timpson and Tom McNally gave evidence, the Chair, Sir Alan Beith MP and his committee members were rather terser in their questioning. The Ministers were vague on the purpose of the clause. When pushed, the Ministers said that the draft clause was designed to change perceptions so Elfyn Llwyd MP (an experienced solicitor) asked: 'Do you know of any other statutory procedure that is adopted to deal with a perception? Do we legislate to deal with perceptions? I have never heard of it before.'[15]

While the committees worked hard on their draft report, meetings inside and outside Parliament continued apace. At an APPG on child protection a terrifying-looking judge prepared to give a talk. I shrank in my seat at the thought of coming before him in his court. But as soon as he spoke, a kind, patient man emerged, clearly utterly dedicated to the welfare of children. He talked about consulting children about their future: 'I very rarely speak to a child without learning something.' A Cafcass[16] manager said sceptically: 'Surely you don't talk to them if they are young?' The judge explained that as long as they can understand that their feelings will not automatically determine the result and that they

---

[15] Mr Llwyd MP, *Pre-legislative scrutiny of the Children and Families Bill*, Fourth report of the 2012–13 session, 12 December 2012, House of Commons Justice Committee, Ev35, Q168.
[16] Children and Family Court Advisory and Support Service.

can't have secrets, they are old enough. Mostly they are over six, but recently he was considering the case of a four-year-old. She was playing in the corner of his court and listening to the judge talk to her older sibling. Then she came over and sat herself on his knee and said: 'You're not going to send us back, are you?' The four-year-old confirmed to the judge the appropriateness of his decision not to return her to her family. The APPG was talking about care proceedings, not private court cases, but the judge got me thinking about children having a say in this law. Those who consult children during their work – whether lawyers or social workers – gave their opinions to the government, Select Committees and APPGs, but children did not do so directly to the House of Commons or government in any systematic way. The Justice Select Committee might have taken evidence from children but was given such a tiny window for producing the report that it would have been impossible to do it properly. Interviewing a few token children would have been worse than relying on their representatives.

Tim Loughton MP (timloughton)

06/11/2012 09:05

Govt presumption shared parenting proposals tinyurl.com/bsvezzl fulfil our 2005 election pledge at last-prepare 4 strong oppo esp in Lords

Tim Loughton has been a Conservative MP since 1997 and was Minister for Children and Families 2010–12

Those campaigning for 'shared parenting' took to the press and social media. However, this had already backfired to some extent, because the press repeatedly misreported the content of the clause. Newspapers had announced the change as the introduction of equal time with their children for both separated parents, although the government did not intend to prescribe a time allocation.[17] The *Telegraph* and BBC claimed that separated fathers were gaining the legal right to see their children when courts already give both parents contact with their children (unless there are welfare concerns), and fathers were not gaining any new 'right'.[18] In January 2013 Channel 4 produced a documentary about parenting; equal time in shared parenting was presented as

---

[17]For example, http://www.theguardian.com/commentisfree/2012/jun/13/fathers-rights-overlooked-law-welcome [accessed 9 October 2014].
[18]http://www.bbc.co.uk/news/education-20223526#?utm_source=twitterfeed&utm_medium=twitter and http://www.telegraph.co.uk/news/uknews/law-and-order/9656507/Absent-fathers-to-get-legal-right-to-spend-time-with-their-children.html [accessed 20 February 2014].

modern and reasonable, while those who were sceptical about equal time were edited to sound old-fashioned. This confused the issue once again by giving the impression that shared parenting was about equal time. It both raised expectations for those who wanted equal time and alarmed those who felt flexibility was better for children's welfare.

Tim Loughton MP (timloughton)

06/11/2012 17:21

BBC getting it wrong- tinyurl.com/clhnasu-shared parenting not about rights of parents but about joint responsibilities 2 their children

---

Towards the end of November 2012 a consortium of organizations and individuals concerned about shared parenting met for the first time at the charity Coram Children's Legal Centre. Whether those attending were representing lawyers' associations, children's charities, family organizations, or interested as academics, they were all worried about the threat to the Children Act 1989, which states 'the child's welfare shall be the court's paramount consideration'. Many were exasperated that the government counted individual submissions to their consultation as equivalent to those made by organizations representing thousands, and that the government sought views on proposals for change but did not ask about keeping the status quo. They feared that a presumption might clash with the paramountcy principle and that people would assume shared parenting means equal time spent with each parent, even though that was not the government's intention. They discussed whether to fight the clause. None of these people working with children thought it would benefit children. It would either have minimal impact (because the explanatory notes are clear that it is not intended to change the division of time) or the impact might be huge if the media continue to misrepresent it. Then people in the shadow of the law might divide up children's time 50:50 between the two parents under the misapprehension that the law demands or at least encourages it. The government's Sorting Out Separation also came in for strong criticism – several found it superficial, vague and difficult to navigate.[19] (This government initiative was launched in November 2012 as a website that aims to offer advice and support for parents who are separating or have separated, mainly by signposting where to go for help.)

The consortium also discussed tactics. If they argued vigorously against the clause it might stir things up and encourage the fathers' rights groups to ask

---

[19] http://www.sortingoutseparation.org.uk [accessed 28 May 2014].

for more; if they said nothing those groups might assume the clause hadn't gone far enough, so they should still ask for more. There was a general feeling that the Minister in charge of the Bill, Edward Timpson MP would understand these concerns, being a family lawyer himself. They discussed what should go into a joint letter to him. It was agreed that the tone should be respectful so as not to antagonize; they should express concerns rather than criticize harshly. They considered which evidence would make the best impression, including some research from the UK and some international studies. For example, the Australian government introduced related but rather different legislation promoting shared parenting and it led to such difficulties that it was amended.

Timpson gave evidence on adoption to the House of Lords Adoption Committee, chaired by Baroness Butler-Sloss. As former President of the Family Court, she might have presided over cases in which he was acting as an advocate. He seemed to be more nervous, more so than when talking to the Justice Select Committee, and was more inclined to take advice. He told me that the Lords tend to be forensic in their questioning so it is necessary to be extremely focused. The more leisurely Lords session went into more detail, and discussed the wider context, in contrast to the shorter, punchier Commons session. The Peers even had time to take evidence from children with the help of the Child Rights Director for England, Roger Morgan.

On 11 December 2012 I sat in on a private session of the Justice Select Committee at which they discussed the first draft of their report on pre-legislative scrutiny of the justice parts of the Bill.[20] I read the draft at the meeting, but it was so confidential that I had to return it at the end of the session. From the viewpoint of the committee, they don't want their disagreements aired in public; like all committees and any political group, it undermines their position if they appear divided. Their assumption is that they have more clout if they appear consistent and united – a challenging proposition when you bear in mind that members come from all the main political parties and represent a wide range of views on justice. But there is another reason for being discreet. MPs on committees (or in political parties, for that matter) know that it will be harder to reach agreements in the future if the shifts, compromises and defeats of individuals are worked through in public.

The changes between draft and final report were not substantial, because members agreed on almost everything, but the draft shared parenting clause was the only sticking point. Most of the private discussion at this committee meeting, at a smaller meeting between two of the MPs arranged to work out a way through an impasse, and a subsequent committee meeting on the following

[20] Inclusion of this account of Justice Committee private meetings is with the agreement of that committee, which hopes that it will further public understanding of the operation of the Select Committee system (3 September 2014).

day, focused on disagreement about this draft clause. The majority favoured a sceptical view towards inclusion of a shared parenting presumption in legislation. However, at the final meeting only three members of the committee were present at the start of the meeting – one sceptic and two rather more in favour of the draft clause. Other sceptics arrived just in the nick of time and sighs of both relief and disappointment could be heard. If they hadn't appeared, and assuming that the government took notice of the committee, then the law on parental separation may have been slightly different as a consequence and that slight difference – in creating perceptions, if not changing legal decisions – could have possibly had an impact on hundreds of thousands of families. Of course pre-legislative scrutiny does not involve the formal amending of bills and the government does not have to act on the recommendations, but the report was likely to influence the debates as the Bill went through both Houses.

During some speedy negotiation the committee deleted a paragraph that criticized the government quite fiercely on the rationale for the draft clause and another that might have been construed as trespassing on the role of the judiciary. They reached another impasse until the Chair suggested a compromise, another was resolved just short of a division (which would have been very unusual for this committee) and a final one was surmounted by a little horse-trading of textual changes. Their conclusion on the draft clause was that they did not really like it, but if it had to be there, then the heading should be changed from 'Shared Parenting' to 'Parental Involvement'.

The government produced the draft Bill in early 2013 (with a version for children produced by the Child Rights Director for England), and the shared parenting clause was there as clause 11 of the Bill. In the process of drafting legislation the politicians determine the broad content, the officials work out detail and Parliamentary Counsel (the government's legislative draughtsmen and women) produce the text. They know that when the opposition crawl over every word of the Bill, they will test, probe and attempt to amend as much as possible. So the government tend to 'over-egg' the first draft, in the words of one civil servant, so they have wiggle room. In relation to parental involvement, Edward Timpson MP told me that since both Norgrove and the Justice Select Committee had been against any clause, it might have been easier to drop it altogether. Although beholden to no one, and not to his predecessor Loughton who was such a fan of shared parenting, he did not want to let it die. I asked what influenced him. The mix was complex. His personal view was partly derived from his professional experience as a lawyer, watching parents fail to get the best outcome because they did not understand the law. Fathers perceive the law as biased, so it made sense to correct this perception. He also paid attention to lobby groups, who are worth listening to even if you expect to disagree: 'Everyone needs the opportunity to make their case, be listened to, and not given a tokenistic ear.' He listened to other MPs in Ministerial positions, in the

Coalition (many with strong views) and in the Opposition, as well as officials and professionals across government.[21] As a consequence, government kept the wording of the clause unchanged from its earlier draft but accepted the Justice Select Committee's recommendation to change the heading (which has no legal effect) from 'Shared Parenting' to 'Parental Involvement'. They even prefaced it with 'Welfare of the Child' to emphasize that children's benefit, and not parents' rights, was their focus, perhaps reacting to misrepresentation by the press. Meantime other MPs remained out of step with the Justice Select Committee and the government's cautious approach. One woman MP on the Coalition government side, but who had not got into the detail of the issue, dismissed the Justice Select Committee's line as the views of the older generation.

I spoke to a representative from a charity in the NGO consortium about the Justice Select Committee report and the Bill. She was impressed by the former but depressed by the latter. Her organization was in a bind about what to do next. They wanted to campaign for the removal of clause 11, or at least for it to be made clearer that it was not about equal time, but they worried that their involvement might undermine the cause. If seen as representing women, would they appear more closely aligned with one side in what was seen by some as a battle between mothers and fathers? After agonizing, they had decided to withdraw from direct lobbying. She added that there is a difference between the academics and the NGOs in the consortium: the academics put their case as strongly as possible, whereas the NGOs tend towards pragmatism and getting the best outcome. The wider consortium was also disappointed that the government had ignored the Select Committee's advice to drop the clause altogether. 'What is the point of consultation if they take no notice?' said one at a later meeting, annoyed that the professionals working with children had been ignored in her view.

A voyage through Parliament

During 2013 the Bill made its way through Parliament. The text of this Bill was formally debated and scrutinized in 23 events in the Commons and 19 in the Lords (not including brief motions about the timetable). In total 1,153 amendments to this whole Bill were 'tabled'. Debate began with Second Reading in the Commons. Just before it the NGO consortium sent a four-page briefing paper to sympathetic MPs. They did not send it to those championing fathers' rights because it would give them an advantage to see their arguments in advance. NGOs knew that the government, and therefore the Commons, would not

---

[21] Interviewed by Emma Crewe, 8 April 2014.

necessarily accept their amendments if they persuaded MPs to put them, but might influence the Lords to do so later. The Bill was introduced to Parliament formally by Edward Timpson with David Norgrove listening from the gallery. When Stephen Twigg MP, Opposition Spokesman for Education, laid out the arguments against clause 11 in some detail, Timpson appeared to judder in frustration. Perhaps he was irritated by the potentially self-fulfilling prophecy of saying that people may assume it encourages equal time for parents.

Sir Alan Beith MP pointed out that the government had accepted all but a few of the Justice Committee's recommendations – one being their advice to remove clause 11 completely – and in doing so might raise expectations or even create harm.[22] Some of those who spoke had personal experience as separated parents. David Blunkett's view was that this strengthened people's wisdom rather than weakened it:

> On part 2 and the subject of family justice, I have a slight disagreement with some of my colleagues. I do not normally speak about this, because it is too raw and sensitive. Although I am not saying that they should not speak, if they have not had experience of the family court and the family justice system they should be wary of taking a view.[23]

Others, such as Charles Elphicke MP, referred to constituents who had been denied access to their children, while the Opposition winding up called for the government to listen to children's voices more closely. As with any Second Reading, different types of evidence – research, personal experiences and consultation – were thrown into the mix with minimal discussion about their source. This stage is a discussion of general principles rather than detail.

The following month, rather late in proceedings, the government produced an 'Evidence Pack', offering arguments in favour of the family justice provisions of the Bill and anticipating its likely impact.[24] This explained the aims of its various clauses. Clause 11 was intended to send a message that it is good for children to stay in contact with both parents and help dispel the perception of bias against fathers in the family courts. They were hoping for a cultural shift. They also hoped it may mean that more cases would be settled out of court even if there may be an initial increase of parents making applications to court, especially fathers anticipating a more sympathetic response from judges once the Bill passes. But the pack acknowledged that anticipating change was difficult: 'It is not possible to reliably quantify the impacts of the measures on

---

[22] Alan Beith MP, *HC Debates*, 25 February 2013, col. 75.
[23] David Blunkett MP, *HC Debates*, 25 February 2013, col. 72.
[24] http://media.education.gov.uk/assets/files/pdf/f/family%20justice%20-%20evidence%20of%20impact1.pdf, pp. 84–6, [accessed 17 February 2014].

these groups because it largely depends on a behavioural response on the part of parents.' So clause 11 was based on trying to influence people by guessing how they were likely to respond to a clarification in the rules. The government were hoping to instil greater responsibility towards children in both parents, especially fathers, and fuller confidence in the court. No amount of evidence could substantiate this desired prediction.

The same arguments for and against clause 11 emerged during the Public Bill Committee, which was assembled to consider the Bill in detail. Public Bill Committees always have a majority of government MPs on them and since Ministers rarely accept amendments and both sides are whipped, many view them as ineffectual. It is as if incorporating opposition amendments would entail a loss of face for the Minister. The government viewpoint is that Public Bill Committee meetings are extremely useful for alerting them to concerns and possible amendments that they might agree to later on. Those they agree with, they often take away for the parliamentary draughtsmen to knock into shape and be re-presented as government amendments. Those they disagree with, they understand better. They can gather powerful arguments for defending themselves against dissenters at the next stage or, if especially threatening, for soothing them in private meetings. Tactically government tend to hold out against amendments for as long as they can to stay in control, one official told me. So perhaps the Public Bill Committee stage is not as futile as it appears to be if you just look at amendments passed – that is, its immediate textual outcomes. When seen in the context of the broader and longer processes, from the government's viewpoint at least, it plays an important role.

Before they considered amendments, this committee took evidence from 32 witnesses, quite a few of them being the same characters sitting before the Justice Select Committee, including the Minister himself. I caught Sir David Norgrove after he gave evidence and asked what he thought of the process. He said it was impressive in comparison to Parliament in the 1970s, when he was a civil servant taking a bill through Parliament.[25] MPs on this committee knew what they were talking about and he generally rates Parliament highly. As the debates in committee began, Edward Timpson and his Opposition counterpart Lisa Nandy settled into dialogue. Their dark suits, black hair, turquoise tie and shirt respectively, and Northern references (one from Cheshire, the other from Lancashire), seemed perfectly suited.

The mood of these sessions was unusually collaborative until they reached clause 11. Lisa Nandy said that the children's charities were unified in opposition to it. Several interventions from the government side sounded impatient; faces

---

[25]Public Bill Committees replaced Standing Committees in 2006, the main difference being their ability to take evidence at some of their first few meetings, before beginning the traditional line-by-line examination of the bill.

became red. Even the customarily gentle Edward Timpson and Lisa Nandy became quite tetchy with each other:

> **Mr Timpson:** I am sorry that the hon. Lady has – perhaps inadvertently – reinforced an impression that I pleaded with her not to create by talking about 50:50 time. The clause is absolutely not about 50:50 time. As my hon. Friend the Member for South Swindon articulated extremely well, we are talking not only about cases that are in court but about many more cases – *[Interruption]*. If the hon. Lady could listen carefully to what I am trying to say, it would be helpful …

Lisa looked thunderous at this point but then she replied:

> **Lisa Nandy:** I am grateful to the Minister for taking time to respond, and for the tone he adopted for the bulk of his response, which was markedly different to the tone of some of the debate. Given how emotive this subject is and how much more agreement there is between us than would be apparent from the tone of some of the remarks, that was extremely important. It is apparent that we are all very much of the opinion that it is the child's right to have parents involved in their lives when they wish to be and when it is safe and consistent with their welfare.
>
> However, it isn't worthy of the Minister, who has such a commitment to children, to suggest that the problem of the perception of shared time has been created by children's organisations and others who are seeking to tackle it. The problem has been created by his own Government, who, by his own admission, are seeking to tackle a perception rather than an actual problem.[26]

They were beginning to sound infuriated. Nandy and her colleague Sharon Hodgson MP withdrew an amendment stating: 'Involvement means any kind of direct or indirect involvement that promotes the welfare of the child, but shall not be taken to mean any particular division of a child's time',[27] knowing that they couldn't win a vote on it yet. They tried again at Report Stage with Stephen Twigg (Opposition Spokesperson for Education) on 11 June 2013, when the Bill returned to the Chamber but the House did not agreed to it or vote on it.

Throughout 2013 those against the promotion of shared parenting continued to be in a bind. They were worried that courts – but even more so, those parents

---

[26] Children and Families Bill, *Public Bill Committee*, 14 March 2013, cols 291–2.
[27] This amendment was originally drafted by Hazel Kent, a family paralegal at Coram Children's Legal Centre, her colleague Kirstin Andersen and its Director, Professor Carolyn Hamilton. See their briefings: http://www.childrenslegalcentre.com/index.php?page=cooperative_parenting_response [accessed 14 October 2014]. This along with briefings sent to both the House of Commons and House of Lords were discussed by the whole consortium of NGOs.

who don't go to court – would assume that the Bill was encouraging separated parents to divide their children's time between them 50:50. But the Bill made it clear in the explanatory notes that the intention was only to encourage 'involvement' but not a specific time split. Rumours persisted that it had high-level Cabinet support, especially from Iain Duncan Smith MP, so it wouldn't be dropped.[28] If they made too much of a fuss, then fathers' groups might retaliate and demand a stronger wording. So most campaigners kept a low profile. Similarly fathers' groups, such as Families Need Fathers, gave quiet support to the clause, not wanting to attract too much attention to it or stir up conflict. They had already spent years building up support for this in both Houses, so a big noise would have been counter-productive.

When the Bill reached the Lords, peers spoke both for and against clause 11. Baroness Perry of Southwark, former Chief Inspector of Schools, was delighted that children would spend more time with their fathers.[29] But Baroness Butler-Sloss took a different view, informed by decades of working as a judge and then President of the Family Division of the High Court. The clause was designed to reduce what was seen as a bias in the courts against fathers, but there was no evidence of bias, she said, only perception. The courts were inclined to give priority to the resident parent – whether mother or father – because it benefits children, so the logical step was to inform people of this rather than change the law. Lord Mackay of Clashfern, not only another lawyer but also an architect of the Children's Act 1989, pointed out that MPs tend to listen to fathers in their constituency surgeries who have lost. They don't hear the good news. However, this opened the way for a counter-accusation of bias: Lord McNally dismissed the objections as reflecting a generation gap; opponents were out of touch, he implied. The government rejected three amendments to the clause: one replacing 'presumption' with 'regard' and two others defining 'involvement'.

The consortium of NGOs met in late November 2013. They continued to discuss the likely impact of the Bill, worrying that parents will bully each other into agreeing an equal split for children of all ages even when it is not in the children's best interests. Research points to the benefits of having one main home for very young children, the children's charity representatives all agreed. The government continued to resist the idea of defining involvement because they claimed the separation website would make the meaning of the clause clear. However, all the NGOs found this site woefully inadequate.[30] They agreed

---

[28] For example, Laura King, 2012, *Supporting Active Fatherhood in Britain*, http://www.history-andpolicy.org/papers/policy-paper-132.html [accessed 17 March 2014].

[29] Baroness Perry of Southwark, *HL Debates*, 2 July 2013, cols 1118–19.

[30] The website can be found here: http://www.sortingoutseparation.org.uk. A subsequent evaluation found that users agreed with their criticisms. Although users liked the idea of a site, they found it difficult to use and were disappointed by lack of detailed information, https://

that it was in the House of Lords that they should persuade parliamentarians to amend the Bill. The campaigners all argued that it was vital for all sympathetic peers to put forward just one amendment to clause 11. More than one would give the appearance of disunity and split potential supporters. So defining 'involvement' was settled upon as the amendment that would most improve the text. They agreed to send out a two-page briefing to the 100 most sympathetic peers – no point in giving notice to their opponents – and to give a briefing to those who might add their name to the amendment.

Meantime the peers prepared for textual battle. Baroness Butler-Sloss hosted a meeting in a small Pugin-decorated room in an out-of-the-way corridor called Residence 1 to which two children's charities were invited, including Coram Children's Legal Centre. I sat on a gilded chair against the wall. The peers explained that in private meetings the government made it clear they would not budge on toning down 'presumption'. Butler-Sloss worried that fighting on that one would be difficult, as non-lawyers will find the arguments about clashing presumptions obscure. Coram Children's Legal Centre proposed the wording of their amendment, explaining that it had been put by the Opposition in the Commons, and suggested that if peers unified around one amendment it would have far more clout. It was agreed that it would be better if fronted by a Crossbencher, especially if it was Baroness Butler-Sloss, and supported by the Opposition led by former Children's Minister, Baroness Hughes of Stretford, who was also present. They discussed why the amendment was needed and one peer emphasized: 'If we all make the same point, they might listen.'

The government sent out a policy briefing on the evening of 16 December to reassure peers that they would communicate widely to explain that clause 11 was not about equal time. On 17 December 2013 the House of Lords convened for the second Report Day. Baroness Butler-Sloss, another Crossbencher (Howard of Breckland) and Baroness Hughes of Stretford moved an amendment to define parental involvement, making it crystal clear that it meant either direct or indirect contact between parent and child and not a particular division of time. Her opening was as sharp as a knife. She complimented the government on their intentions but expressed a regret that the clause contained a 'presumption'. Behind the regret lurked the terrible possibility that if provoked, she might move an amendment to remove the clause altogether. But she wasn't doing that. She was merely defining involvement particularly for the benefit of families in the shadow of the law – that is, for those who don't go to court and come to an arrangement between themselves.

The peer replying for the Opposition, Baroness Hughes of Stretford, supported the Crossbench amendment, saying that despite the government's policy

www.gov.uk/government/uploads/system/uploads/attachment_data/file/289400/863summ. pdf [accessed 3 August 2014].

briefing, the original title (Shared Parenting) and press coverage had created a belief that the clause was about equal time. So definition of 'involvement' was a necessary corrective. An almost identical one had been put to the Commons Public Bill Committee on 14 March 2013 by Lisa Nandy MP, at Commons Report stage by Nandy and colleagues, and in Grand Committee by Baroness Hughes, so this was also an Opposition amendment from the Commons, originally drafted by the Coram Children's Legal Centre (see footnote 27), and influenced by discussions with various charities and others concerned or affected by the clause. But Hughes did not mention its source. She allowed the amendment to be fronted by the one woman who was most difficult for government to ignore: Baroness Butler-Sloss, the legal giant of family law. Another champion of children, Baroness Walmsley, called on the government to explain what Ministers had said in private meetings – that this is not about equal division of children's time – so that it is on the record for parents and judges to note. Following these supremely articulate speeches, Lord McNally sounded hesitant and uncertain. He said that this amendment might over-correct the perception of bias by creating another one. If he attacked the amendment too harshly and lost the vote, then it might create problems later. How could you then defend it in the Commons? Butler-Sloss put it to a vote and won by four votes – the only division that the government lost on this Bill. The NGO consortium were delighted; Coram Children's Legal Centre emailed the members: 'Following the consortium's efforts, on Tuesday 17th December 2013, the government suffered a defeat as peers in the House of Lords voted by 225 to 221, majority four, to make clear that the presumption of parental involvement shall not be taken to mean "any particular division of a child's time".'[31]

The amendment was sent to government lawyers and Ministers and civil servants met with Baroness Butler-Sloss to do a deal, as she put it.[32] The government accepted the amendment and agreed not to reverse it in the Commons, but proposed their own slightly adjusted wording. Without this agreement, the Bill might have ping-ponged between the two Houses – with Baroness Butler-Sloss refusing to back down – and the government would have had to use the Parliament Act to force it through, which she knew they did not want to do. On Third Reading Baroness Butler-Sloss even added her name to the government's amendment to her amendment, musing: 'I am happy to accept the revision that the Government have made. I am well aware that any amendment that is not a government amendment has to be rewritten; that seems to be a given part of parliamentary life.'[33] A powerful combination of

[31] http://www.childrenslegalcentre.com/index.php?page=children_and_families_bill [accessed 17 March 2014].
[32] Interviewed by Emma Crewe, 13 October 2014.
[33] Baroness Butler-Sloss, *HL Debates*, 5 February 2014, col. 206.

forces – Baroness Butler-Sloss, the Crossbenchers supporting her, the Labour Party, charities and academics – had defeated the government.

On 10 February 2014 Lords Amendments to the Bill arrived in the Commons to be considered there. The government began by moving to accept new anti-smoking amendments introduced by the Lords, including a prohibition on smoking in cars when children are present. This caught the attention of the press, leaving the government little choice but to accept it. Several Tories complained about the triumph of the nanny state and Philip Davies MP complained that his party was abandoning the idea that people can do as they wish on private property.[34] Ian Paisley MP characterized the anti-smoking in cars as a PR stunt, while some saw it as unenforceable. But others spoke fervently in favour. All this debate and voting took up a large chunk of the time allocated for the Bill.

The Commons reached amendments to other clauses two hours into debate. Edward Timpson, looking tired after 18 months of intensive work on the Bill, said about clause 11 that the Lords accepted the principle of parental involvement but addressed some concerns about it with an amendment that clarified it doesn't mean a division of time. He thanked the pro-shared parenting MPs who had championed this cause. While the Lords debate saw women championing the interests of children, this Commons debate was dominated by men representing the interests of fathers and children, with a few exceptions. Tim Loughton MP seemed to be trying to reinstate the idea of shared parenting by repeating the phrase. Caroline Nokes MP tried to defend it by complaining about its dilution: 'That is the core of my concern with the amendment. It appears to erode the positive steps that the clause originally made towards a culture of shared parenting.'[35] She even got elected promising that she would campaign for a presumption of shared parenting and made a plea for not ignoring the welfare of parents. Charlie Elphicke MP put his support for shared parenting in terms of children's rights and claimed that those against it don't understand how much the world has changed. They are not young.[36] But the fight was all over. So the Bill moved swiftly to thanks by Minister Timpson in the presence of a tiny contingent of aficionados. He concluded:

> We have had some excellent debates in this House on the Bill. I would like to thank hon. Members for their participation and for how supportive they have been in helping the Government to develop the Bill. An illustration of how much work has been done is that, in both Houses together, 1,153 amendments have been tabled and debated. The Bill started off as a very good

---

[34] Philip Davies MP, *HC Debates*, 10 February 2014, col. 614.
[35] Caroline Nokes MP, *HC Debates*, 10 February 2014, col. 659.
[36] Ibid., col. 661.

piece of legislation; with all the constructive and well-meaning work that we and Members of another place have done on it, I believe it is now a great piece of legislation. We should all be very pleased about that and the benefits that children, young people and their families will see as a consequence.'

Table 6.3 Final version of section 11 in the Act

* The changes are underlined.

Welfare of the child: parental involvement
(1) Section 1 of the Children Act 1989 (welfare of the child) is amended as follows:
(2) After subsection (2) insert –
"(2A) A court, in the circumstances mentioned in subsection (4)(a) or (7), is as respects each parent within subsection (6)(a) to presume, unless the contrary is shown, that involvement of that parent in the life of the child concerned will further the child's welfare."
"(2B) In subsection (2A) "involvement" means involvement of some kind, either direct or indirect, but not any particular division of a child's time."
(3) After subsection (5) insert:
"(6) In subsection (2A) "parent" means parent of the child concerned; and, for the purposes of that subsection, a parent of the child concerned –
(a) is within this paragraph if that parent can be involved in the child's life in a way that does not put the child at risk of suffering harm; and
(b) is to be treated as being within paragraph (a) unless there is some evidence before the court in the particular proceedings to suggest that involvement of that parent in the child's life would put the child at risk of suffering harm whatever the form of the involvement.
The circumstances referred to are that the court is considering whether to make an order under section 4(1)(c) or (2A) or 4ZA(1)(c) or (5) (parental responsibility of parent other than mother)."

The Bill received Royal Assent in March 2014 and most of the family justice provisions came into effect on 22 April. The government press release made no mention of parental involvement, highlighting that the change of law includes 'New child arrangements orders that will encourage parents to focus on the child's needs rather than what they see as their own "rights"'.[37] Section 11 commenced in October 2014 but its impact will not be known for some time; the sentences in the final version of section 11 may have huge consequences, positive for some and negative for others. Perhaps some parents who have been the main carers before separation may feel more confident about arguing

---

[37] https://www.gov.uk/government/news/family-justice-reforms-to-benefit-children   [accessed 30 May 2014].

that children do not necessarily benefit if their time is split equally. Perhaps some less accustomed to caring for their children may zone in on the encouragement of involvement by both parents and demand more time with their children. No one really knows. Making laws is about 'reading the runes', as Edward Timpson put it to me – divining the future based on one's understanding of the present.

Social life under legislation

Section 11 has been described in detail so that I could have a careful look at what scrutiny means in relation to both consultation and evidence. No one could accuse the government of failing to allow scrutiny of this Bill. It was chewed over, sometimes in minute detail, by four Select Committees, one Public Bill Committee and one Grand Committee, in many events in two debating Chambers, and huge (but unknown) numbers of experts outside Parliament. If you take the process as a whole, scrutiny was thorough. On the other hand, the one body you might think would influence the shape of the Bill – the Public Bill Committee of the House of Commons that is charged with going over each clause in depth – only passed government amendments. Section 11 received the attention of hundreds inside and outside Parliament and was changed by government after consultation and after pre-legislative scrutiny and by peers during the final stages of the passage of the Bill. These two sides of the argument about the quality of scrutiny were articulated by the government and the Opposition:

> **Mr Buckland:** … I think that the Bill's passage through this House offers a very positive example of how scrutiny can work. The length of time we took – the Committee's proceedings were extended by several sittings to allow all the debates – allowed us to lay a good foundation so that their lordships could consider our concerns and act upon them.

> **Mrs Hodgson:** I am grateful to be in the Chamber tonight to hear the hon. Gentleman's contribution. Does he agree that it was the hundreds of amendments and the hundreds of hours – it felt like hundreds – of debate in the Commons that laid the groundwork that allowed the Lords to bring forward the amendments that the Minister is able to accept today? If that is how it has to be, then we did our job, but it is a shame that more amendments could not have been made in the Commons.

> **Mr Buckland:** I agree that it would have been nice to have made some of the amendments in the Commons, but I understand that in the other place

there is more time for deliberation and for votes, so the fact that we reached this stage in that way does not trouble me.[38]

So when assessing the scrutiny of legislation should the whole of Parliament, or just the lower house, or even one stage of Commons scrutiny, be judged? Evaluating the outcomes of the Public Bill Committee on section 11 gave a negative view. But if you consider the whole process of airing views, reconsidering the text in private, and then eventually conceding changes, then even the Public Bill Committee looks more positive. The consensus seems to be that the Bill was improved through consultation and debate. But thorough scrutiny of one clause doesn't prove that Parliament always does a good job, merely that it can.

So, what makes good scrutiny more likely? Maclean and Kurczewski describe four case studies of family law between 1985 and 2010 that range from superb to catastrophic, with the Children Act 1989 at one end and the Child Support Act 1991 at the other. The success of the Children Act is attributed to its base of careful research and absence of political interference. In contrast, the Child Support Act was pushed forward by Mrs Thatcher, against the advice of officials, to extract payments from non-resident parents for the care of their children. Their view is that haste, political interests and flimsy evidence made this law a disaster.[39] While the damage caused by haste seems self-evident to any process of legislative scrutiny, the entanglement of evidence with politics makes it hard to sustain an anti-politics, pro-evidence argument. Looking at politics and evidence underneath section 11 illustrates this entanglement. I have described how shared parenting had ferocious political backing at the highest levels, on the one hand. On the other hand, both pro- and anti-shared parenting had various types of evidence supporting their case. During the passage of the Bill social scientific surveys, legal cases and personal testimonies were brought into debate to substantiate contradictory positions. Judging by attitudinal surveys, while the promotion of shared parenting or involvement by both parents tends to be in the interests of non-resident parents as individuals, the majority of whom are fathers, the collective interest of those women and men as parents bumps up against fraught feminist-informed debates.[40] Child and family care is seen by some feminists at one end of a continuum as a source of women's oppression, so sharing the workload is pro-women for women seeking to change gendered roles in society. Other feminists focus on women's interests as mothers in the

---

[38] *HC Debates*, 10 February 2014, col. 650.
[39] Mavis Maclean with Jacek Kurczewski, *Making Family Law* (Oxford: Hart, 2011).
[40] Belinda Fehlberg and Bruce Smyth with Mavis Maclean and Ceridwen Roberts, 'Caring for children after parental separation: Would legislation for shared parenting time help children?', *Family Policy Briefing 7* (Department for Social Policy and Intervention, University of Oxford, 2011).

present. If they are the main parent, or particularly if victims of domestic violence, then the government should not undermine their position, some argue.

The evidence about where the interests of children lie is even more complex. First, their age makes a difference. According to some psychological research, children under four years old benefit from having one main home and one main carer, whereas older children are more flexible.[41] Secondly, for a minority of children, whatever their age, promoting shared parenting may increase the risk of harm – for example, if one parent is violent or negligent. So a solution that benefits one child will harm another. While researchers make convincing claims that a positive relationship with both parents, and harmony between parents, improves children's sense of well-being, the impact on children's outcomes of different scenarios is fraught with methodological difficulty. Separating different variables (contact arrangements, quality of relationships, impact of separation, age of child, income level, risk of violence and so on) of a hugely diverse group makes meaningful generalization challenging, to put it mildly. On-going societal changes in attitudes towards parenting further complicates the picture. Furthermore, some might argue that children's interests can only be properly assessed by a far more thorough consultation with different groups of children. If we wanted to fulfil our commitments to the United Nations Convention on the Rights of the Child, then such consultation would require far more attention. No amount of weighing up the research will lead to an easy 'evidence-based' solution because it always requires interpretation and prioritizing. The making of law entails political judgements.

Philosophers have been musing on political judgement since Ancient Greece. Political judgement is about using imagination to decide what is good for a wider public – a group, community or whole society – so entails a mix of evidence, politics and morality. As Aristotle pointed out, making a decision about what is good for others is always an ethical process, one he advised needs practical wisdom rather than the application of universal rules. John Dunn warns that modern political theory focuses on intention but gives inadequate weight to practical skill.[42] Part of the practical skill is about deliberating on the plurality of interests affected by law directly or in its shadow. Since what is good for some will be bad for others, reading the runes – imagining the future on the basis of the present – is fraught with danger for politicians. Their decisions will always be

[41] J. McIntosh, B. Smyth, M. Kelaher, Y. Wells and C. Long, *Post-separation Parenting Arrangements and Developmental Outcomes for Infants and Children* (Canberra: Attorney-General's Department, 2010).
[42] John Dunn, 'Trust and Political Agency', in Gambetta, Diego (ed.), *Trust: Making and Breaking Cooperative Relations*, electronic edition, Department of Sociology, University of Oxford, chapter 5, 2000, pp. 73–93, http://www.sociology.ox.ac.uk/papers/dunn73-93.pdf [accessed 11 October 2014]

distasteful to some and in this sense we might even be grateful to politicians for courting inevitable unpopularity. According to Dunn:

> The very purpose of political society itself is precisely to stand in – by clear and predictable legal and judicial arrangements, backed by effective powers of enforcement – for the erratic and dangerous conditions generated by the collision of institutionally unrestrained human partiality.[43]

So it is not impartiality we should demand of our politicians; it is honesty about their partiality – inevitably and continually privileging the interests of one group above another – that helps democracy. Politics can never *just* be the rational assessment of evidence; it would lack morality if it was or pretended to be so.

Part of the point of democratic politics is to give voice to arguments about evidence and truth. Watching the passage of section 11 was not so much a process of politicians mechanically weighing up the evidence, but listening to different groups of people deliberate, discussing their plural and partial views and taking sides. The social organization of the people involved was structured in complex ways. The changes to the text were directly accomplished by those most closely involved on a day-to-day basis – the politicians and officials – either in highly ritualized events (committees and debates), in policy discussions within their party and across government, or behind the scenes on computers that are never seen by outsiders. Every change to the Bill required agreement across government departments. The Cabinet Office co-ordinates the process of policy approval and while this used to be deeply secret, they have published documents explaining exactly how this works.[44] During the Coalition Ministers had to err towards getting approval even more than usual, due to the persistent disagreements between Conservative and LD, especially for changing any proposals that were in the Coalition Agreement. Changes to the Children and Families Bill proposals qualified for cross-government approval for three reasons: proposals were clearly in the Coalition Agreement, they involved three government departments, and they aroused considerable public interest, so any amendments to this Bill had to go to the Cabinet. Section 11, and its amendments, received approval from the whole top tier of government.

More fluidly, politicians and officials were involved in a series of relationships with groups of people who had a stake in the clause. As Minister Edward Timpson put it: 'It is as much about tapping into the human element as it is about getting into the nitty gritty. It is a very human process, it's about

[43] Ibid., p. 84.
[44] https://www.gov.uk/government/uploads/system/uploads/attachment_data/file/224997/Guide_to_Cabinet_Committees_2012.pdf [accessed 24 April 2014].

relationships, not just texts.' Those potentially affected were the imagined beneficiaries of the clause: the children and parents in families that separate. The cases that go to court might involve over 40,000 in a year but families that don't get to court (120,000 in 2013), the ones in the shadow of the law, may be as much or more dramatically affected. Between these families and the politicians/officials are a range of professionals who represent or work with or for parents, women, mothers, fathers or children: judges, magistrates, lawyers, social workers, Cafcass guardians, children's charity workers, women's organizations and fathers' groups. The less formally ritualized events, such as All-Party Parliamentary Group meetings, political party meetings and meetings to lobby politicians, consisted of freer discussion and debate or less antagonism. These were perceived as less political, but that doesn't make them so. Politics entails agreement and co-operation, as much as disagreement and conflict; depending upon who is in the room, the disagreement is either part of the discussion or its backdrop, but it is always at the least implied.

Despite the hundreds of debates, section 11 was only changed by an adjustment to its heading and 30 new words defining the title. But scrutiny within Parliament should not be judged only by the extent to which the formal process results in an end product – that is, an amended text of a bill. The debates between parliamentarians and with those affected or interested are as important. It is the framework of scrutiny enabling parliamentary and public debates to take place around an issue that matters as much. Some calls for 'evidence-based policy' give the impression that a rational process of weighing up research findings and expert testimony should lead linear-fashion to clear priorities. But the circulation of 'evidence' for and against the idea of putting a statement about parental involvement in legislation was far from linear. The 'evidence' had within it contradictions (about the statistics), conflicts of interests (e.g. between some fathers and mothers) and huge shifts in patterns of family life. Assuming that the evidence could tell you about the past was difficult enough. Using it to predict what might happen in the future was even harder. So while even more public discussion of these contradictions, conflicts and changes in the evidence would have been useful, politicians will necessarily be in the business of making political judgements rather than merely rational assessments. The balance between private and public discussion, and elite and wider consultation, is moving towards the latter in both cases. This means that the opportunities for more rigorous scrutiny are expanding.

Section 11 was presented as if it was apolitical. But it was deeply political, even if not in a narrow party political sense. It was a statement about parenting within a context of changes in the relationship between the family and the state. While legal aid has been cut in private law cases, the state is being pushed (or pulled) out of family life and replaced with mediation and technology in the guise of a website guiding parents about how to handle separation. The text was fought over with some vigour because it could redefine family life for hundreds of thousands of people. As Timpson says, like any political change it is all about relationships.

7
Reading the Runes

Making sense of the work of our politicians is only possible if you consider all the contradictory strands of their job. Then what looks like unreliability and concealment becomes honourable compromise. MPs cope with contradictions through riffs, rhythms and rituals. But some contradictions at the core of our democracy are unresolvable. If we fail to appreciate the paradox in which MPs find themselves, then we are doomed to misunderstand them.

****

Its faults strike one at first approach, but its qualities are only discovered at length ... Democracy does not give the most skillful government to the people, but it does what the most skillful government is powerless to create; it spreads a restive activity through the whole social body, a superabundant force, an energy that never exists without it ... [it] can bring forth marvels. These are its true advantages.

Tocqueville

In this book I have tried to explain why our democracy is not as hopeless as the pervasive refrain in public and media commentary implies – or at least not in the sense that attackers usually claim. Even MPs sometimes join in the attacks, perhaps partly to distinguish themselves from other lazy, greedy and power-hungry politicians. But strong defence of democratic politics can only be easily made if we consider the links between different aspects of MPs' work and the parliamentary democracy that they lead, rather than looking at particular strands of their work in isolation. To take one example, apparently Margaret Hodge MP complains that this government arranges too few sittings so that 'it hardly feels as if we are working'.[1] But if MPs attend Parliament for 140–50 days a year that still only leaves another 100 for government/opposition, constituency, party,

---

[1] As quoted by Rajeev Syal, 'MPs look lazy with short parliamentary hours, says Margaret Hodge', *Guardian*, 21 April 2013, http://www.theguardian.com/politics/2013/apr/21/mps-lazy-hours-margaret-hodge [accessed 5 May 2014].

staff, campaigns and overseas trips that take place outside Parliament if they don't work at weekends. Most do. Some MPs work flat out and rarely take a day off, even at weekends; others take a slightly more leisurely approach to their various roles; but most work long hours. The average working week for new MPs is almost 70 hours.[2] So studying sitting hours gives you one piece of the jigsaw, which tells you little on its own, but if you look at all the pieces together it looks far prettier. But that example is a relatively trivial detail. The common criticisms that I drew attention to in Chapter 2 – that MPs are all the same, preserving the status quo and in it for their own gain – misunderstands the work of our elected representatives as well as their motives. They are diverse, obsessed with modernization and driven by multiple motives. The criticisms blind many to what is really going on in Parliament and distracts us from the vital scrutiny and criticism that should be angled at government.

Table 7.1 Twitter conversation about political cynicism on 2 June 2013 between the researcher and an account called 'Politics Worldwide'

Politics Worldwide:	'Remember. MPs hate you more than you hate them. Otherwise they wouldn't behave as they do.'
Emma Crewe:	'I disagree. I've been studying them for 18 mths and aside from a few rotten apples, vast maj have v. honourable intentions.'
Politics Worldwide:	'In which case, institution itself must be rotten – good men & women prevented from doing good for institutional reasons.'
Emma Crewe:	'Parliament is not rotten – MPs do good and hard work, esp in select committees & constituencies. Gov struggles not parliament.'
Politics Worldwide:	'Which means MPs failing in their first duty: control executive.'
Emma Crewe:	'Not their job, surely, & imposs cos gov has maj. They do hold gov to account and even gov MPs rebel more than 50 years ago.'
Politics Worldwide:	'Controlling executive precisely their job. Social worker-type constituency work is secondary. They're legislators.'
Emma Crewe:	'Scrutiny not control. Few noticing parliament under going revival while effective Gov gets harder. Cynicism bad for democracy.'

[2]Matt Korris, *A Year in the Life*, p. 5.

In this final chapter I will probe further the most neglected aspects of MPs' work that have arisen out of this research to fill in some of the gaps in our understanding. The most obvious omission in many studies and commentaries of British politics concerns agency. MPs are written about as if they are *only* individuals or members of political parties. They are both but many other social relationships are central to all aspects of their political work as well, from canvassing to getting things done in government. To give examples, when Select Committees take evidence from experts, when MPs write to housing officers to ask them to help a constituent or when backbenchers across parties make alliances to campaign for civil liberties or against airport expansion, they are making and maintaining social relationships as part of the process of doing politics. Agency is not merely something that adheres to autonomous individuals with total freedom, or to an abstract political system or structure that determines people's behaviour, but is found in these relationships – or, to be more specific, in processes of humans relating through action. Griffin escapes from stultifying choices between freedom and determinism by putting a paradox of human agency at the centre of his understanding rather than trying to eliminate it.[3] He points out that people are both free to make choices, and constrained by others, at the same time. This is true for MPs as much as others. So the cliché that 'all politics is local'[4] may not be literally true – although it is at election time – but all politics is certainly both political and social.

My point about how relationships thread through all MPs' roles is easy to make. Who could disagree with the observation that at every turn politicians are spying on each other, winning support, and articulating co-operation or antagonism? Every day they meet old friends, opponents and supporters as well as strangers who they need to woo. To get along in your party, get re-elected in your constituency, govern the country, hold government to account or contribute to lawmaking, all these roles require MPs to listen, persuade or pressurize others in various ways according to context. So they not only engage in relationships but in an usually varied range of them. It is worth saying more about these relationships, how MPs communicate and perform across them and the cultural meanings and hierarchies that they create, and are created by, along the way.

---

[3]Griffin, *The Emergence of Leadership*, pp. 7–14.
[4]This has been attributed to the former Speaker in the USA, Tip O'Neill, but was probably said first by Byron Price, according to a US writer Barry Popik: http://www.barrypopik.com/index.php/new_york_city/entry/all_politics_is_local/ [accessed 9 October 2014].

Culture and hierarchies

Relationships among MPs and with others outside are hierarchical, but in complex and changeable ways. Class distinctions are alive in well in the UK with the result that policymaking and lawmaking arenas are dominated by middle- and upper-class social groups, while the number of working-class MPs has declined. Women make up less than a quarter of parliamentarians and although one in four people in a YouGov poll expressed an interest in standing as an MP, twice as many men as women were keen to do so.[5] Those women who rise towards the top make terrible sacrifices or arrange their lives so that politics can consume all their time. The public have to make a choice: do we want a more diverse group of politicians, including those with a hinterland, or a socially narrower group of MPs who do nothing else but politics?

Those giving evidence to Parliament do not represent the diversity of Britain either. In October and November 2013 the gender split among witnesses giving evidence in the House of Commons was 76 per cent men and 24 per cent women – a slightly worse balance than committees in the House of Lords.[6] Among those categorized as 'experts', as many as 83 per cent were men. Children, youth and the elderly scarcely get a look-in at all during consultations, although the Select Committee on Education and the Department of Education do try. Consulting people under 18 years old deserves particular attention, partly because they do not have the vote, but also because the UK government has pledged to do so under the UN Convention on the Rights of the Child (1989). The Youth Parliament holds debates and campaigns on issues – influencing the government to introduce sex and relationships education in schools, for example, in 2008 – but their representatives' capacity to fully represent the views of all young people in the UK will always be circumscribed. While it is difficult for youth and various other groups to visit Westminster, which is partly why committees have stepped up their outreach and hold sessions around the country, a systematic approach to ensuring diversity of experts, witnesses and those consulted is a long way off. In view of the rampant and increasing cynicism towards politics and politicians, it seems highly likely that MPs will increasingly find ways to consult with young people through social media, outreach and inviting them into Parliament and constituency meetings.

Power hierarchies are not just about numerical participation or decision-making but about value too. So a gendered hierarchy is not merely revealed by the absence of women from influential or decision-making forums, but by

---

[5]http://labourlist.org/2013/01/exclusive-nearly-a-quarter-of-people-would-be-interested-or-enthusiastic-about-becoming-an-mp/ [accessed 24 June 2014].
[6]The Democratic Audit, www.democraticaudit.com/?p=2278 [accessed 9 October 2014].

the denigration of their ideas when they do articulate them. While white men feel more easily entitled to be our representatives, women and black or Asian people can be treated in subtle ways as if they are space invaders in Parliament, as Nirmal Puwar puts it.[7] Sometimes women's ideas go unnoticed, but when repeated by a man – especially a senior one – are taken up as masterful. Many women feel uncomfortable and hesitant in the Chamber. One woman MP said more specifically that while most MPs are only 'OK' at gladiatorial Chamber performance, it is mostly men and only a very few women who excel; men have more confidence, aggression, deeper voices and relish the quick repartee. Women MPs tend to do better in the less aggressive and visible debates. The weakness in our democracy is not so much found in inadequate individuals but in a perennial political deficit: the quieter voices in our Parliament, and in our wider society, get ignored. Rather than inviting them to shout louder, perhaps our politicians should listen differently, including to each other?

The more precise value that attaches to different groups of witnesses, their knowledge and their views is unknown. It would be worth probing the assumptions MPs make about different people based on the witnesses' experience and status. Are MPs more impressed by witnesses with a long experience of performance at public speaking – academics, lawyers, other MPs and those in corporate public relations – and less dazzled by people who rarely speak in public? Does this further exacerbate the social hierarchies mentioned above, given that older, white men are over-represented in these professions? It is quite likely that practice and confidence at the skill of public performance gives certain people an advantage when trying to impress MPs and influence their conclusions. But hierarchies are not formed by the charisma or skill of individuals; they emerge out of relationships between people, in this case the relationships between MPs and witnesses. When MPs find an older male barrister sitting before them they will reveal a host of assumptions as they converse with him in their tone, body language and the content of their questions. As an example, they may variously assume – rightly or wrongly – that he is intelligent, knowledgeable about the law, but protecting his financial interests, not because of his personal qualities but due to their past experience of and relationships with barristers and the law. So the value MPs attach to different witnesses emerges out of their past experiences (as well as that of the witnesses) as much as it is influenced by how witnesses talk in the specific session.

The discipline of anthropology has always been concerned with the denigration of the culture and knowledge of particular groups of people partly because it emerged at the beginning of the last century during the era of British colonialism. Since the 1960s anthropologists' response to Euro-American

---

[7] Nirmal Puwar, *Space Invaders: Race, Gender and Bodies Out of Place* (London: Berg, 2004).

claims of racial, cultural or political superiority has been to point out the intel-
lectual and moral equality in value of cultures globally.[8] These days many social
scientists may take for granted that all bodies of knowledge around the world
should at the least be treated with respect. But both lawyers and scientists, two
groups that have huge influence on politics in most societies globally, are under
pressure to present their objectivity, detachment and 'evidence' as superior to
other ways of producing knowledge. The more senior they are, the more they
are taken seriously and so is their knowledge. So the old adage that knowledge
is power is only partly true. Everyone has knowledge but it does not necessarily
make you powerful; often it works the other way around: power can appear as
wisdom.[9]

If knowledge doesn't make you automatically powerful, what does? There
is nothing automatic about power. Power is not something that individuals or
institutions wield in a fixed way as if it were a commodity. Power is a character-
istic of relationships between people that is continually on the move, sometimes
malign and sometimes benign. The MPs who are whips are not powerful people
in all situations, for example. They are in a powerful position in relationship to
most backbenchers in their party if the latter aspire to Ministerial office; they
are little different in terms of power to other MPs in relation to highly rebellious backbenchers. As the power of whips diminishes in general in the UK
Parliament, which it has since the 1950s, their position in relation to ambitious
backbenchers in their 'flock' also shifts. At the same time, individual whips may
improvise to be more persuasive or threatening and develop relationships of
rapport or conflict, whether intended or not, so the power of particular whips
over particular backbenchers may also vary at one given time.

The power of MPs in relation to citizens varies in even more complex ways.
For those MPs who are representatives of the state (that is, Ministers within the
government), the potential of their power to do good or evil to citizens is huge
(as I discussed in Chapter 4). But most MPs are not in government. Those
holding government to account are potentially in co-operative relationships with
citizens challenging the power of the state and part of it at the same time. It
is this neglected relationship that I will take a look at in more detail in my final
sections.

---

[8] As examples, see the work of Evans-Pritchard in the 1960s, Stephen Lansing in the 1980s
and 1990s, and Paul Sillitoe in the 1990s onwards.
[9] Emma Crewe and Richard Axelby, *Anthropology and Development: Culture, Morality and
Politics in a Globalised World* (Cambridge: Cambridge University Press, 2004), pp. 150–6.

Communication: Concealment and truth

People in all cultures have a tendency to distrust strangers. This presents a problem for rulers unless people believe God has put them there. While an autocracy can more easily rely on secrecy to consolidate their power, democracy demands publicity from politicians because to get re-elected they need people to trust them. Politicians wish us to think highly of them, partly also because they wish to think well of themselves, and paint a picture of themselves and their achievements in the sunniest light. If we like their party, or those they associate with, we are more likely to have a favourable opinion. But we can never really know strangers, or anyone else for that matter, as Simmel explains:

> Since one never can absolutely know another, as this would mean knowledge of every particular thought and feeling; since we must rather form a conception of a personal unity out of the fragments of another person in which alone he is accessible to us, the unity so formed necessarily depends upon that portion of the Other which our standpoint toward him permits us to see.[10]

This makes it extraordinarily difficult for MPs to represent themselves or others. Add to this that politicians have to engage in various forms of communication that inevitably erode trust, and they have a serious PR problem on their hands.

One kind of communication that damages trust comes to the fore during elections in the form of promises. The parties write their manifestoes as if they were going to win a majority and form a strong enough government to make decisions and introduce the policies and laws they choose. There are various reasons why these manifesto promises can't ever be totally fulfilled. Circumstances change locally, nationally and globally so that, for example, the promise not to raise taxes made in better times becomes unwise. There is so much that will always be impossible to predict. The two parties in the 2010–15 Coalition Government did not know they were going into government together when they wrote their manifestoes, most of which each coalition partner probably heartily dislikes. The Minister who championed 'shared parenting' before getting into government was replaced by another who preferred 'parental involvement' (see Chapter 6). 'Evidence-based policy' can only ever be provisional because manifestoes can be no more than a guess – a form of divination that politicians would be unwise to rely on too rigidly. All plans require adaptation and further innovation to take account of the inevitability of social change.

---

[10] Georg Simmel, 'The sociology of secrecy and secret societies', in *American Journal of Sociology*, vol. 11, 1906, p. 442, http://www.brocku.ca/MeadProject/Simmel/Simmel_1906.html [accessed 9 October 2014]

How to best represent constituents' views is also impossible for MPs to predict. The plurality of voices within any constituency means that literal representation of its residents is impossible. Occasionally they may all agree that they don't want an airport near their town, for example. But mostly some want one thing, others want another, and either can subsequently change their mind. So what should an MP do when communicating their constituents' interests in Parliament? She has no choice but to filter out some voices, privilege others and thereby represent different sections of her constituency at different times. This communication task is further complicated by the contradictory nature of constituents' reactions. They may tolerate their MP articulating views that are different from their own and respect them for having their own mind, or they may not and see it as betrayal, but what does this depend upon? It seems to be more to do with the nature of the relationship between MP and constituents than a rational assessment of the value of their views or even their actions. If the MP is seen as actively interacting within the locality, and communicating about the constituency to Parliament with a sense of loyalty and pride, then they will be forgiven for saying things that some constituents don't agree with.

Communication by MPs on behalf of individuals or families with a grievance also follows a pattern of selectivity. The MP will nearly always do something on hearing about a problem. They (or their staff) will explain the issue on the phone or in writing and put the case for their constituent, rather as a lawyer might advocate their interests. They copy the correspondence to the constituent. Also like a lawyer, they take care with what they reveal in this communication and how they articulate the problem to others. MPs convey in the subtlest form the degree of severity and the extent to which they perceive the grievance to deserve urgent action. This is concealed if you only see the letter that concerns you, but by reading across a variety of several MPs' constituents' files, it becomes obvious that some MPs develop a code for conveying the merits of each case. The people receiving the letters are grateful for this because it helps them prioritize and avoid wasting too much time on constituents who can't be helped.

Changeable communication might potentially erode trust with constituents, but they forgive all this if they respect their MP. What they truly despise is the generic tribal communication between MPs in their gangs. The public are turned off by the aggressive verbal bashing at PMQs and on TV shows such as *Newsnight*. 'Typical politician', they say when the parties mock and attack each other. Some backbench rebels can afford to eschew ferocious party politics, but our aggressive media, first-past-the-post electoral system and competitive mode of interaction between MPs make tribal communication an integral part of our parliamentary culture for MPs with any ambition. So frontbenchers, and those aspiring to join the upper echelons, feel they have little choice but to join the fray, choosing to exacerbate general distrust of MPs rather than exposing their own individual weaknesses.

These patterns of communication have been more evident in recent years, but another development transformed politics more abruptly in 2005. The new Labour administration wanted to introduce a law to increase the transparency of information produced and held by public authorities. The result was the Freedom of Information Act passed in 2000 and active five years later. This allowed the public sight of information, with certain exceptions, by merely making a request. The intention of increasing trust through transparency has been described by some as backfiring. Former Cabinet Secretary Gus O'Donnell[11] is one of many who tells us that it created uncertainty because civil servants and politicians never quite knew when something was FoI-able (as the requests became known). Since the Act Ministers have avoided saying anything experimental or controversial in minuted meetings in case it might be published and might not play well with the public. Rather than holding formal meetings, government communication at senior levels has become more informal, ad hoc and frequently held on the phone. So a bid for public trust has ironically created greater secrecy and distrust among those running the government.

The work of politicians, and especially those in government, is about concealment as well as communication. As Simmel points out, if you suspend moral indignation about lying for a moment, then you notice that concealment and keeping secrets is part of all social relationships. It is felt as a greater betrayal the nearer the person is to you.[12] On the other hand, since it can be extremely difficult to distinguish between someone lying and making an error (or possibly both) when you have no direct relationship to the person and little knowledge about their character or the circumstances of the lie/error, then accusations of immorality tend to flow. When backbenchers are holding government to account, or citizens are challenging politicians, care has to be taken not to assume that a mistake was an intentional lie.

But that should not dissuade anyone from relentlessly putting government Ministers and politicians on the spot in specific contexts and criticizing them if found lying. You can get into trouble if you do so bluntly in the parliamentary Chamber. In September 2012 Paul Flynn MP accused Minister for Defence, Philip Hammond MP of lying about government policy in Afghanistan. Paul Flynn is a Labour MP who argues against war at every opportunity partly because his father was incapacitated by wounds from the First World War and he sees history repeating itself for others. It is so serious to accuse a Minister of lying in the Chamber that the Speaker had no choice but to 'name' Mr Flynn, label his behaviour as disorderly and, with the consent of the House, evict him from Parliament for a few days. Mr Flynn subsequently told me that he had never had so many letters of support from constituents as he did following this episode.

---

[11] http://www.cabinetsecretaries.com [accessed 9 October 2014].
[12] Simmel, 'The sociology of secrecy and secret societies', p. 446.

But most MPs would prefer not to be evicted and so choose their words carefully when making allegations of lying. Winston Churchill's phrase 'terminological inexactitude' has been taken up as a handy euphemism for lying. But others are forced to be more precise about what their accusation consists of rather than relying on the bald concept of lying.

The inevitability of concealment by people working in teams or organizations is not peculiar to politicians. When I work for international aid charities, which I have done for much of my career, we are grilled by potential donors about our projects and organization. It is not possible to fully explain the track record of even a tiny organization, so you filter out some of your knowledge and privilege the stories that put your team in a better light. Personally I would assume that no intelligent, experienced grant-maker will believe you if you pretend that your results are 100 per cent positive, so I would include some of the 'challenges', as negative news is euphemistically called. But I would conceal the bitter argument we had the day before about whether to keep working in Peru, the £350 wasted when we had to reprint a document and an allegation of corruption from one of our partners in Cambodia until I have had time to deal with it. Potential donors do not want to hear about these until they are sorted; they want to collude in your sanitized version of perfect organizational life so that they can have confidence that their money will be well spent. They do not want their superiors saying in three years' time: 'You knew that they were struggling with x, why did you approve their grant?' There is surely no established charity, grant-maker or government that tells the whole unvarnished truth to their donors and supporters in a timely fashion with absolutely no delay. In a world where the explosion of audit culture makes truth-telling impossible, it would jeopardize your ability to meet charitable objectives and breach the confidentiality of colleagues and other organizations. On the other hand, I would never knowingly distort what I knew in order to gain an advantage and to those I knew well I would tell the whole messy and imperfect truth. Is this so different from politicians?

In the corporate world, too, managers are expected to voice completely contradictory versions of reality – doublethink, in Orwell's phrase – especially when public relations is the order of the day. One executive told sociologist Robert Jackall: 'We lie all the time, but if everyone knows that we're lying, is a life really a lie?'[13] Only those corporate managers with discretion will be thought of as worthy of trust and promoted, so they keep quiet about the mistakes of their superiors and peers. And they conceal their own mistakes by getting promoted as fast as possible so that by the time errors become obvious they have moved to another department or even country. Truth is disguised with the use of euphemisms, judicious silence and giving different explanations for different contexts.

---

[13] Robert Jackall, *Moral Mazes* (Oxford and New York: Oxford University Press, 2010), pp. 197, 127.

A professed belief in 'facts' as opposed to 'interpretation' allows corporates to create the impression of truth while undermining research that doesn't fit with their commercial interests.[14]

Political parties are probably not as bad – in part because they are so exposed to public view and under constant attack from opponents – but they, too, try to conceal the minor misdemeanours of their Members, the arguments between factions and the experimental ideas that do not yet have the approval of those who matter in the party. The difference is that despite their appeals to their Members to be discreet, increasingly MPs can't resist the pressure to appear independent, transparent and better than the rest. So they leak. Tories tweet about the deeply private 1922 Committee meetings of backbenchers, Labour tweet from Parliamentary Labour Party meetings or tell hacks about the foibles of their rivals and LDs criticize their Coalition partners. Unlike corporate and charity worlds, where people can be sacked for indiscretion or awkward truth-telling, MPs can only be kicked out by the voters or local associations. It may be that underlying the distrust towards politicians we find not so much secrecy or lies but indiscretion and a cult of transparency.

The only group in our political world that are almost 100 per cent discreet are the parliamentary Clerks. If they betrayed the trust of the politicians they serve, they would be instantly sacked, so they take the greatest care not to reveal what they know unless they have a cast-iron guarantee that they are talking to someone equally discreet or they have retired. They know all manner of secrets. They hear gossip about MPs doing things they shouldn't, whether it might be bullying their staff or rubbishing their leader. As the only people allowed into private MPs' space along with other senior officials they observe which MPs are working hard or merely killing time in the tearoom. When asking the Clerks for advice, MPs reveal their dastardly plans for outwitting the other side. If an MP presents them with a proposal and asks for guidance, the Clerk may have a good idea that it won't work but can't say why she thinks that because it could reveal what others are up to. They can't even say why they think what they think, so MPs sometimes find them obfuscating and assume they don't like change. The proportion of Clerks who favour innovation is surprisingly high, but even this can't be revealed to all MPs because it implies criticism of the status quo. The protection of secrets of politicians was greater and more tolerated in the past. In the modern era it is scrutiny, exposure and transparency that is the order of the day. It is partly this transparency that makes our politics so messy.

---

[14] Jackall, *Moral Mazes*, p. 184.

Facing many ways

The results of politics are messy and contradictory, but the process has an energy running through it that can't be achieved by any other way of doing politics, as Tocqueville wrote. The energy derives in part from intense emotion. The political commitment of one local politician was so strong that she was persuaded to induce her baby early so that the need to give birth would not keep her away from a vital vote. And that was only a local council meeting. The strength of emotion is evoked despite the messiness.

Richard Bacon MP comments on the ambiguity in our democratic politics:

> Politics is complex, subtle, messy and ambiguous ... It is one thing to point out that the current system involves supervising a deeply ambiguous set of relationships, but it is another not to acknowledge that they are bound to be deeply ambiguous. This is called politics ... It is true that with more clarity there would be less politics – and sometimes that might be a good thing – but there would also be less democracy, leaving ministers even more circumscribed than they are now, facing civil servants who refused to do as they were asked because it was 'not in the contract' ... Economics has seen a big shift towards studying how people actually behave, rather than how they are supposed to behave. We need a similar shift in government and politics.[15]

The public want simplicity and certainty but instead they get contradictions and conflicts. Party because of this, MPs are no longer objects of respect and deference; en bloc they are despised and distrusted. To be an MP was once an accolade but those two letters have become an albatross.[16] They lose security – as they can be thrown out at any election or due to a boundary change – privacy, and any decent amount of time with their family. And yet curiously the role of politician remains addictive for most MPs. When I asked Sir George Young why he enjoyed being an MP he replied that he could not think of another job with as much variety. It is three jobs in one: (1) the constituency job involves representing over 50,000 people, being there to help them and being their voice in Parliament, as a cross between an ambassador and social services; (2) the parliamentary job means considering bills, getting legislation through and being in the cockpit of debate; (3) the Ministerial job involves running things. The combination of these three makes being an MP highly addictive. Add to those roles continual social interaction on Twitter and the drama of elections and you

---

[15] Richard Bacon MP, *Accountability Under the Spotlight*, Institute of Government, 27 March 2013, http://www.instituteforgovernment.org.uk/blog/5578/guest-blog-accountability-under-the-spotlight/ [accessed 3 December 2013].
[16] So writes backbencher Paul Flynn, *How to Be an MP*, p. 1.

have an irresistible combination. It is perhaps this that makes the ambiguity and exposure bearable.

Andrew Percy (andrewpercy)

10/09/2012 22:09

The rock and roll MP lifestyle. One min it's speaking in the Mother of Parliaments, next it's a visit to a Chicken Cottage.

Andrew Percy was a history teacher and has been a Conservative MP since 2010

So why does the ambiguity arise? The audiences and sites that MPs adjust to create a kaleidoscope of ingredients so that it is as if MPs have to learn to perform in a multitude of theatres with different players and scripts every day. While your aim on the floor of the House is a political debating victory involving the humiliation, or at least outwitting, of opponents and enemies, Kaufman recommends abandoning any overt conflict in committee. Since the opposition can speak repeatedly and for as long as they like, it is best to pacify and placate.[17] These sites are public, within which political parties have to feign consensus and unity, while others are private, where contestation and endlessly divergent views within parties are aired. In the words of a former Labour backbencher: 'You can say completely different things to different people and you believe them at the time. You convince yourself of contradictory things. So you say "I fully support my Leader" to the media and then you go to the tearoom and discuss how to get rid of him. This is politics. What we say is different from what we actually do.'[18] That is not just politics: that is how people are, responding to different contexts and relationships.

MPs have no choice but to worry about appearances. All develop extraordinary skills at adapting to different relationships. While I was interviewing a Clerk in Portcullis House café a prominent Conservative MP walked up to us and started joking with the Clerk, pretending to treat him as if he was unstable.[19] They had been on a work trip together so knew each other well. The Clerk kept trying to intervene and finally managed to say: 'Do you know Dr Crewe from the University of London, who is doing an academic study of MPs?' The MP appeared visibly shocked and in a second was transformed from jovial, chatty mate leaning over our table into upright, back-straight, highly dignified important person showing respect to an academic – an outsider – with formality, politeness and reserve. In the blink of an eye his face was transformed from twinkling to sombre. Successful MPs develop an ability to adapt to different social situations without even thinking about it.

---

[17] Ibid., p. 81.
[18] Interviewed by Emma Crewe, 15 December 2011.
[19] Interviewed by Emma Crewe, 18 September 2012.

Politicians find themselves facing what Goffman called the dilemma of expression versus action: 'Those who have the time and talent to perform a task well may not, because of this, have the time or talent to make it apparent that they are performing well.'[20] Most MPs tend towards either one or other – geniuses at performance on the front stage or at getting things done out of the public gaze backstage. As politicians relying on the support of party and voters, ignoring the front stage is dangerous to your party and individual prospects. So this problem is not going away. But it is at least worth appreciating that when politicians focus on the front stage, from their viewpoint it is to create the possibility of doing useful things backstage. At the same time, seeing MPs meeting individuals in their constituencies and achieving results for them that they can never brag about in public shows that they are more than mere attention-seekers.

The final fragmentation that MPs navigate is the past/present/future. During any study of documents, conversation or debate in the present, they are influenced Janus-like by past and future.[21] Janus is the god of entrance and exit, beginnings and endings, and he looks backwards and forwards simultaneously. In a similar vein MPs are not shaped by past/future consecutively but in the same moment. Social scientists tend to offer deterministic explanations about how the past has shaped the behaviour of people in the present, but most have given less attention to how people are influenced by the future,[22] and especially politicians. To understand what MPs are up to, it is important to consider the way they see the future in their aspirations for continuity or change. It was a desire to understand how MPs dwell on the future that drew me to follow them arguing about one clause in one bill.

When governments propose a change in the law, what they are doing is reading the runes, as Edward Timpson MP, Minster for Children and Families put it, and thereby imagining the future based on the present. He took a huge bill through Parliament – the Children and Families Act 2014 – one clause of which I followed as it passed through both houses of Parliament and across the desks and into the conversations of hundreds of professionals. The clause instructed the courts to assume that children should have contact with both parents in the event that they separate. This statement sounds obvious and inane; of course both parents are responsible for looking after their children. But when you study the patterns of the past and predict the likely impact, then this clause becomes charged with significance: take into account that the courts already assume that children should see both parents; that one main and one subsidiary home is said to be better for many children, especially when young; that 30 per cent of non-resident parents (mainly

[20] Goffman, *The Goffman Reader*, p. 100.
[21] Nicholas Sarra, a colleague at the University of Hertfordshire, suggested this analogy (2013).
[22] Exceptions include Arjun Appadurai, Chris Mowles and Henrietta Moore.

fathers) lose contact with their children when families split; and that women still tend to take responsibility for most childcare. MPs listened to professionals anticipating the likely effects of the Bill based on their past experience of current law and practice. Some felt the clause would bring about positive cultural change while others looked into the future and saw more conflict, confusion and a shift from children's welfare to fathers' rights. So lawmaking may be based on research and consultation that considers the past and present, but the past is always seen by people through experience and assumption. As we reflect, learn and improvise, our past changes. Since the aim is to influence an unknowable future, there has to be a magical-like process of divination. Policymaking or lawmaking can never be a rational assessment of 'evidence' on its own.

MPs have to cope with being in several imaginary and real places at one time – past and future as well as present, the audience in front of them but also the other audiences mediated through the television or Twitter. They adapt to multiple audiences and deal with conflicts and contradictions between their various roles. So what happens to their sense of self? How do they cope? Some don't. Alcohol consumption and divorce among MPs is relatively high.[23] But many do, judging by the skill with which they adapt their performance to multiple sites, audiences and demands. MP can bear the hard work, media exposure, loathing and fractured lives due to a combination of the continual drug of social interaction and emotion evoked by the heady possibility of making a mark on the world. Underlying this emotion, there are three processes that provide some continuity for MPs between and across all this chaotic diversity and dynamism. The first process is the riffs that MPs develop to make sense of ideology and communicate as policies and arguments, each improvised for different audiences. The second is rhythms that organize the work of MPs by creating repetition in time and space but allow for variation at the same time. The third is the rituals – as examples, debates in parliamentary Chambers, interviews in TV studios and speeches in party conferences – which punctuate the daily routine with riffs and rhythms of particular political, social and cultural significance. They deal with the contradictions and conflicts in the everyday present through shared riffs, rhythms and rituals.

If riffs, rhythms and rituals create a sense of continuity for MPs over time and across their various sites and audiences, then what to make of the fact

---

[23] Alcohol Concern carried out a survey in 2013 and one-quarter of the 150 MPs who responded believed that there is an unhealthy drinking culture in Parliament http://www.alcoholconcern.org.uk/media-centre/news-archive/mps-admit-to-unhealthy-drinking-culture-in-parliament-new-survey-reveals [accessed 9 October 2014]. According to Conservative MP Charles Walker, around one-sixth of the 2010 intake of Conservatives had divorced, separated or had long-term relationships break down by early 2013. Nicholas Hellen and Jack Grimston, 'One in six new Tory MPs suffer split', *The Times*, 3 February 2013, http://www.thesundaytimes.co.uk/sto/news/Politics/article1206644.ece [accessed 9 October 2014].

that MPs' work continually changes? After all, social and political life always has both patterns of continuity and of change. Rather than Kant's dualistic 'both/and'-type explanations, or splitting these into different times or contexts as scholars of Parliament have a tendency to do, we need to recognize the paradoxes that people live out in everyday relationships.[24] MPs are living more exacting paradoxes than most. They are both constrained and enabled by power, emotion and values, the past and future *in the same moment.* For each MP their identity is bound up with their own individual history, their role as parliamentarians and their embodiment of their constituency. The last of these creates a paradox: although they cannot logically both represent themselves and embody their diverse constituency, practically speaking they do. They do not choose between these roles but accomplish them at the same time, and the contradictions created thereby ensure continual change. The dynamism and adaptability of parliamentary democracy flow from this. It may always infuriate but it has the unique virtue that it can, and does, constantly renew itself in an ever-changing world.

---

[24] Griffin, *The Emergence of Leadership*, pp. 9–17.

Bibliography

Abélès, M., *Quiet Days in Burgundy* (Cambridge: Cambridge University Press, 2007).

Adonis, A., *Parliament Today* (Manchester: Manchester University Press, 1993).

Alexander MP, D., *ITV 1's Agenda*, 11 February 2013.

Ashe, J., Campbell, R., Childs, S. and Evans, E., '"Stand by your man": Women's political recruitment at the 2010 UK general election', *British Politics*, vol. 5, no. 4, 2010, pp. 455–80.

Ashton MP, J., *HC Debates*, 4 June 1997, col. 507.

Bacon MP, R., Accountability under the spotlight, Institute of Government, 27 March 2013, http://www.instituteforgovernment.org.uk/blog/5578/guest-blog-accountability-under-the-spotlight/ (accessed 3 December 2013).

Balls, E., tweet, 20:41, 05/07/2012.

Banks MP, T., http://news.bbc.co.uk/1/hi/uk/4047123.stm (accessed 17 September 2014).

Barrett, M., 'The Government's attempt to fix the Backbench Business Committee would take back power for the executive', 12 March 2012, http://www.conservativehome.com/platform/2012/03/the-governments-attempt-to-fix-the-backbench-business-committee-would-take-back-power-for-the-execut.html (accessed 9 December 2012).

Beattie, J., '"You'll never be a surgeon if you go to a state school": Tory by-election candidate rubbishes education system', *Daily Mirror*, 16 February 2013, http://www.mirror.co.uk/news/uk-news/eastleigh-by-election-conservative-candidate-maria-1712534 (accessed 12 April 2013).

Begg MP, A., http://annebegg.wordpress.com/westminster-work/ (accessed 2 July 2013).

Beith MP, A., *HC Debates*, 25 February 2013, col. 75.

Bernstein, G. L., *The Myth of Decline, the Rise of Britain since 1945* (London: Pimlico, 2004).

Berry, J., tweet, 19:59, 08/07/2012.

Bevan MP, A., *HC Debates*, 3 November 1959, col. 862.

Bevan, A., *In Place of Fear* (London: Simon and Schuster, 1952).

Blair MP, T. *HC Debates*, 27 February 2002, col. 698.

Blair, T., *A Journey* (London: Hutchinson, 2010).

Blunkett MP, D., *HC Debates*, 25 February 2013, col. 72.

Bone, P., *HC Debates*, 12 September 2013, col. 1153.

Bourdieu, P., *Outline of a Theory of Practice* (Cambridge: Cambridge University Press, 1977).

Brake, T., *HC Debates*, 12 September 2013, col. 1153.

Brogan, B. 'Clegg's tit-for-tat retaliation could bring about the Coalition's end', *Telegraph*, 5 November 2012, http://blogs.telegraph.co.uk/news/benedictbrogan/100187967/cleggs-tit-for-tat-retaliation-could-bring-about-the-coalitions-end/ (14 November 2013).

Burke, E., *The Works of the Right Honourable Edmund Burke. Vol I* (London: Henry G. Bohn, 1854).

Burns MP, C., *HC Debates*, 10 April 2013.

Butler, R., http://www.cabinetsecretaries.com/ (accessed 29 May 2013).

Butler-Sloss, Baroness, *HL Debates*, 5 February 2014, col. 206.

Cameron MP, D., *HC Debates*, 10 April 2013, p. 1615.

Campbell, R. and Childs, S., 'Parents in Parliament: "where's mum?"', *Political Quarterly*, vol. 85, issue 4, pp. 487–92.

Carswell, D., 'Voters have turned against politics-as-usual', *Telegraph*, 6 October 2014, http://blogs.telegraph.co.uk/news/author/douglascarswellmp/ (accessed 11 October 2014).

Childs, S., 'A feminised style of politics? women MPs in the House of Commons', *British Journal of Politics and International Relations*, vol. 6, 2004, pp. 3–19.

Childs, S. and Krook, M. L., 'Critical mass theory and women's political representation', *Political Studies*, vol. 56, 2008, pp. 725–36.

Churchill MP, W., *HC Debates*, 23 January 1948, col. 557.

Clark MP, A., *Dairies: In Power 1983–1992* (London: Phoenix, 2003).

Collins, P., 'Labour can't win if it's on Mick Philpott's side', *The Times*, 5 April 2013, http://www.thetimes.co.uk/tto/opinion/columnists/philipcollins/article3731420.ece (accessed 8 May 2013).

Commonwealth Parliamentary Association seminar, House of Commons, 24 October 2012; Crewe, Lords of Parliament, pp. 126–28.

ComRes, *MPs Pay and Pensions, A Public Verdict* (London: Independent Parliamentary Standards Authority, 2012).

Cooke, R., 2007, 'Oh Babe, just look at us now', *Observer*, Sunday 22 June, http://www.guardian.co.uk/politics/2007/apr/22/women.labour1 (accessed 20 May 2013).

Cowley, P., 'Why not ask the audience? Understanding the public's representational priorities', *British Politics*, vol. 8, 2013, pp. 138–63.

Cowley, P. and Childs, S., 'Too spineless to rebel? New Labour's women MPs', *British Journal of Political Science*, vol. 33, no. 3, 2003 pp. 345–65.Cowley, P. and Stuart, M., http://www.conservativehome.com/platform/2013/05/philip-cowley-and-mark-stuart-for-1000am-tuesday.html (accessed 7 October 2013)

Cowley, P. and Stuart, M., 'Five things about the gay marriage vote', 2 May 2013, http://nottspolitics.org/2013/02/05/five-things-about-the-gay-marriage-vote/ (accessed 10 October 2014); table taken from Mike Simpson (accessed 8 May 2013).

Crewe, E., *Lords of Parliament* (Manchester: Manchester University Press, 2005).

Crewe, E. and Axelby, R. *Anthropology and Development: Culture, Morality and Politics in a Globalised World* (Cambridge: Cambridge University Press, 2004).

—*Anthropology and Development, Culture, Morality and Politics in a Globalised World* (Cambridge: Cambridge University Press, 2013).

Crick, B., *In Defence of Politics* (Chicago: Chicago University Press, 1962).

Davies MP, P., *HC Debates*, 10 February 2014, col. 614.

Dixon, H., 'Nadine Dorries attacks newly promoted colleague on Twitter', *Telegraph*, 8 October 2013, http://www.telegraph.co.uk/news/politics/conservative/10362614/

Nadine-Dorries-attacks-newly-promoted-colleague-on-Twitter.html (accessed 9 October 2013).

Duffy, L., interviewed by journalist John Harris, in 'The Battle for Britain', *Guardian Weekend*, 18 May 2013, p. 28.

Dunn, J. (ed.), *Democracy: The Unfinished Journey, 508 BC to AD 1993*, (Oxford: Oxford University Press, 1992).

—'Trust and Political Agency', in Diego Gambetta (ed.) *Trust: Making and Breaking Cooperative Relations*, electronic edition, Department of Sociology, University of Oxford, Chapter 5, 2000, pp. 73–93, http://www.sociology.ox.ac.uk/papers/dunn73-93.pdf (accessed 11 October 2014).

Eagle MP, A., *Building a Better Politics, Speech to the Hansard Society*, 24 April 2013, http://www.labour.org.uk/building-a-better-politics,2013-04-24 (accessed 2 May 2013).

Edensor, T., 'Introduction', in T. Edensor (ed.) *Geographies of Rhythm* (Farnham: Ashgate, 2010), pp.1–20.

Elias, N. and Scotsman, J. L., *The Established and the Outsiders* (London: Sage, 1994).

Elliott, L. and Treanor, J., 'MPs assessed. Chummy to chastening: how the committee measured up', *Guardian*, 5 July 2012, pp. 4–5.

Engel MP, N., *HC Debates*, 26 April 2012, col. 331WH.

Family Justice Review, November 2011, https://www.gov.uk/government/uploads/system/uploads/attachment_data/file/217343/family-justice-review-final-report.pdf (accessed 18 February 2014).

Feargal McGuinness, F., *Social Background of MPs* (House of Commons Library, SN/SG/1528, 2010).

Fehlberg, B. and Smyth, B. with Maclean, M. and Roberts, C., 'Caring for children after parental separation: would legislation for shared parenting time help children?' *Family Policy Briefing 7* (Department for Social Policy and Intervention, University of Oxford, 2011).

Fenno, R., *Home Style, House Members in their Districts* (New York: HarperCollins, 1978).

Fitt MP, G., *HC Debates*, 29 March 1979, col. 521.

Flynn MP, P., *The Unusual Suspect* (London: Biteback Publishing, 2010).

—*How to Be an MP* (London: Biteback Publishing, 2012).

Forsyth, J., ' Tim Loughton vs the Department for Education', *Spectator*, 17 January 2013, http://blogs.spectator.co.uk/coffeehouse/2013/01/loughton-vs-dfe/ (accessed 30 May 2013).

Foster, D., 'Going "Where Angels Fear to Tread": How Effective was the Backbench Business Committee in the 2010 – 2012 Parliamentary Session?', *Parliamentary Affairs*, published online 9 June 2013, (accessed 4 December 2013).

Fox, R. and Korris, M., *Making Better Laws, Reform of the Legislative Process from Policy to Act* (London: Hansard Society, 2010).

Geertz, C., *The Interpretation of Cultures* (New York: Basic Books, 1973).

Gilmour MP, I., *Dancing with Dogma, Britain under Thatcherism* (London: Simon and Schuster, 1992).

—*The Body Politic* (London: Hutchinson, 1969).

Goffman, E., 'Social Life as Drama', in Charles Lemert and Ann Branaman (eds), *The Goffman Reader* (Oxford: Blackwell, 1997).

Goodman, P., 'Jacob Rees-Mogg becomes the first Tory MP to back a Conservative-UKIP pact', 8 May 2013, http://conservativehome.blogs.com/

parliament/2013/05/jacob-rees-mogg-becomes-the-first-tory-mp-to-back-a-conservative-ukip-pact.html (accessed 5 June 2013).

— 'Mitchell: This evening's 22 meeting "was divided 50:50"', 17 October 2012, http://www.conservativehome.com/parliament/2012/10/mitchell-this-evenings-22-meeting-was-divided-5050.html and http://www.theguardian.com/commentisfree/2012/oct/21/andrew-rawnsley-tories-made-andrew-mitchell-go (both accessed 11 February 2014).

— 'Mrs May might – why Tories are tipping Theresa May for the very top', *Telegraph*, 22 October 2012, http://www.telegraph.co.uk/news/politics/conservative/9373105/Mrs-May-might-why-Tories-are-tipping-Theresa-May-for-the-very-top.html (accessed 11 February 2014).

— 'Tomorrow's 1922 Committee Elections – nominations in full', 2012, http://conservativehome.blogs.com/parliament/2012/05/tomorrows-1922-committee-elections-nominations-in-full.html (30 May 2013).

— 26 October 2010, http://conservativehome.blogs.com/thetorydiary/2010/10/by-paul-goodman-during-the-summer-there-was-a-kerfuffle-about-the-work-of-the-whips-office-and-i-wrote-a-defence-of-whips.html (accessed 1 June 2013).

Grice, A., 'Exclusive: Reform Lords – or it will cost you 20 MPs, David Cameron told', 6 July 2012, *Independent*, http://www.independent.co.uk/news/uk/politics/exclusive-reform-lords--or-it-will-cost-you-20-mps-david-cameron-told-7917993.html (accessed 13 November 2013).

— 'The homophobic campaign that helped win Bermondsey', *Independent*, 27 January 2006, http://www.independent.co.uk/news/uk/politics/the-homophobic-campaign-that-helped-win-bermondsey-524703.html (accessed 2 May 2013).

Griffin, D., *The Emergence of Leadership, Linking Self-organisation and Ethics* (London: Routledge, 2002).

Guido Fawkes [blog], http://order-order.com/2013/09/03/tory-twitter-bitch-fight-philip-davies-v-kris-hopkins/ (accessed 9 October 2013).

— 'Quote of the Day', 4 March 2013, *Guido Fawkes' Blog*, http://order-order.com/2013/03/04/quote-of-the-day-605/ (accessed 9 October 2013).

Hain MP, P., 'We need to up our game', *Progress On-line*, 8 May 2013, http://www.progressonline.org.uk/2013/05/08/we-need-to-up-our-game/ (accessed 30 May 2013).

Halfon MP, R., in Norman, *Lessons from the Marginals*, 2012.

Hansard Society, *Audit of Political Engagement, The 2012 Report: Part One* (London: Hansard Society, 2012).

— *Tuned In or Turned off? Public Attitudes to Prime Minister's Questions* (London: Hansard Society, 2014).

Hattersley, R., 'The Party's Over', *The Observer*, 22 March 2009, http://www.guardian.co.uk/politics/2009/mar/22/james-callaghan-labour-1979-thatcher (accessed 23 May 2013).

Hellen, N. and Grimston, J., 'One in six new Tory MPs suffer Split', *The Times*, 3 February 2013, http://www.thesundaytimes.co.uk/sto/news/Politics/article1206644.ece (accessed 9 October 2014).

Hennessy, P., 'Whitehall men told what not to disclose', *The Times*, 22 May 1980, pp. 361–3.

— http://www.cabinetsecretaries.com (accessed 2 October 2013).

— *The Prime Minister: Its Office and its Holders since 1945*, (New York: Palgrave, 2000).

HM Government, *The Coalition: our programme for government: Freedom, Fairness, Responsibility*, 2010, http://www.instituteforgovernment.org.uk/sites/default/files/ publications/The%20Challenge%20of%20Being%20a%20Minister.pdf (accessed 2 October 2013).

Hope, C., 'David Cameron faces biggest ever rebellion by Tory MPs over Lords reform', *Telegraph*, 6 July 2012, http://www.telegraph.co.uk/news/politics/9382313/ David-Cameron-faces-biggest-ever-rebellion-by-Tory-MPs-over-Lords-reform.html (accessed 14 November 2013).

House of Commons, Children and Families Bill, *Public Bill Committee*, 14 March 2013.

—*Rebuilding the House, House of Commons Reform Committee*, First Report of Session 2008–09, 12 November 2009, HC 1117, p.7.

House of Commons Justice Select Committee, *Operation of the Family Courts, Sixth Report of Session 2010-12,* HC 518–1.

Howard, A., (ed.), *The Crossman Diaries*, (Basildon: Magnum Books, 1979).

Howe, G., *Conflict of Loyalty* (London: Macmillan, 1994).

Hunt, J. and Macleod, A., *Outcomes of Applications to Court for Contact Orders after Parental Separation or Divorce* (London: Minister of Justice, 2008).

Ian Gow MP, *HC Debates*, 29 November 1989, col. 7.

IPSA, *Reviewing MPs; Pay and Pensions: A Consultation, October 2012* (London: Independent Parliamentary Standards Authority, 2012), http:// parliamentarystandards.org.uk/payandpensions/Documents/2.%20Reviewing%20 MPs'%20Pay%20and%20Pensions%20-%20A%20Consultation.pdf (accessed 8 May 2013).

—*Reviewing MPs' Pay and Pensions, A First Report – January 2013* (London: Independent Parliamentary Standards Authority, 2013), http:// parliamentarystandards.org.uk/payandpensions/Documents/1.%20Reviewing%20 MPs'%20Pay%20and%20Pensions%20-%20A%20First%20Report.pdf (accessed 8 May 2013).

Jackall, R., *Moral Mazes* (Oxford and New York: Oxford University Press, 2010).

Joseph, K., *Stranded on the Middle Ground, Reflections on Circumstances and Policies* (London: Centre for Policy Studies, 1970), http://www.cps.org.uk/files/cps/Keith_ Joseph_files/634_ProductPreviewFile.pdf (accessed 9 May 2013).

Kaufman MP, G., *How to be a Minister* (London: Faber and Faber, 1997).

Kelly, R. and White, I., *All-women Shortlists* (House of Commons Library Note, SN/ PC/05057, 2012).

King, A. and Crewe, I., *The Blunders of our Governments* (London: OneWorld, 2013).

King, L., 2012, 'Supporting Active Fatherhood in Britain', http://www.historyandpolicy. org/papers/policy-paper-132.html (accessed 17 March 2014).

Latour, B., 'What if we talked politics a little', *Contemporary Political Theory*, Vol. 2, 2003, pp. 143–64.

—*Making of Law. An Ethnography of the Conseil d'Estat* (London: Polity Press, 2010).

Leveson Inquiry, 14 May 2012, http://webarchive.nationalarchives.gov. uk/20140122145147/http://www.levesoninquiry.org.uk/hearing/2012-05-14pm/ (accessed 15 May 2014).

Lloyd MP, S., http://gallery.mailchimp.com/cdaa010d3f3b37bc5da7e5592/files/ Casework_Summary_2_.pdf (accessed 28 June 2013).

—website, http://stephenlloyd.org.uk/en/article/2010/453897/lloyd-votes-against-rise-in-university-tuition-fees (accessed 28 June 2013).

Llwyd MP, E., *Pre-legislative scrutiny of the Children and Families Bill*, Fourth report of the 2012–13 session, 12 December 2012, House of Commons Justice Committee, Ev35, Q168.

Lodge, G. and Gottfried, G., *Worst of Both Worlds. Why First Past the Post no Longer Works* (London: IPPR briefing, 2011).

Loughton MP, T., http://www.timloughton.com/tims_track_record/aweekinthelife.htm (accessed 2 October 2013).

Maclean, M. with Kurczewski, J., *Making Family Law* (Oxford: Hart, 2011).

Major, J., *The Autobiography* (London: HarperCollins, 1999).

Marshall-Andrews, B., *Off Message* (London: Profile, 2011).

Matt Korris, M., *A Year in the Life: From Member of Public to Member of Parliament*, Interim briefing paper (London: Hansard Society, 2011).

McAlpine, A., *The Servant* (London: Faber and Faber, 1992).

McBride, D., *Power Trip: A Decade of Policy, Plots and Spin*, (London: Biteback Publishing, 2013).

McCluskey, L. 'Mandelson's argument is about politics not procedure', 21 May 2013, http://www.unitetheunion.org/news/unitenewsdigest/mandelsonsargumentisaboutpoliticsnotprocedure/ (accessed 29 May 2013).

McDougall, L., *Westminster Women* (London: Vintage, 1998).

McGuiness, F., *House of Lords Statistics* (House of Commons Library Standard Note SN/SG/3900, 2012).

McIntosh, J., Smyth, B., Kelaher, M., Wells, Y. and Long, C., *Post-separation Parenting Arrangements and Developmental Outcomes for Infants and Children* (Canberra: Attorney-General's Department, 2010).

McWalter MP, T., *HC Debates*, 27 February 2002, col. 698.

Mensch, L., tweet, 17:32, 04/05/2013.

Montcrieff, C., *Wine, Women and Westminster, Behind-the-scenes True Stories of MPs at Play over 50 Years* (London: JR Books, 2008).

Montgomerie, T., 'Tories must deliver at least "tiny" elected element to Lords or lose boundary changes, Cameron tells 1922 meeting', *conservativehome*, 11 July 2012 http://www.conservativehome.com/thetorydiary/2012/07/tories-must-deliver-tiny-elected-element-to-lords-or-lose-boundary-changes-cameron-tells-1922-meetin.html (accessed 14 November 2013).

—tweet, 17:34, 04/05/2013.

Mooney, A. Oliver, C. and Smith, M., *The Impact of Family Breakdown on Children's Well-Being, Evidence Review*, Research Report DCSF – RR113 (London: Institute of Education, 2009).

Moore, C., 'David Cameron's lonely Ministers have been abandoned by Down Street', *Telegraph*, 15 February 2013, http://www.telegraph.co.uk/news/politics/david-cameron/9873325/David-Camerons-lonely-ministers-have-been-abandoned-by-Downing-St.html# (accessed 2 October 2013).

Mouffe, C., *The Democratic Paradox* (London and New York: Verso, 2000).

Mullin, C., *Decline and Fall, Diaries 2005–2010* (London: Profile, 2011).

—*The Diaries of Chris Mullin*, vols 1–3, (London: Profile, 2010, 2011, 2012).

Nokes MP, C., *HC Debates*, 10 February 2014, col. 659.

Norman MP, J. (ed.), *Lessons from the Marginals* (ConservativeHome, 2012) http://conservativehome.blogs.com/files/4121-lesson-from-the-marginals.pdf (accessed 23 May 2013).

Norman, J., tweet, 02:42, 04/10/2013.

—tweet, 17:56, 06/07/2012.

—tweet, 08:03, 09/07/12.

O'Farrell, J., 'Why I'm standing for Labour in the Eastleigh byelection', *Guardian*, 13 February 2013, http://www.guardian.co.uk/commentisfree/2013/feb/13/john-ofarrell-why-standing-eastleigh-labour (accessed 12 April 2013).

— 'How Eastleigh gave me reasons to be cheerful about the next election', *Guardian*, 4 March 2013, http://www.theguardian.com/commentisfree/2013/mar/04/eastleigh-reasons-cheerful-general-election (accessed 30 May 2014).

Parry, K. and Gay, O., *Parliamentary Private Secretaries* (House of Commons Library Standard Note, SN/PC/04942, 2012).

Patsoe-Watson, G., 'John Reid's brain is missing', *Sun*, 7 September 2007, http://www.thesun.co.uk/sol/homepage/news/29723/John-Reids-brain-is-missing.html (accessed 11 February 2014).

Perry of Southwark, Baroness *HL Debates*, 2 July 2013, cols 1118–19.

Peston, R., *Who Runs Britain?* (London: Hodder and Stoughton, 2008).

Pickles MP, E., *HC Debates*, 12 March 2013, cols 12, 15, 20.

Pierce, A., 'Is Ed's pal the sickest man in politics', *Daily Mail*, 22 February 2013, http://www.dailymail.co.uk/debate/article-2283026/Is-Eds-pal-sickest-man-politics.html?ito=feeds-newsxml (accessed 12 April 2013).

Political and Constitutional Committee 'Revisiting Rebuilding the House: the impact of the Wright reforms' HC 82, 18 July 2013 http://www.publications.parliament.uk/pa/cm201314/cmselect/cmpolcon/82/82.pdf (accessed 5 May 2014).

Pound MP, S., *HC Debates*, 15 April 2013, col. 137.

Puwar, N., *Space Invaders: Race, Gender and Bodies out of Place* (London: Berg, 2004).

Rai, S., 'Disruptive democracy: analysing legislative protest', *Democratization*, vol. 20, 2013, pp. 385–91.

Reed MP, J., a series of tweets, between 15:02 and 15:16, 23/07/12.

—tweets, 20:20 and 20:21, 15/08/12.

Rees-Mogg MP, J., *HC Debates*, 8 May 2014, col. 344.

Rhodes, R. A. W., *The Everyday Life in British Government* (Oxford and New York: Oxford University Press, 2011).

Richards, S., The battle over Thatcher's legacy is a battle for the future, *Guardian*, 10 April 2013, http://www.independent.co.uk/voices/comment/the-battle-over-thatchers-legacy-is-a-battle-for-the-future-8567289.html (accessed 9 October 2014).

Ricoeur, P., *History and Truth* (Evanston: Northwestern University Press, 1965).

Rifkind MP, M., *HC Debates*, 9 July 2012, cols 52–3.

Robinson, N., 'Lords reform: now its handbags', 11 July 2012, http://www.bbc.co.uk/news/uk-politics-18793452 (accessed 12 November 2013).

Rogers, R. and Gay, O., 'Suggestions for possible changes to the procedure and business of the House – a note by the Clerks, House of Commons Standard Note', 18 June 2009, SN/PC/05110 www.parliament.uk/briefing-papers/SN05110.pdf (accessed 28 May 2014).

Rogers, R. and Walters, R., *How Parliament Works* (London: Routledge, 2006).

Runciman, D., *The Confidence Trap* (Princeton: Princeton University Press, 2013).

Russell, M., '"Never Allow a Crisis to Go to Waste": The Wright Committee Reforms to Strengthen the House of Commons', *Parliamentary Affairs*, vol. 64, no. 4, 2011.

Sainty, J. C., 'Sir Charles Harris and the management of the business of the House of Commons', *Parliamentary History*, vol. 21, 2002, pp. 233–9.

Saner, E., 'Why don't we trust politicians', *Guardian*, 19 October 2012, http://www.guardian.co.uk/commentisfree/2012/oct/19/why-public-dont-trust-politicians (accessed 6 June 2013).

Sarra, N., personal communication, 2013.

Saward, M., 'The representative claim', *Contemporary Political Theory*, vol. 5, 2007, pp. 297–318.

Seldon, A., http://www.cabinetsecretaries.com (accessed 15 May 2014).

Shapps MP, G., *HC Debates*, 12 March 2012, col. 13.

Shrapnel, N., *The Performers: Politics as Theatre* (London: Constable, 1978).

Silvester, C. (ed.), *Pimlico Companion to Parliament* (London: Pimlico, 1997).

Simmel, G., 'The sociology of secrecy and secret societies', *American Journal of Sociology* vol. 11, 1906, http://www.brocku.ca/MeadProject/Simmel/Simmel_1906.html (accessed 9 October 2014).

Simpson MP, A., *HC Debates*, 30 March 1994, cols 1041–2.

Stratton, A. 'Darling admits in memoirs "deposing" Brown might have saved government', *Guardian*, 4 September 2011, http://www.guardian.co.uk/politics/2011/sep/04/alistair-darling-memoirs-gordon-brown (accessed 11 February 2014).

Straw MP, J., Speaker's Lectures, Great Offices of State, http://news.bbc.co.uk/democracylive/hi/house_of_commons/newsid_9688000/9688423.stm (accessed 15 May 2014).

Street, J., 'Celebrity politicians: popular culture and political representation', *British Journal of Politics and International Relations*, vol. 6, pp. 435–52.

Syal, R., 'MPs look lazy with short parliamentary hours, says Margaret Hodge', *Guardian*, 21 April 2013, http://www.theguardian.com/politics/2013/apr/21/mps-lazy-hours-margaret-hodge (accessed 5 May 2014).

The Democratic Audit, www.democraticaudit.com/?p=2278 (accessed 9 October 2014).

Theakston, K., as cited by Peter Riddell, Zoe Gruhn and Liz Carolan, *The Challenge of Being a Minister*, The Institute for Government, 2011, http://www.instituteforgovernment.org.uk/sites/default/files/publications/The%20Challenge%20of%20Being%20a%20Minister.pdf (accessed 2 October 2013).

Tyrie MP, A., *HC Debates*, 22 February 2010, col. 100.

Walker MP, C., *HC Debates*, 14 June 2012, col. 517.

Walpole J. and Kelly, R., *The Whip's Office* (House of Commons Library Standard Note, SN/PC/02829, 2008).

Walters, S., 'Fury over "moral reprobate" Labour candidate who wrote of disappointment that Mrs Thatcher didn't die in the Brighton bomb', *Daily Mail*, 17 February 2013, http://www.dailymail.co.uk/news/article-2279886/My-disappointment-Mrs-Thatcher-didnt-die-Brighton-bomb--Labours-Eastleigh-candidate.html (accessed 12 April 2013).

Wilson, A., *Clement Freud: Unusual Achievements*, http://bishopalan.blogspot.co.uk/2009/04/clement-freuds-extraordinary.html (accessed 18 April 2013).

Wintour, P. 'Lords reform committee divided over key issues', *Guardian*, 23 April 2012 http://www.theguardian.com/politics/2012/apr/23/lords-reform-committee-divided-reports (accessed 14 November 2013).

Wynne-Jones, J., 'Gordon Brown launches thinly-veiled attack on Tony Blair', *Telegraph*, 19 February 2011, http://www.telegraph.co.uk/news/politics/8335843/Gordon-Brown-launches-thinly-veiled-attack-on-Tony-Blair.html (accessed 9 October 2014)

YouGov, *Boundaries update*, 24 October 2012, http://ukpollingreport.co.uk/blog/
archives/category/boundary-review (accessed 8 November 2013).

Young MP, G., 'The Reshuffle', http://www.sirgeorgeyoung.org.uk/articles/newsitem.
cfm?newsid=4120 (accessed 2 October 2013).

—*HC Debates*, 12 July 2011, cols 200–1.

Ziegler, P., as quoted by Peter Hennessy, *The Hidden Wiring: Unearthing the British
Constitution* (London: Phoenix, 1996).

Zolotow, M., 'Alec Guinness discusses his role in play by T. S. Eliot', *New York Times*,
26 February 1950, http://www.nytimes.com/books/97/08/24/reviews/guinness-
party.html (accessed 11 October 2014).

Index